D1256893

WITHDRAWN

A Behaviorist Looks
at Form Recognition

Books by William R. Uttal

- *Real Time Computers: Techniques and Applications in the Psychological Sciences*

- *Generative Computer Assisted Instruction* (with Miriam Rogers, Ramelle Hieronymus, and Timothy Pasich)

- *Sensory Coding: Selected Reading* (Editor)

- *The Psychobiology of Sensory Coding*

- *Cellular Neurophysiology and Integration: An Interpretive Introduction*

- *An Autocorrelation Theory of Form Detection*

- *The Psychobiology of Mind*

- *A Taxonomy of Visual Processes*

- *Visual Form Detection in 3-Dimensional Space*

- *Foundations of Psychobiology* (with Daniel N. Robinson)

- *The Detection of Nonplanar Surfaces in Visual Space*

- *The Perception of Dotted Forms*

- *On Seeing Forms*

- *The Swimmer: An integrated Computational Model of a Perceptual-Motor System* (with Gary Bradshaw, Sriram Dayanand, Robb Lovell, Thomas Shepherd, Ramakrishna Kakarala, Kurt Skifsted, and Greg Tupper)

- *Toward a New Behaviorism: The Case Against Perceptual Reductionism*

- *Computational Modeling of Vision: The Role of Combination* (with Ramakrishna Kakarala, Sriram Dayanand, Thomas Shepherd, Jaggi Kalki, Charles Lunskis Jr., and Ning Liu)

- *The War Between Mentalism and Behaviorism: On the Accessibility of Mental Processes*

- *The New Phrenology: The Limits of Localizing Cognitive Processes in the Brain*

- *A Behaviorist Looks at Form Recognition*

A Behaviorist Looks
at Form Recognition

WILLIAM R. UTTAL
Arizona State University

LAWRENCE ERLBUM ASSOCIATES, PUBLISHERS
2002   Mahwah, New Jersey   London

Lawrence Erlbaum Associates, Inc., Publishers
10 Industrial Avenue
Mahwah, NJ 07430

Cover design by Kathryn Houghtaling Lacey

Library of Congress Cataloging-in-Publication Data

Uttal, William R.
    A behaviorist looks at form recognition / William R. Uttal.
          p. cm.
    Includes bibliographical references and index.
    ISBN 0-8058-1482-2 (alk. paper)
1. Form perception. 2. Behaviorism (Psychology). I. Title.
BF293 .U853   2002
152. 14´23—dc21   2001055591
                                                                   CIP

Printed in the United States of America
10 9 8 7 6 5 4 3 2 1

For Mit-chan

Contents

Preface

For a number of years, indeed, a larger number than I like to count, I have been working on a series of books that present my personal answers to the question— How do we see? I have gone through a number of changes in my interpretations of what the vast data accumulated over the past century means. I am now convinced that I am converging on a consistent and coherent perspective about the nature of human vision. As I progressed along this path, I have used tools that have ranged through the armamentaria of psychophysics, neurophysiology, and computer modeling as well as the conceptual aides of taxonomic classification and even a kind of metascientific approach that was once called speculative psychology (without pejorative intent). That is, I have tried to define the critical questions in our field, what empirical evidence speaks to these questions, suggest the best possible answers to some of them, and finally, to suggest what might be the most useful future research efforts. This task has resulted in a series of books, a series I consider to be my major career contribution.

More important in the long run, however, is that by self-consciously pursuing such synoptic tasks instead of concentrating on the details of the next experiment, I feel I have achieved more progress toward a general appreciation of the status of our perceptual science than I would have otherwise. I wish I felt as confident that my personal point of view on these matters was a consensus view, but this is probably not the case. Idiosyncratic methodologies can often lead to idiosyncratic sets of conclusions. Nevertheless, I do feel that my emerging point of view is internally consistent if not externally in agreement with what others may have concluded about the state of this science.

The series of books I have written about sensation in general and vision in particular has covered a number of different topics and approaches. First, in my neuroreductionist phase were the *Psychobiology of Sensory Coding* (1973) and then the *Psychobiology of Mind* (1978). These were followed by a transition volume entitled *A Taxonomy of Visual Processes* (1981) in which I first encountered a set of barriers that seemed to separate vision science into two quite distinct parts: A "lower level" portion concentrating on more or less peripheral transmission codes that seemed to be closely correlated with observed neurophysiological findings, and a "higher level," more cognitively penetrated, portion that is dependent on neural networks of such complexity that it seemed unlikely they could ever be unraveled to the point of providing a complete neuroreductionist explanation of the observed perceptual phenomena.

What we know about these higher level phenomena was explored in a fourth book entitled *On Seeing Forms* (1988). By this time I was convinced that the Zeitgeist in contemporary vision science with its heavy emphasis on neuroreductionist and cognitive modular theories was moving in the wrong direction. Many complex visual phenomena, in particular, were rather cavalierly being associated with the abundant neurophysiological data coming from laboratories in which that powerful tool, the single cell microelectrode, was being exploited so elegantly. Although the microelectrode is one of the most important tools for studying the behavior of single cells, it also provided a compelling but misleading force toward interpreting complex visual phenomena in terms of the activity of single neurons. Many of us, on the other hand, were becoming more and more convinced that an ensemble of a very large number of neurons was the true equivalent of perceptual experience. Given the complexity of these ensembles, the hope of a valid neuroreductive theory of perception seemed to be ever more elusive.

My next book, Toward a New Behaviorism: The Case Against Perceptual Reduct*ionism* (1998), was a review of the issues involved in neural reductionism as well as in the reductionist ideas offered by today's computational modelers and cognitive psychologists, clearly the majority movements in current experimental psychology. All three categories of reductionist theory seemed to me to have made serious conceptual errors that needed some clarification. This iconoclastic and, admittedly, somewhat contentious title covered an attempt to show that the classic nonreductive behaviorisms were perhaps closer to some fundamental truth than was the nearly overwhelming body of reductive theory that characterized our science today.

From there, I felt I had responsibility to review just what behaviorism had been in the past and suggest what a modern version might be in the future. That book entitled *The War Between Mentalism and Behaviorism: On the Accessibility of Mental Processes* (2000) was essentially a historical and philosophical effort, but necessary one if I was to maintain the logic of this set of synoptic reviews.

I returned to the topic of reductionism in my next volume, *The New Phrenology: The Limits of Localizing Cognitive Processes in the Brain* (2001). This book was written in an effort to call attention to some of the questionable assumptions of the new imaging approach to localization. This new macroscopic kind of neuroreductionism has become the vehicle for a substantial part of current psychobiological thinking. However, as with so many of the earlier approaches to localization of cerebral mechanisms more central than the sensory and motor systems, there seemed to be some serious conceptual errors that had crept into this attractive and much desired noninvasive approach to cognitive analysis.

Having completed these tasks, I am now free to move back to my main interest—vision—and, in particular, to one of its most difficult problems—form recognition. This present work is an extension and sequel to *On Seeing Forms* (1988) and includes a few updated excerpts from it. I deal here with a topic that was only a small part of that earlier book and concentrate more on the theories than on the psychophysical findings emphasized there. Admittedly, my new approach is different from the one that dominated my earlier thinking. I have become much more of a behaviorist than I could have imagined early in my career and much less willing to consider as valid some of the more imaginative reductive theories of the past. All three reductive approaches, cognitive, neurophysiological, and computational, with their various kinds of explanatory theories, now seem to me to be inappropriate. The reasons for this change in my personal view were detailed in my earlier works; at this point my goal is to show how the scientific study of form recognition can be carried out within the constraints of a modern behaviorism and still be a productive and informative scientific enterprise.

The problem of form recognition in particular and form perception in general is enormously complicated for many different reasons. However, there are three main points that make questions concerning this topic particularly difficult to answer. First, it is clear that some of the most fundamental psychophysical experiments necessary to define the basic nature of form perception have not yet been carried out. In other words, there is still no adequate description of the form recognition process at even a phenomenological level. Theories of even the best-known phenomena are diverse and controversies concerning their origins have raged for decades, if not centuries, without being resolved. Second, many of the supposed neural correlates of form perception are fanciful at best. Third, and finally, computer models and mathematical theories (and, especially, the connectionist or neural net models) that purpose to describe how we see shapes, although sometimes interesting and even enlightening analogs, seem destined to be based on totally different principles, functions, and mechanisms than those likely to account for organic form perception. Although most of my colleagues may be unwilling to accept the presumption, I argue here that most computational models are constrained *not* by the psychobiological facts they presume to model but, instead, by the conceptual limits of today's computer science. However well they *simulate,* and despite some designer's strong arguments, most current developments in the computational theory of form recognition are based on tools available from computer engineering rather than from psychophysical or neurophysiological concepts and data.

The psychology of form recognition, therefore, calls out for a review of what has been accomplished empirically and theoretically in the past, an analysis of what is the current status of the field, and to the extent to which I am capable, an estimate of what can effectively be accomplished in the future. The purpose of this project, therefore, is to bring together what we know (as well as what we do not know) about form recognition. Most of all, however, I reconsider the fundamental questions, consider the usual assumptions, and establish a unified point of view regarding this exciting problem area. Such an interim summary is presented in the final pages of this book.

This book also considers some epistemic questions of what we can know and what we cannot know. One should not talk these days about any aspect of human mentation and behavior without focusing at least at some point in the discussion on what barriers to progress are insurmountable. To suggest that some of the questions that can be asked in this field (or any other) cannot be answered, however, does not imply any supernatural mystery, only that there may be real physical and formal mathematical "in principle" constraints to some of the things perceptual scientists are trying to do. I believe that an appreciation of the limits of a science contributes as much to its maturation as do its empirical findings and theories. As I showed earlier in *Toward a New Behaviorism* (1998), profoundly influential constraints, barriers, and limits do exist in this field as well as in any other science. To deny or ignore them is to slide down a slippery slope to misunderstanding, misdirection, and wasted effort; in short, to a false science that does not truly represent our visual processes.

A final note: It is very easy to characterize this critical consideration of form recognition as being overly pessimistic. In this work as well as in my other books, I have tried to transcend such subjective issues and, in their place, provide as much hard scientific evidence as is available. That there may be some limits to the psychological enterprise is not necessarily "pessimistic" as much as it is "realistic" and scientifically hard-nosed. Unfortunately, there is a powerful vested interest in ignoring questions of this genre as well as some of the already available answers provided by well-accepted science and mathematics that should make us appreciate the real and demonstrable limits of our science. At the very least, it seems to me that critics of the point of view presented here have an obligation to consider the arguments and avoid the personification of any point of view as either pessimistic or optimistic.

ACKNOWLEDGMENTS

I would like to acknowledge at the outset the important personal contributions of a number of people to the completion of this book. This project was initiated while I was a summer visitor in the Psychophysics Laboratory directed by Dr. Lothar Spillman at the University of Freiburg's Institute of Biophysics and Radiation Biology in Germany. Lothar's energy, hospitality, and intellectual vigor all contributed to my interest and enthusiasm for attacking this problem, one that is of continuing interest and excitement for both of us. We have major disagreements about theory and interpretation of data but this has not deterred either of us from appreciating the value of a deep consideration of these matters.

The Department of Industrial Engineering chaired by Professor Gary Hogg under the leadership of Dean Peter Crouch at Arizona State University continues to support my work well beyond my official retirement in 1999. This support is greatly appreciated.

I also want to thank Sondra Guideman, the production editor, and an anonymous copyeditor at Lawrence Erlbaum Associates for their efforts in the production of this book.

As usual, it is my dear Mit-chan who makes it possible for me to make any progress in my professional life. It is to her, as is usual, that this book is dedicated.

—*William R. Uttal*

1

The Form Recognition Problem: Introduction and Preview

1.1. A BEHAVIORAL VIEW OF PERCEPTION

- Behaviorists eschew the study of subjective processes.
- Perception is a subjective process.
- Therefore, behaviorists should not study perception.

This pseudo-syllogism lay at the heart of what was perceived by many as a dark age of perceptual research during the mid 20th century. Instead, the foundation empiricist assumptions of the traditional behaviorist enterprise were interpreted to mean that explicit behavior and the changes in behavior occurring as a result of experience (i.e., studies of learning) should be the main objects of study for a scientific psychology.

A major goal of this book is to demonstrate that the conclusion drawn by this syllogism is incorrect; adherence to an appropriately revised version of behaviorism creates no intrinsic barrier to the study of perception (and, in particular, form recognition) any more than it does to any other aspect of human psychology. Rather, if one operates within the confines of a proper and sound behaviorism, understanding of the relationships between stimuli and perceptual responses can be as illuminating as studies of learning, decision making, or development to name but a few places where psychological science has made many important contributions. To do so, requires that we appreciate the limits on analyzability, reducibility, and accessibility that constrain any attempt to scientifically study how people mentally respond to the complex environment of which they are a natural part. In short, an emphasis on observable behavior is offered as a substitute for the unobtainable reductive goals of current cognitive mentalism.

As the history of mid 20th century psychology is reviewed, it is quite clear that studies of perception did not disappear completely from the scientific scene, even if the main thrust of experimental psychology at the time was directed elsewhere. Studies pursued by European psychologists (especially the German Gestaltists) and related work in such countries as Japan that had been strongly influenced by that European tradition, kept perceptual research at a high level of intensity even as it was more or less quiescent in the United States.

Considerable American progress, however, was made during this same period in what were labeled "sensory" studies. The measurement of visual and acoustic thresholds, both absolute and differential, the study of color mixture, the discovery and formularization of the properties of stimuli (e.g., spatial frequency spectra), and the codes used by the peripheral nervous system made this an exciting time for that subdivision of scientific psychology. Many other of the basic parameters of vision regarding visual space, adaptation to light, and sensitivity to movement were first measured between the 1930s and 1960s. Two books stand out as summaries of the Zeitgeist of the time—Graham's (1965) incorrectly double-titled *Vision and Visual Perception* and Stevens' (1951) *Handbook of Experimental Psychology*. Obviously, perceptual research was not in the mainstream of American psychology during that period. Where "learning and adjustment" deserved seven chapters in Steven's great handbook and four were devoted to human performance, only one was devoted to visual *perception* and one to the *perception* of speech. There is no doubt that implicit acceptance of the syllogism presented at the beginning of this chapter was having a significant chilling effect on perceptual studies even though it had not completely exterminated interest in these topics.

The study of the supposedly more complex responses denoted as perceptual phenomena was, thus, stymied by the reluctance of the kind of behaviorism that dominated psychology during the mid 20th century; phenomenological or mental responses were just not considered valid targets for research. Although most psychologists today would argue that the distinction made between *sensation* and *perception* is a false one, the tradition of using both categories of cognitive experience persists in today's textbooks, many of which have titles such as *Sensation and Perception* (Coren, Ward, & Enns, 1999; Goldstein, 1998; Matlin & Foley, 1996).

An alternative view asserting that what might have heretofore been considered to be the simplest sensory phenomenon is actually no less complicated than the most complex perception is still not generally accepted. If this extreme sensation–perception dichotomy is rejected, however, then the lack of enthusiasm for perceptual studies during the glory days of American behaviorism becomes even more difficult to understand. In that context, it can be argued that the same techniques and approaches that were used to study *sensory* topics might as well be applied to the *perceptual* ones. To do so, however, requires that we understand that the intrinsic limits on studying mental processes are roughly the same for both fields of study (which are really the same field). The special reasons that mental qua perceptual responses were ignored, at the same time that sensory research topics were vigorously pursued, were simply not justified then any more than they are today.

It must be reiterated, however, that a new view of the limits on how any mental process can be studied is required to pursue this logic to its ultimate conclusion. Within the limits of a new, more robust behaviorism, perceptual topics that were of virtually no concern to an older form of behavioral psychologists, can and should now be attacked. Another major goal of this book is to spell out the details of this new approach to the general study of perception and how a specific topic—form recognition—can be attacked in a way that opens new doors to understanding without violating certain fundamental epistemological assumptions that guide a modern behaviorist approach to psychological science.

The specific topic of *form recognition* appears infrequently in Graham's (1965) and in Stevens' (1951) books and then most often only as a name for a method used to explore learning phenomena. Other perceptual phenomena of broad interest in contemporary experimental psychology appear mainly in the form of mostly unexplained and inadequately described demonstrations akin to those provided by the Gestalt psychologists.

Why should this lack of interest in the recognition of forms have been the case given how obviously important a part of visual perception it was? To answer this question in general, we must note it was impeded by the same antiphenomenological philosophy that was embedded in the false syllogism opening this chapter. However, the historical fact that the topics simply had not matured sufficiently for psychological science to be much concerned with them was also important. Nevertheless, vestiges of interest in how we see and recognize objects and forms can be found long ago in the philosophical musings of Plato and Aristotle. Obviously, its roots go back to the origins of natural philosophy. However, the topic did not leap full grown into scientific consciousness until the second half of the 20th century.

Another particular reason for the inattention to form recognition until the middle years of the 20th century was that the developments in computer technology that are currently providing such important new heuristics for studying and theorizing about such areas of human perception were still only the most preliminary glimmers in the eyes of the psychologists and engineers of those times. Therefore, passive forces such as untimeliness and the low level of development in cognate sciences also played a major role in the general disinterest in form recognition research.

However, there were also some very active (as opposed to passive) forces at work from the 1920s through the 1960s that specifically argued against the study of such "mental," "cognitive," "phenomenological" processes exemplified by form recognition. Some of these forces become very obvious when one considers certain of the foundation assumptions of traditional behaviorism. Behaviorism of the time, as noted, was a strongly antimentalistic approach to psychology. Foremost among these assumptions was the rejection of the accessibility, if not the reality, of mental processes. Some behaviorists argued that although the mental processes were "real," they were private and, thus, inaccessible; other philosophers of the time championed the idea that the phenomena of conscious awareness simply did not exist (e.g., Ryle, 1949; Wittgenstein, 1953) and, therefore, any search for it would be futile.[1] Both epistemological and ontological arguments, therefore, coalesced in agreeing that researching perceptual phenomena would be a wasted effort.

Although a modern behaviorist would not dispute the assumption of inaccessibility, the earlier champions of this approach to psychology went on to make a much more expansive (and ultimately destructive) claim that perception was beyond the pale of scientific inquiry. Regardless of which particular rationale drove decision making, the study of perceptual responses was categorized as a mentalist enterprise that could not be achieved and should, therefore, be ignored. In its place, the emphasis should be on the directly observable responses and, in particular, their dynamics over time.

It is a thesis of this book that this conclusion was ill-taken and that visual perception can be and should be studied, albeit within the same epistemic limits confronting any other kind of psychological inquiry; that is, by accepting the same constraints defined by a modern, reformulated behaviorism. This new behaviorism is based on a number of assumptions; some of which are germane to the present discussion and some not. Let us first put to rest some of the irrelevant ones before attending to these that do speak to the topic of perceptual research.

Traditional behaviorism had been afflicted by its critics with extrascientific and extraneous "deficiencies" that have long been a source of confusion and weakness in interpreting its potential as a valid approach to psy-

---

[1]Some "behaviorists," it is also to be appreciated, were actually mentalists. Tolman (1932), for example, was clearly in search of the mental components and structures. His behaviorism was only a methodological one producing objective observations from which he was convinced that he could infer the underlying mental structure.

chological inquiry. Some of these have been in the form of long-term debates between psychologists and philosophers about issues that probably cannot be resolved. For example, a view long (incorrectly) associated with the more radical versions of behaviorism was that there was no such thing as "free will." Rather, it was argued by "radical" behaviorists such as B. F. Skinner and J. B. Watson that all behavior was determined solely by the sequence of stimuli that were presented to the individual. Human behavior, from this perspective, was said to be merely reactive, responding not to conscious and active decision making, but instead only to the probabilities and contingencies that were generated by previous experiences. Mind, if its existence was accepted at all, was assumed to be merely an epiphenomenon, passively following the sequence of motor responses dictated by previous experiences, but incapable of influencing that behavior. In short, humankind was driven by *learned contingencies*, not by any kind of thoughtful reasoning to choose among possible alternatives of various degrees of adaptive utility. It is not at all clear that such an issue, clouded as it is with religious and theological overtones, can ever be resolved.

Closely associated with the denial of free will was the matter of consciousness and its efficacy in determining behavior, a topic of renewed interest in recent years despite the absence of any new scientific findings that speak to the issue.[2] Consciousness, and the method that has traditionally been used to study it—introspection—were rejected on the basis of a presumed inaccessibility. Again, there was a dichotomy of theory—some arguing against the reality of consciousness and others simply asserting its inaccessibility. The result in either case was that topics dealing with conscious responses to stimuli or even endogenously produced experiences such as imagery were de-emphasized. Again, however, it is not at all clear that there is a scientific route to resolving this issue.

Another argument against behaviorism was that it was trivial. In particular (Suppe, 1984) argued that because of its long association with what he considered to be the "rejected" positivist philosophy, it produced an "impoverished science" in which its observations, no matter how empirically correct, were meaningless. He went on to argue that the important questions were simply ignored by behaviorism. The counterargument, of course, is that neither behaviorism nor any other kind of psychology is capable of answering some of the questions humans want to ask. Rakover (1986) responded to the accusation of "triviality" by citing some of the important empirical facts produced by this science and asserting what I be-

---

[2]There are likely to be many who disagree with this statement. However, there are still no scientific answers to the question of how a net of neurons can give rise to consciousness or what is the role of consciousness. In the place of science, we have had to do with fantastic speculations and rampant euphemisms and metaphors that do not provide the barest glimmering of answers to such fundamental questions as those asked here.

lieve is a compelling reminder of the past history of psychology when he said:

> While empirical discoveries in psychology seem to stay invariant over time, theories and explanations change constantly. In fact, what we have [in all of psychology] is no more than a set of very interesting discoveries which we understand only partially. (p. 306)

Thus, trivial or not, and in spite of the enthusiastic desire to provide answers to some deeply important questions, perhaps all that is available to a valid psychological science is behaviorism—a scientific approach that deals with the interpersonally observable and avoids reductive or speculative inferences about what internal processes may be at work.

Finally, radical behaviorists, it was argued, overemphasized the empiricist side of the argument between rationalism and empiricism. Unfortunately, both Watson, and Skinner went so far as to argue that the human infant was born with minimal innate psychological proclivities; everything was learned and heredity played little or no role in the development of the individual. Both argued that a child could be trained to be any kind of a person given the proper training regime. It seems obvious nowadays that such an extreme empiricism was overblown. However, there is still no resolution of the relative influence of heredity and experience respectively, again suggesting the possible existence of another irresolvable controversy.

The fact is that many of these positions, supposedly held by all behaviorists but actually held only by the most extreme adherents, were exaggerated in a way that misrepresented the truly central assumptions of a pure form of behaviorism. Few behaviorists were actually as radical as these "assumptions" suggested. Furthermore, science has marched on in a way that provides a sounder foundation for a new kind of behaviorism. Today, any arguments against genetic or hereditary influences on human behavior are no longer tenable. Modern genetics, whether based on statistical or macromolecular studies, unequivocally demonstrates that our genes are potent contributors to both our cognitive processes and our behavior. The distribution of mental illness in family lines, and the identification of specific genes associated with behavioral tendencies make it clear that the radical empiricism that was sometimes attributed to behaviorists is no longer acceptable.

The concepts of free will and consciousness, however, continue to perplex scientific psychology. Debates about their reality or influence still rage concerning the nature or reality of consciousness (Fodor, 2000; Pinker, 1997) as well as whether or not we have free will. Recently, four articles appeared in a single issue of the journal *American Psychologist*. Kirsch and Lynn (1999), Gollwitzer (1999), Wegner and Wheatley (1999), and Bargh and

Chartrand (1999) presented an interesting new take on the subject. The theme throughout was that rather than freely choosing our own behavioral responses, much that we do is automatically determined. Free will, according to this group of authors, is mainly an illusion due to the *ex post facto* error of thinking that a priori thoughts were the causes of the emitted responses. Such an illusion is based on the implicit assumptions "that people are consciously and processing incoming information in order to construe and interpret the world and to plan and engage in courses of action" (Bargh & Chartrand, 1999, p. 462). The problem for a scientifically sound psychology is that the observed behavior is fundamentally neutral. Either free will or automaticity could account for behavior—there is no way to tell!

It is argued here that, because these controversies are in large part not resolvable, they represent false issues for a scientific psychology. Many proposed resolutions of such debates are dependent on the resolution of a more fundamental problem—*the accessibility of mental processes*. If it is determined that the privacy of mental life is, in point of scientific fact, inviolate either because mind does not exist or because it is not accessible, then such derivative topics as the existence of free will or the efficacy of consciousness in influencing behavior simply become "red herrings." The resolutions of these pseudoissues then, by definition, become unachievable and, therefore, are a priori wasted and misdirected efforts. Consciousness might or might not exist; it might or might not have influence over our behavior; we might or might not be free to determine our own behavior; but, if mental activity is truly inaccessible, then there would be no way to resolve these controversial and woefully persistent issues. In point of fact, although often clothed in what is superficially scientific language, discussions of these classic arguments are usually founded on extrascientific assumptions (e.g., the dehumanization of humankind, value judgments, thinly veiled dualistic concepts, and sociopolitical agenda) as well as the one irrefutable, but curiously unconvincing, piece of evidence—our own personal self-awareness and its attendant illusion of free will.

The bottom line of any discussion of these controversies is that they are probably unresolvable. There is not likely to be any compelling "Turing test" (Turing, 1950) that can distinguish between conscious and automatic behavior (Searle, 1980) even if consciousness does exist. Therefore, let us set them aside and deal only with the interpersonally observable issues. I argue that there are some fundamental scientific issues that can be attacked that transcend the red herrings of consciousness and free will. By considering the foundation assumptions, the case can be made that perception, like sensation and learning, is susceptible to the traditional methods of science if and only if they are tempered by a modern form of behaviorism and our expectations limited by realistic and generally acceptable epistemological constraints.

Now that we have disposed of the unresolvable, the chimerical, the illusory, let us consider some of the assumptions and issues that more accurately represent the conceptual challenges faced by a new behaviorism. I have argued (Uttal, 1998, 2000) that some other controversies and issues are not only germane to the current discussion, but are also fundamental to the development of a perceptual science that does minimal violence to the methodological and philosophical tenets of a modern behaviorism. The following list distills from these earlier works what I am convinced are the necessary assumptions of not only a modern science of perception, in particular, but also a modern psychological science, in general. It is the basis of a realistic science of psychology—one that includes topics like form recognition—and yet is still responsible to the conventional scientific standards of the simpler sciences.

1. Psychophysical data are neutral with regard to underlying mechanisms and can only describe the behavioral functions and transforms carried out by the brain. This is a basic principle of all "black boxes" that can only be examined with input (i.e., stimulus)–output (i.e., response) methods, whether they be organic or inorganic.

2. In principle, a closed complex system can be decomposed into a very large number of equivalent mechanisms. Similarly, a very large number of mechanisms can be designed to produce the same behavior. Therefore, neither definitive bottom-up synthesis nor definitive top-down analysis is possible.

3. Computational, mathematical, and other kinds of formal theories and models are, at best, process descriptions and are also neutral with regard to the underlying mechanisms no matter how well they may describe the process. This a basic principle of all such representational systems—they can only produce descriptive analogs and metaphors, but not unique statements of internal structure. In other words, hypotheses concerning internal processes and mechanisms are separable from descriptions of the system's behavior in any theory striving to "explain" a closed system.

4. The neurophysiological mechanisms that actually underlay all kinds of mental processes are so complicated that they are completely intractable to analysis. Mental processes can never be reductively explained in such terms.

5. Perception is just as real or just as unreal, just as accessible or inaccessible, just as analyzable or nonanalyzable, as any other psychological or mental process and is subject to the same constraints and limits on our understanding as any other.

6. By adopting the psychophysical strategy that allowed substantial progress to be made in what were previously called sensory processes, equiva-

lent progress can also be made in measuring certain aspects of perceptual responses. The psychophysical strategies that continue to be successful include:

   a. Stimuli must be well anchored to independently defined physical measures and attributes.
   b. Responses must be simple (Class A responses as defined by Brindley, 1960) such as same–different discriminations[3] in which "cognitive penetration" is minimized.

7. Because of the irreducibility of mental processes to either cognitive or neural components, we should emphasize a global, molar, configurational approach to the study of form recognition rather than a local or feature oriented one. Perception, in general, is likely to be driven more by relations among a set of components parts than by the nature of the parts.

8. The central goal of any valid psychophysical behaviorism in studying perception should be to determine which attributes of stimuli influence behavior and the functional relationships (hereafter referred to as the *transforms*) between well-defined stimuli and the equally well-measured patterns of responses that are produced by them. The transforms so produced are process descriptions, not reductive explanations, and only formalize what changes occur between stimuli and responses, not how the changes are instantiated. Transforms may be made concrete in the form of functional graphs or mathematical formulae.

9. Psychophysical techniques are powerful tools for identifying the salient dimensions and determining their influence on perception.

A behavioral approach to perceptual science, therefore, should be framed in the context of a search for the descriptions of the transforms that occur between well-defined stimuli and tightly controlled responses. In that context we are able to move ahead from the general properties of a perceptual behaviorism to the specific target of inquiry in this book—the recognition of form.

1.2. ON THE RECOGNITION OF VISUAL FORMS

The human visual system is an extraordinary image processing system. It can detect amounts of electromagnetic energy that are as small, or as

---

[3]Of course, adequate experimental designs such as two alternative-forced choice or SDT procedures must be used to guard against uncontrolled or unmeasured variations in criteria level, a particularly insidious form of cognitive penetration.

nearly so, as they can possibly be (Hecht, Shlaer, & Pirenne, 1942; Sakitt, 1972). It can discriminate between at least tens of thousands of different hue-saturation-intensity combinations. It can detect misalignments in lines that are one fifth the diameter of the eye's receptors (Westheimer & McKee, 1977). However, perhaps the most amazing thing that the visual system does is to recognize the virtually infinite number of possible images that can be projected onto the retina. The images may be distorted, rotated, displaced, magnified, embedded in, camouflaged by, or occluded by distractors of all kinds and yet humans are able to respond appropriately in an overwhelmingly large proportion of instances when confronted with exceedingly complex visual scenes. The exceptions (e.g., illusions) are so unusual and so infrequent that they become curiosities subject to special attention.

The ability to recognize shapes and interpret scenes is indispensable for animals to adapt to their environment. Without it no creature could survive. Predators and other hazards would be ignored until too late. The necessities of life would be bypassed at times that they are desperately needed. Social interaction would be impossible. In fact, unless evolution had provided some adequate kind of form recognizer, the very existence of complex species like ours would probably not have been possible. Visual form recognition is probably as important as any neural process with the possible exception of our cutaneous sensitivity to noxious stimuli. Given that we are visual organisms, however, it is clear that our ability to survive is mainly dependent on our form recognition skills. Certainly we would be hard pressed to have any kind of a civilization without our ability to write and then read—one of the most salient of our form recognition capabilities. Recognition of members of one's tribe, family, or even of one's spouse is required for an ordered society. How could you pick an edible berry, distinguish between prey and predator, or carry out any of the many visual tasks that are required for daily existence in either simple or complex life styles without some kind of form recognition? The point is that accurate form recognition is an extremely important part of the necessary behaviors that determine the success or failure of the evolutionary experiment that mankind represents.

In spite of this central role played by visual form recognition in human history and prehistory as well in the behavior of any other organism that is reasonably high on the evolutionary tree, it is surprising to note that the level of understanding we have achieved of the organic process is so modest. This fact is not always obvious given the extensive mass of scientific and engineering effort that has been directed at mimicking organic form recognition with computers. Form recognition is a central part of the effort to develop artificial intelligence (AI) tools capable of taking over some of the repetitive visual tasks now challenging our industrial and information processing society. Indeed, moderate progress has been made in developing devices and algorithms that do a creditable job in specific applications such as character recognition or simple inspection tasks.

Three intellectual forces have driven the high level of current interest in form recognition research and development. The first is our continuing amazement with the ability of the organic visual system to accurately categorize the nature of an incoming image with enormous speed and accuracy. The second is the need for understanding and simulating such systems. The third is the progress, limited it may be, that has been made in what, heretofore, has been called pattern recognition. Interest has broadened in recent years as computers began to show some promise that they, too, might be able to process images in a way that can substitute for human vision in some well-controlled situations.

However facile humans may be and however easy it is to define the task of recognizing forms, it also must be appreciated that it is an awesomely difficult task to understand exactly how the process is being carried out. More than 25 years ago Bremermann (1971), among others, clearly understood the difficulties involved in what seemed to be even simple form recognition tasks. He pointed out that the problem is not the number of bits in an image (which itself may be reasonably large) but the number of combinations of those bits—a number that may be astronomically high. He further noted that all the mathematical work that had been done had not been able to solve even some of the simplest problems when a device (i.e., a computer vision system) is asked to recognize forms. In his words, "In fact, most theoretical papers on pattern recognition are quite worthless" (p. 31). Bremermann further asserted that at the time he wrote his article, most pattern (i.e., form) recognition problems had not yet been solved.

Speaking more generally of computational complexity and the difficulty in solving some kinds of problems a few years later, Bremermann (1977) noted:

> In another area, artificial intelligence, the excessive computational costs of known algorithms has been the main obstacle to having, for example, computers play perfect games of chess (or checkers, or Go). . . . All known algorithms involve search through an exponentially growing number of alternatives and this number, when search is pursued to the end of the game, exceeds the power of any computing device. . . .
>
> In summary, many mathematical, logical, and artificial intelligence problems cannot now be solved because the computational cost of known algorithms (and in some cases all possible algorithms) exceeds the power of any existing computer. (p. 171)

Bremermann (1977) concluded by making an important point (also made by Casti, 1996) that even though a problem may be "transcomputable" (i.e., the costs of the computation exceed the abilities of digital computation), this does not mean that the real system is not possible. Analog computers may carry out computations that are beyond the abilities of digital computers. Bremmerman continued:

> In that case, if an analog of the system can be obtained, put in the proper initial state, and if the state of the system can be observed, then the system trajectories are predictable, provided that analog system runs faster than the original. If no such analog system is obtainable, then prediction becomes impossible, *even if all of the parts and the laws governing their interactions are know.* (Italics added, pp. 173–174)

The implications of this last italicized statement should be obvious (and a warning) to anyone hoping to understand the myriad of neural interactions that are the psychoneural equivalent of mental activity.

Bremermann (1971) was not alone in raising the complexity issue. An important corollary of *in principle* intractable problems is that many easily stated and superficially simple problems may be impossible to solve *in practice.* Stockmeyer and Chandra (1979) and Meyer (1975) were among those who commented on the difficulty of solving certain kinds of problems with computational algorithms. Stockmeyer and Chandra in particular made the following comment—one that still is worth repeating even giving due consideration to the enormous improvements in computing speed since their time:

> Some kinds of computational problems require for their solution a computer as large as the universe running for at least as long as the age of the universe. (p. 140)

Today, a quarter of a century later, it does not seem we have progressed much further toward the solution of some of the same problems these prescient scholars highlighted then. The combinatorial reasons that they highlighted were inhibiting progress then are as salient now. Although there has been a substantial amount of theorizing about form recognition, there is no question that most of the problems faced by computer vision engineers as well as perceptual psychologists are as refractory to analysis and imitation now as they were 25 years ago. In the following sections, some of these unresolved issues are discussed.

1.2.1. Features Versus Wholes

Perhaps the main reason for the continuing difficulty in developing a universal artificial form recognizer is that the most popular research approach in this area—feature analysis—is just incorrect in terms of its most basic assumptions. Much more is said later in this book about this problem. In brief, however, there is increasing evidence that the human vision system works on the basis of a holistic rather than a feature approach. Currently, however, virtually all computer systems still utilize what are essentially elementalist, local feature-based, techniques. Although the emphasis on parts may be the only strategy available to computer vision engineers (and, thus, a practical necessity), an overemphasis on this form of "elemental" theory may be misdirecting our psychobiological theories away from a more valid explanation of how people seem to so effortlessly recognize forms.

One aspect of the whole versus part issue concerns the relevance of computer-based pattern recognition theories and algorithms as theoretical "explanations" of the organic brain. It is unlikely, I argue here, that any current computer algorithm operates on the basis of techniques, algorithms, and procedures that are the same as those the organic nervous system uses to accomplish similar tasks. We know enough about computers to invent powerful algorithms that permit some useful work to be done. However, it is crystal clear that these useful machines have not achieved the same level of performance as the human visual system. Indeed, there are ample suggestions that the computer vision industry uses techniques and strategies that are constrained more by the nature of the computer and its software than by the nature of the organic system. Current "neural net" or connectionist recognition systems are only distantly related to the great networks of organic neurons that carry out the form recognition process in us. Thus, an important question arises—Do even the most successful computer algorithms function in a way that is sufficiently close to the action of the brain so that they can be assumed to be useful theoretical models for psychologists and other neuroscientists? The major problem in answering this deeply important theoretical question is that we do not have even the glimmerings of understanding of how the brain accomplishes its wonderful recognition feats.

It is surprising to appreciate, therefore, that although the basic facts are not yet at hand, a vigorous controversy has developed and continues to rage concerning the way the organic visual system works. Resolution of this controversy would not only be important because of the promise of better computer vision systems, but also because of the important theoretical understanding that would accrue should we be able to penetrate the actual functioning of the recognition functions of the brain. The specific theoretical controversy is: Does the process of recognizing a form depend more on the general organization of the image or the specific features of which it may be composed. I review the psychophysical and theoretical literature pertaining to this topic later. However, in preview, I must point out that the available findings are not yet definitive and possibly cannot be. Nevertheless, this controversy between the organizational aspects of an image and its local features is a major focus of the discussion in this book and it is important to, at least, define the alternative positions.

There is no point to avoiding the obvious, so let us put it on the table right away: At the present time, most researchers in this field support the idea that recognition, if not all of perception, is mediated by the elemental features of the image. The Gestalt tradition that held otherwise in the more holistically oriented psychology of an earlier time is held in low repute these days by a majority of the scholars who are actively studying this problem. One reason that the feature-oriented perspective is so strong today is that it is reciprocally supported by the dominant reductionist and elemental traditions of cognitive psychology, neurophysiology, and computer programming on the one hand and the difficulty of producing a formal definition of "arrangement" on the other.

The argument presented here is that, even though most of our current theory and development work in form recognition is based on some kind of analysis into features, this is the wrong direction in which to proceed. A more valid explanation of how people see would better be framed in global or configural rather than local elemental terms. Making this case requires that we examine the form recognition process in detail from several different points of view.

It is somewhat surprising that the molar nature of human form recognition was clear from the beginning of the information-computer revolution during the last half century. Dreyfus (1992) called our attention to a comment made by Shannon (the person usually given credit for introducing information theory into modern engineering and science) that was discussed in an article by Rosenblith 40 years ago (1962):

> Efficient machines for such problems as pattern recognition, language translation, and so on, may require a different type of computer than we have today. It is my feeling that this is a computer whose natural operation is in terms of patterns, concepts, and vague similarities, rather than sequential operations on ten-digit numbers. (pp. 309–310)

Dreyfus also made the same point himself throughout both the 1992 and the original version (Dreyfus, 1972) of his iconoclastic book. Repeatedly he refers to the need for global knowledge and the need for a holist rather than an atomist or elementalist approach as we attempt to solve the problems of artificial intelligence. He argued simply that no current theory or model of pattern recognition, applied or arcane, is functioning in the same way as the configuration sensitive brain. Although, as I mentioned earlier, we have no "killer argument" to prove this conjecture since we do not know how the brain works, we see in Chapter 3 that an increasing body of indirect psychophysical evidence generally supports this molar hypothesis.

1.2.2. The Neutrality of Mathematics, Neurophysiology, and Behavior

A related premise of this present work is that success in mathematical simulation or in engineering useful devices is sometimes misunderstood as a valid theoretical explanation of the information-processing mechanism underlying the analogous human recognition process. As noted, virtually all of our technology is based on a feature oriented, elementalist approach to the problem. Indeed, pattern recognition (the words of choice among engineers and computer scientists) is often defined exclusively in the terminology of feature analysis and subsequent identification by a process of comparison or matching of these features. Sometimes such a simulation may be successful in superficially imitating some limited aspect of human performance. However, the review of the basic perceptual literature presented in Chapter 3 strongly suggests that an algorithmic, feature processing approach is not the correct direction from which to seek understanding of the organic process. What has all too often happened in this field is that the available tools and techniques of mathematics, science, and engineering are carelessly and glibly metamorphosized into psychobiological theories of organic form recognition in total disregard of what perceptual research on living organisms tells us. Students of the artificial intelligence movement such as Dreyfus (1972, 1992), in addition to challenging the feature approach, have repeatedly stressed the need for the knowledge-based processes that characterize form recognition processes in humans.

There are some other general reasons for this state of affairs. One to which I have frequently called attention is that form recognition is a mental process and mental processes and the mechanisms that account for them are extremely difficult, if not impossible, to access and analyze (Uttal, 1998, 2000). It is impossible to directly measure or even define the internal mental processes that account for form recognition simply because we have only overt and observable behavior to use as an assaying tool. I argued in these earlier books, as well in the introduction to this chapter, that both behavior and mathematics, however excellent they are as a means of describing the outcome of some cognitive activity, are intrinsically incapable of reductively explaining the specific mechanisms that account for that behavior. In other words, a basic premise of a modern behaviorist psychology must be that any of a very large number of different internal information-processing mechanisms could account for identical external behavior and, as a corollary, there is no way to distinguish between them. In other words, any behavior can be interpreted as the result of many different mechanisms *and* many mechanisms may produce the same behavior.

In addition, it now becoming appreciated that although some would argue that neurophysiology can and has provided an entrée into explaining the cognitive mechanisms accounting for form recognition, it is much more likely that both the salient neural networks and the cognitive structures are so complex that they are forever beyond our grasp. The difficulty of analyzing redundantly encoded systems that may involve hundreds of thousands of neurons to represent even the simplest perceptual experience is vastly misunderstood. It is only recently that the difficulty of solving some very simple problems has begun to be appreciated (see the discussions of Bremermann, 1971; Stockmeyer & Chandra, 1979; Casti, 1996, p. 12). "Reverse engineering" of psychologically significant neural networks is at very least an extremely difficult, and probably an impossible one.

In short, mathematical and computer models, behavior, and neurophysiology are all incapable of specifying the underlying structure and function of cognitive processes. They are, in one vocabulary, neutral on this matter. However pessimistic such a conclusion may seem to some reductively oriented cognitive psychologists, others of us believe it is a more realistic expression of the enormous problems encountered when one attempts to study such a complex mechanism as the brain.

1.2.3. Lexicographic Difficulties

The study of perceptual process has also been continuously hindered by inadequate definition of many of the terms involved in cognitive or mental activity. What exactly is it that we mean by the term *recognition?* Is this the best term to both denote and connote the process? What other theoretical baggage does such a term have? It does not take long to realize that the mentalist vocabulary generated for use in this field of science is very resistant to lexicographic precision and uniqueness. Indeed, there is a continuing problem concerning whether or not the terms we use actually denote specific psychobiological realities. It is entirely possible that looking for a *recognition* mechanism would be futile. The word may actually describe the design of the psychologist's experimental procedure rather than some kind of psychobiological reality. The scientific literature is filled with experiments that purport to study recognition. However, a close inspection of this literature suggests that the denotative boundaries of this research topic are so broad as to include many topics and processes that are only distantly related to each other. The word *recognition*, like so many other psychological terms, simply may not be precisely enough defined to avoid carrying an excessive amount of connotative and theoretical baggage. Thus, it may not adequately guide research in this field. Achieving a more precise definition of some of these central terms, therefore, is also an important task for this book.

In the absence of precise definitions and the extreme difficulty, if not impossibility, of either directly or indirectly examining covert psychological mechanisms, psychologists often wander from the most germane goals.

Sometimes this wandering leads them to uncritically adopt ideas and theories from other fields of science as putative explanations or theories of form recognition. In some other cases "studies of form recognition" turn out to be studies of other psychological activities unrelated to the actual subject of interest and far distant from what I designate later in this chapter as the critical questions of this field of research. Indeed, a good bit of the form or pattern recognition literature seems to be what the ethologists would call "displacement activity"—activity carried out just because it *can* be carried out in place of the activities that *should* be carried out. Uhr (1966) went even further when he said:

> The bulk of experimental work on perception has studied what seem to me peripheral problems. Whereas the whole perceptual process is directed towards recognition, most psychologists have chosen to examine the ancillary processes whereby an image can be distorted and, conversely, the processes that the brain uses to regularize distorted images. (p. 57)

The quotation from Bremmerman (1971) at the start of this book makes the same point.

The ethological analogy is—birds often collect stones when they should be fighting off competitors or seeking a mate or food. Fish sometimes circle about aimlessly when confronted with challenges to their territory rather than taking the necessary defensive actions. In an analogous way, psychologists often study memory or visual form discrimination or detection when they should be trying to identify the basic factors involved in form recognition. In fact, there is a surprising paucity of instances in which even the most fundamental questions concerning form recognition are asked. Little research is directed to the specific questions revolving around the problem of form recognition and how much is research "displacement activity." Although some of this misdirected research may be useful in solving some other problem in psychology, much of it shoots off research arrows that do not even go in the approximate direction of the target labeled—"How do we recognize forms?"

An additional problem is that exactly what is the form or shape or pattern or configuration of the physical stimulus is usually not adequately defined. Just what is a form or a pattern? How, precisely, does one term differ from another? How do we go from a picture to a quantitative description of a stimulus that allows us to use the same powerful psychophysical techniques that are available when one is trying to relate other more easily defined aspects of the physical stimulus (such as its wavelength) to the observed response? In other words, how do we represent stimuli? Form recognition is a compelling concept that is intuitively satisfying, but one that has inadequate quantitative anchors to the physical stimulus world because of the absence of a solid objective measure of that elusive property—form. The task in this case is to determine what kind of a representation system and what dimensions are best suited for the study of form.

Several interesting attempts have been made to provide a quantitative coding scheme or language (i.e., a representation system) for shape and form, some of which are discussed in Chapter 2. It must be acknowledged at the outset, however, that none is completely satisfactory. Some fail because they simply do not work well. Others produce representations that may not be the ones actually used by the nervous system and, thus, may either introduce attributes that are irrelevant to the perceptual process or ignore others that are essential. For example, the analysis of an image into its Fourier or spatial frequency components sometimes loses the psychophysical essence of the image as the procedure converts qualitative arrangement into a numerical representation. Unfortunately, such a transformation from the spatial domain to the frequency domain results in a new form that itself must be recognized. The problem has hardly been solved in this situation; rather, the key issue has merely been deferred. This generation of what may become an infinite regress is reminiscent of the historical invocation of the homunculus as a solution to other kinds of cognitive problems. This holds true even if there are spatial frequency analyzers in the periphery of the nervous system; only the representation task has been carried out, not the classification, conceptualization, or recognition one that is the heart of the problem.

1.2.4. Some Contrasting Strategies

A closely related issue concerns the plausible alternative strategies that may be used to achieve form recognition by the nervous system. What has now become the standard feature oriented model implicitly, if not explicitly, assumes a two-step process. First, stimulus images are usually supposed to be decomposed into sets of geometrical components or features and represented as lists of those features in some appropriate coding scheme. This first step, as I have noted, is referred to as the process of *representation*. The feature lists are then supposedly compared in a second step against a set of patterns or templates using the same representation scheme and stored as a result of previous experience or training in the various memory stores presumed to exist in the cognitive system. This second step is variously referred to as the process of *comparison*, *matching*, or *correspondence*. Whenever a system of this kind is invoked, the processes of representation, on the one hand, and matching or correspondence, on the other, are considered to be essential, but separate, parts of the form recognition process. A further fundamental, but infrequently expressed, premise of this point of view is that the comparison or correspondence matching process is the essential part of the classification or recognition process.

Furthermore, it is usually assumed by the proponents of the feature comparison process that the establishment of the library of comparison forms required previous "learning," a process that is considered by some psychologists to be a necessary prior preparatory step in the recognition process. The question posed there becomes: How do we create a library of templates should that be the strategy that is actually used by the nervous system? The problem faced by any template comparison model, of course, is overcoming the ponderous combinatorics of the matching process. That is, the number of comparisons that must be made between a form and all members of the supposed library of comparison forms, even if they are to be carried out in parallel, must be enormous for a form to be recognized. It can be argued, that the time required to carry out such a process in sequential order would be so great that no information-processing system, including our brain, could conceivably operate on this principle. Real-time operation using a sequential or serial comparison would be unthinkably slow. Parallel processing ameliorates the time handicap of serial processing, but does not reduce the enormous computational load required by a template system.

The "break into pieces, represent, and compare with a library of previously learned images" approach, which is the primary standard contemporary model of the recognition process, is based on concepts and ideas that are relatively easy to invent and to implement in the form of computer programs. It is also, furthermore, easy to suggest experimental psychophysical research protocols that may superficially support this point of view.[4] However, it is important to reiterate that the results forthcoming from these experimental designs, like all psychophysical findings, are neutral with regard to the actual form recognition processes being carried on in the brain. Furthermore, some of the best known and classic demonstrations of form recognition suggest that the feature oriented approach may be completely incorrect in terms of its most fundamental assumptions—particularly those incorporating serial sequencing of the analysis-into-features and template comparison stages.

It is possible that much of the difficulty in either developing a good computer vision system or understanding the form recognition process in humans arises because our theories are still not evolving in the right direction. That is, the feature oriented-comparison model that permeates both psychology and computer science may be inadequate to deal with the enormous complexity and inaccessibility of the processes actually carried out by the brain. Although there is no question that the human visual system serves as an indisputable existence proof that precise, real-time form recog-

---

[4]It is equally easy to suggest experimental designs that support virtually any other approach. Indeed, a fundamental problem faced by psychophysicists is that any theory can find empirical support if the conditions of the experiment and the stimuli are judiciously chosen.

nition is possible, there is no evidence yet in either theory or practice that we have managed to identify those process and procedures that underlie this powerful organic data processing ability. Simply to carry the current paradigm forward, however useful it may be in filling journals with esoteric and arcane mathematical derivations or highly speculative and unlikely cognitive or neural constructs, may not be the most expedient way to solve the problem. I believe that a breakthrough can come only when a new paradigm is provided. To understand the advantages of any new approach, the fundamentals of the old one must be appreciated. That is the main purpose of the next section.

1.3. A BRIEF HISTORY OF THE CONCEPT OF FORM

In this section, a brief history of the concept of form is presented. This section simply highlights a few of the major milestones but does not exhaustively review the topic. Many other authors (including Boring, 1942; Klein, 1970; Marx & Hillix, 1963; Zusne, 1970) have discussed some of the historical and philosophical issues that antedate current views of the form recognition problem. I have already pointed out one great gap in the historical continuity of research that has occurred as a result of what I believe was a misunderstanding of what behaviorists said about perceptual research. Nevertheless, there are other historical milestones prior to the behaviorist "perceptual dark ages" that are especially important as we consider the problem of form recognition. Some of these are now briefly discussed.

1. First consider the nature of form by the classic Greek philosophers. Much of their concern revolved around abstract concepts of what was meant by a *form*. Although some of their thoughts seem distant and even naïve from a contemporary perspective, one can often discern an early intuitive insight into their use of the term that helps us even today to understand some part of the form recognition problem. Plato and Aristotle, for example, considered forms to be the "universal unchanging aspects" of something that absolutely defined or even created its existence. Although this seems far from the geometrical manner in which we think about form today, it is far closer to the modern connotations of the word than is immediately apparent. The classic idea of what constituted the "essence of something" comes close to the concept of the primacy of "organization" or "configuration" with which many contemporary scholars are comfortable. It replaces the "essence of a thing" (phrased in terms of the parts of which it is made) with the notion that there is some essential aspect that transcends a simple list of those parts. Aristotle and Plato could have used Fig. 1.1 to make this point if it had been available

FIG. 1.1. This figure, which has become a classic, is among the strongest a priori evidence that the local features of which a global form is constructed matter less than the global form itself. Many other similar pictures (e.g., Green & Courtis, 1966, Blesser et al. 1973, and many illustrations in Hofstadter, 1985, make the same point. This one is from Kolers (1970). Reprinted with permission from Academic Press.

to them. This figure presents a set of exemplars of a single form in which no individual member of the set shares any of the local features or component parts with another. Nevertheless, all are immediately "recognized" or "conceptualized" as members of a particular class. Obviously this is because of some configurational aspect that transcends the nature of the particular individual parts that make up each form. It is this universal overall property—analogous to the Platonic and Aristotelian form—that ties them together within the confines of a single rubric. There are, of course, other subtleties of Aristotle's use of the word *form* that differ from this interpretation. His assertion that form persists indefinitely both before and after the life time of the object[5] must be considered a somewhat extreme, and from the point of view of a contemporary physicalist materialism, an unsatisfactory part of the defi-

---

[5] The form of an object can be preserved in some other medium (a drawing or a story) but the notion of an independent existence of a form without some instantiating medium is what was being proposed here. This extra-materialistic premise is rejected.

nition. His use of form in this sense was a metaphysical statement rather than a physical one. Implicit in Aristotle's philosophy, on the other hand, was something with which many of us are quite comfortable—his holistic approach to form. Klein (1970) noted that Aristotle, perhaps reflecting the views of many of his contemporaries, was a proto-Gestaltist when he (Aristotle) asserted that "The whole is of necessity prior to the part" (Klein, p. 92).

2. Another important influence on the shaping of our concepts of form came from the Arab philosophers of the 10th and 11th centuries when Europe was intellectually quiescent. Of these, two are of special importance. Avicenna (980–1037) dealt with form as a property of a material objects, a property comparable to the matter of which it was composed. His distinction was based on a theological need to differentiate an immaterial God (who could be characterized totally by form alone) from material objects (which had the properties of both matter and form.) The distinction between matter and form made by Avicenna was a subtle and largely unappreciated precursor of later thought concerning the nature of form. It distinguished between the material aspects and the organizational aspects of a form in a way that is currently quite acceptable in modern scientific circles once it is stripped of its theological baggage. Indeed, an analogy can be drawn between Avicenna's "form" and Shannon's information theory. There is no question, however, that Avicenna and many philosophers of later times and other places were more concerned about the theological implications of form than about its role as a measure or property of objects in the material world. In this regard, the Greek's nontheological and naturalist approach actually should be considered to be conceptually more advanced than the Arab theological philosophers. Avicenna's successor Averroes (1126–1198) followed in these same intellectual footsteps. He argued that although God was defined by pure existence and man by both matter and form, that man could hope for some kind of a spiritual immortality because the matter and the form that defined human existence could exist separately from each other—an idea that is also quite inconsistent with modern materialism. Incidentally, Averroes was among the first to question reductionism—a concern that has arisen anew in contemporary science.

3. Albrecht Dürer (1471–1528), the great medieval artist was also fascinated by form and actually wrote one of the first mathematical studies of geometry (Dürer, 1525). Indeed, some consider him to be the grandfather, if not the father, of the modern quantitative geometry of form called morphometrics.

4. Francis Bacon (1561–1626) took an entirely different tack than did the theologically oriented Arab philosophers. He was one of the first true materialists when he described his concept of the meaning of "form." To him, form was not some kind of a trans- or metaphysical concept but, rather, was another measure of the true physical essence of an object, even taking priority

over the matter of which it might be composed. Thus, form took on a whole new role, not as a secondary property of an object, but as the primary one.

5. The concept of form was further developed by John Locke (1632–1704) when he championed a point of view that was similar to that expressed by other empiricists of the 17th century, particularly his colleagues in the British school. In developing his notion of primary and secondary qualities, it seems clear that Locke placed form among the primary qualities of an object. *Extension* and *figure* were the terms he used, but these are transparent synonyms for *form*. Other properties of objects such as color and smell were deemed to be secondary. Implicit in the distinction made by the empiricists between the primary and secondary attributes was a difference between the actual physical attributes of an object and its perceived or interpreted properties. The primary properties were extant regardless of being observed or not. The secondary ones were interpretations constructed by the observer and thus completely dependent on the act of observation. The classifications of primary and secondary attributes, therefore, suggested to him the thoroughly modern idea that there is a difference between the measurable dimensions of the physical stimulus and the dimensions of the perceived experience. (This is, of course, a distinction that often seems to be opaque to beginning students when first introduced to sensory psychology.) It is important to appreciate however, that Locke dealt with form as a composite of other more elemental features. Although form is a *primary* attribute, Locke believed that it had to be created by combining simpler parts of the stimulus by a process of association resulting from experience. The "associationist" position taken by Locke and other later British empiricists, however, is quite contrary to the holistic use of the word *form*. It introduced the component or feature-based line of thinking that has obviously maintained considerable influence among reductionist psychologies even today.

6. Gottfried Wilhelm Leibnitz (1646–1716), on the other hand, treated form quite differently than did Locke. Leibnitz, another one of the very special intellects whose interests ranged broadly across philosophy and the natural sciences, had been strongly influenced by both the writings, inventions, and discoveries of biologists such as Marcello Malpighi (1628–1694) and Antonie van Leeuwenhoek (1632–1723) and by the philosophers René Descartes (1596–1650) and Benedict de Spinoza (1632–1677). He was, therefore, a rare combination—more biological than the philosophers and more philosophical than the biologists. Leibnitz' attitude toward form was very holistic. As a rationalist, he was more interested in the nature of the entire mind than of percepts, but clearly his holist notions are precursors of the Gestalt school with its heavy emphasis on perception per se.

7. Immanuel Kant (1724–1804), on the other hand, had quite a different view of what form was. He suggested that form was not a material property at all. It had no external existence, but was purely a manifestation of mental

processing. One could not find form in the external world but only in terms of the order that was imposed on the elements or components of an external scene by the observer. In championing this idealistic viewpoint he was, it seems, back-tracking from the emerging 16th and 17th century materialism of Leibnitz, Locke, and Bacon to a version of Berkeleyian idealism.

8. George Santayana (1863–1952) and Georg Simmel (1858–1918) were both very much in the tradition of their predecessor George Berkeley (1685–1753) as well as being influenced by Kant. All were idealists supporting the idea that the form of an object was something that was constructed only as we mentally processed some stimulus scene. Berkeley, for example, proposed that such geometrical forms as lines and angles do not really exist until mathematicians described them or humans perceived them. The reality of form to him was purely a mental construction, not a property of the physical stimulus. Indeed, to Berkeley, the reality of the external world was very much in doubt. Santayana, writing two centuries later reflected some of these same views. He distinguished between the *medium*, the *expressiveness*, and the *form* of an object. To him medium and expressiveness were innate attributes of the object but that form arose a result of mental processes and was not "of the object." Simmel, less well known than Santayana, also followed the idealist principle that form arose out of our experiences; that form was created by the observer. Clearly this idealist viewpoint is contrary to the materialist physicalism of contemporary science. It unfortunately tends to take percepts, in general, and percepts of form, in particular, outside the domain of science by denying them a role as measurable properties of an object.

9. Ernst Mach (1838–1916), another Leonardian polymath by any one's standards, was one of the intellectual sources that led both to modern behaviorism and to modern psychophysical research. He also had a powerful influence on modern operational and positivistic philosophy and argued strongly that description was the best possible, if not the only possible, kind of explanation. His influence was felt on so many fields of science that it is hard to limit any discussion of Mach to any single topic, but clearly he was one of the strongest proponents of the point of view that the external world is available to us only through our sensations. In doing so, Mach may also be considered to be the first authentic psychophysicist. He clearly supported the idea that there existed a close correlation between the physical stimuli and the resulting sensations. Indeed, the only things we can measure about the external world, he suggested, were our sensations. One does not have to go to deeply into the literature to realize that the functional correspondence that he identified between the physical stimulus and the psychological response is also the fundamental assumption of virtually all of modern psychophysics and a necessary part of any successful scientific psychology. Mach also championed the idea that all objects were made up of elements such as

color and texture. In the context of this present work, perhaps his most important contribution was to include as a separable element that we now call *form*, but in a very modern sense of the word. Mach's thoughts, therefore, about the nature of reality contributed to the elementalist view that culminated in Wundt and Titchener's structuralism. Surprisingly, however, given his notion of form as a separate element, he must also be considered one of the major contributors to the holistic idea of indivisible form that was later to be called Gestalt theory.

10. Christian Von Ehrenfels (1859–1932) developed Mach's ideas of form as a separate element or attribute of objects to the extreme. Von Ehrenfels' work went so far as to give precedence and priority to the "global form" or the "Gestalt" attribute of an object or a melody. The first use of the term *Gestalten* is usually attributed to him. He went much further than Mach's simple acceptance of the existence of just another attribute called *configuration* or *form* when he suggested that the other elements of an object (such as the components or parts of which it is constructed and their properties) are secondary in determining our perceptual experience. His concepts of the Gestalt of an image or the melody of a musical piece transcends the earlier notions of the accumulation or even the organization of the parts. Rather, the Gestalt is an independent property in its own right. To the degree that the word *Gestalt* is at least partially synonymous with the word *form*, Von Ehrenfels can be considered to be the immediate precursor of the Gestalt school of German psychologists. However, although strongly emphasizing the importance of the Gestalt, Von Ehrenfels still considered it as only one of many influential elements in defining the nature of our perceptual experiences. It was left to the Gestalt psychologists of the next intellectual generation to make the next great step and reject elementalism and elemental properties altogether.

11. The Gestalt School was obviously the culmination of ideas as old as those of Aristotle and as recent as those of Mach, Von Ehrenfels, and numbers of other psychologists who were influenced by them. Both Zusne (1970) and Marx and Hillix (1963) detailed the rich intellectual history of those times and described the contributing role of William James (1842–1910) and John Dewey 1859–1952) in the United States and a group of German psychologists at the University of Gottingen including G. E. Muller (1850–1934), David Katz (1884–1957), and Edgar Rubin (1886–1951). The full blown Gestalt approach to form perception, however, came into its own in another German university—the one at Frankfurt. There Max Wertheimer (1880–1943), Wolfgang Kohler (1887–1967), and Kurt Koffka (1886–1941) created the modern version of a holistic, molar, Gestalt psychology. The main principle of their approach to the study of form perception was that the elements or parts just do not matter when a stimulus figure leads to a perceptual response. The parts were just place markers that provided indicators of spatial arrangement—the

primary stimulus attribute. No longer was the Gestalt or the configuration just another property or element of an acoustic or visual object; from their point of view it was the predominant factor in defining our perceptual experiences. It is important to appreciate that the Gestalt approach is also a relativistic one—a part was important only in terms of its relationships to other parts, not in itself. Whether this is merely a pun on the words *relation* or *relativity* or whether the fathers of the Gestalt school were really influenced by the rise of relativism in the physical sciences is uncertain. However, it does seem possible that there was some intellectual influence exerted on the development of Gestalt psychology by the new relativistic physics that was gaining such credibility in other areas of science. This possibility is enhanced by the fact that both movements occurred in the early part of the 20th century and in the same general region. Frankfurt, Germany and Bern, Switzerland are close in space and Einstein's work preceded that of the Gestalt psychologists by only a few years. Whatever the exact connection, the idea that what was seen was dependent mainly on the configuration or form of the stimulus fell on fertile grounds. In this same vein of relativistic thinking, the Gestaltists also specifically rejected the then popular idea that the perceptual significance of the points of the retina remained constant. This idea had been called the "local sign" by Rudolf Hermann Lotze (1817–1871), another one of the remarkably broad intellects of psychological history. The Gestalt psychologists argued, to the contrary, that what the stimulation of a particular location on the retina ultimately would mean perceptually was dependent on the role that that point played in the overall form. This is now a widely accepted premise of modern perceptual psychology as we see in Chapter 3. Gestalt psychology had a number of other philosophical ramifications that are outside the realm of topics considered in this book. Nevertheless, the tradition that emerged at the University of Frankfurt in the early part of the 20th century, perhaps more than any other, brought the idea that the primary aspects of a figure were its configurational properties to the fore. Furthermore, the Gestaltists, the radical configurationists that they were, enunciated a system of principles that included laws of grouping that still remain a central part of psychology's basic facts. On the other hand, Gestalt psychology may have been somewhat ahead of its time. The typical research paradigm they used was the critical demonstration. This methodological propensity, along with the total failure of the erroneous physiological model that the Gestaltists adhered to, led to a diminution in interest in their approach in the second half of the 20th century. One can only imagine what might have been the course of modern psychological theory if the early Gestalt psychologists like Wertheimer, Koffka, and Kohler had had computer controlled displays with which to work and had known some more about the actual physiology of the brain.

12. Another trend in the study of form was going on at virtually the same time as psychologists and philosophers were examining it from a qualitative

point of view. The mathematization or quantification of form studies was gaining both popularity and power. Its roots could be traced back as far as Durer, as noted earlier, but the mathematical trend was long inhibited by the absence of the appropriate mathematics. Even Thompson's (1917) geometric approach, as seminal to thinking about form as anything, was essentially a nonmathematical one. It took many additional developments in statistics, biometrics, and computation (specifically factor analysis and multidimensional mathematics) to bring *morphometrics*—the mathematical study of form per se—to its current state of development. I discuss this important topic extensively in Chapter 2.

13. In recent years, the molar approach of the Gestalt psychologists has been submerged under a cognitive and essentially elementalist landslide. As I have already noted virtually all current theories invoke some sort of feature analysis. The reasons for this theoretical onslaught are clear and are worth highlighting again. First, computer modeling is, of necessity, an approach that depends on the analysis of global forms into isolatable and computer interpretable components and sequential steps. Second, advances in neurophysiology have centered on the activity of individual neurons and their sensitivity to relatively simple, but separable, trigger features. Third, we still do not have a good mathematical way to describe organization and form. Our mathematics is predominantly analytic, rather than synthetic.

This, then, in a nutshell is a brief history of the development of the idea of form and a list of some of the main contributors to its study. Many scholars, other than those listed here, have participated in the development of the concept of form and the definition of the term. However, these are the major historical players. We now have arrived at a point where modern times begin concerning the study of form recognition from an increasingly empirical perspective. In some ways it is sad that the philosophers are less likely to contribute to this discussion today than are the barefooted empiricists. The sheer abundance of the data makes it clear that the value of philosophers as organizers and systematizers would be of great value. Perhaps this book partially fills that role until more technically trained philosophers can attend to this problem area. Now, however, I turn to the remarkably difficult task of trying to unravel the tangled meaning of the terms *form, recognition*, and other related ones that are germane to the topic at hand.

1.4. DEFINITIONS OF TERMS

The investigation of any mental process, no matter what the instigating circumstances or motivating interest, is always confounded by the difficulty of specifying a sufficiently precise denotation as well a consensual connotation of the words used to represent particular concepts, constructs, or objects of interest. The difficulty in studying cognitive functions, of which form recognition is only one component, is no different than in any other field of psychology. Indeed, as the science has prospered and the techniques have matured, it is not always clear that the hypothetical mental entities (see MacCorquodale & Meehl, 1948 for a consideration of the meaning of the critically important term "hypothetical constructs") we identify are real entities or only manifestations of the design of our experiments or the theories that have been proposed. The problem is that there is no a priori reason that any perceptual function (e.g., detection, discrimination, or recognition) need necessarily be a demarcatable process that can be assigned exclusively to a particular part of the brain or attributed to an independent cognitive component. It could as well be an attribute of the overall functioning of the brain or the collective action of a group of components of a coherent and heavily interconnected and thus, in principle, unanalyzable cognitive system. Nevertheless, an enormous effort has been directed in recent years toward the localization of a wide variety of sometimes ill-defined and falsely isolated mental processes in particular parts of the brain.[6] New tools of enormous power such as the functional Magnetic Resonance Imaging technique (fMRI) have offered new opportunities to examine brain anatomy and activity and have promised to relate metabolic differences to psychological processes. Although there are a number of purely technical problems involved in the application of this device (Uttal, 2001; Van Orden & Papp, 1997; Van Orden, Pennington, & Stone, in press; Vishton, personal communication, 2000) the lexical problems involved in defining the mental processes to be localized, usually considered to be the easiest, may actually be the most problematic.

The psychobiological reality of virtually any mental concept (e.g., mind, learning, planning, emotion, thinking, and so forth) is always subject to question, if not precise definition. The historical analysis presented in Uttal (2001) is not encouraging. Virtually all the terms used to denote mental activity have been transient throughout that history and there is no evidence that we are converging on a consensus of what constitutes an acceptable taxonomy of mental processes. Each psychologist seems to invent his or

---

[6] The problem of the localization of psychological processes in the brain is dealt with in another book (Uttal, 2001) and I do not want to belabor the point here. Let it be sufficient to summarize the arguments presented there in the following skeletal form:

1. The psychological processes to be localized are so vaguely defined that the entire process is questionable.
2. The statistical methods and hardware devices that are used in an effort to localize mental processes, however direct they may superficially seem, are actually highly problematic.
3. The chain of logic used in associating psychological processes with particular sites in the brain is fragile and built on assumptions that cannot always be justified.

her own hypothetical construct in an ad hoc or a priori manner that is often highly idiosyncratic. Many of these constructs are simply artifacts of method or imprecise, however necessary, artifices of verbal communication. Clearly, the meanings of many of the psychological terms that we use are all too often taken for granted and the difficulties involved in their precise definition ignored as we submerge them under the superficialities of technology and methodology.

At the present time, therefore, it is not clear, that any hypothetical psychological function, should it exist, is uniquely or even mainly associated with a particular region of the brain. The difficulties in untangling the components of a highly interactive and nonlinear system are well known in engineering but usually ignored in psychobiology.

Very often, in psychology in particular, vigorous controversies between different schools of thought eventually are ultimately resolved by agreement between the contending theories on a joint acceptance of the meaning of some term. It is for this reason that I prefer to set the stage for the discussion to follow with a minilexicon in which my use of a few of the critical words is clarified to the maximum possible extent. The following paragraphs provide a shortlist of the key words I feel are especially important in the discussion presented in this book. It must be acknowledged, of course, that word definitions are only what people agree them to be. Nevertheless, the main point I make in discussing the following definitions is that some of the traditional meanings assigned to some of these words may actually preempt the answers to what are still controversial questions. This happens because there is often sufficient extraneous meaning attached to each of these words that can actually force theoretical thinking in directions not supported by robust data. It is for this reason an effort must be made to determine the nature of this superfluous semantic content.

1.4.1. Form

Because this is a book about *form* recognition, lets begin with a consideration of the meaning of this central concept itself. If one takes the time to review the literature in this field it quickly becomes obvious, even at this cursory level of examination, that there have been a number of different words with roughly the same meaning regularly substituted for *form*. *Pattern, shape, configuration*, and even that elusive-to-define Germanism—*Gestalt*—have been used over the years to designate this key term. There are subtle differences, however, in the connotation or denotation of each of these words that should have, but did not, inhibited their more or less careless use as synonyms for *form*. To make this point, let us look at some dictionary definitions of each one. My computer dictionary (The American Heritage Talking Dictionary, Version 4.0 1995) offers the following major definitions for these terms:

pat·tern *n.* **1. a.** A model or an original used as an archetype. **b.** A person or thing considered worthy of imitation. **2.** A plan, diagram, or model to be followed in making things: *a dress pattern.* **3.** A representative sample; a specimen.

con·fig·u·ra·tion *n.* **1. a.** Arrangement of parts or elements. **b.** The form, as of a figure, determined by the arrangement of its parts or elements. See note at **form. 2.** *Psychology* Gestalt

Ge·stalt *n.* **1.** A physical, biological, psychological, or symbolic configuration or pattern of elements so unified as a whole that its properties cannot be derived from a simple summation of its parts.

shape *n.* **1. a.** The characteristic surface configuration of a thing; an outline or a contour.

form *n.* **1. a.** The shape and structure of an object. **b.** The body or outward appearance of a person or an animal considered separately from the face or head; figure. **2. a.** The essence of something. **b.** The mode in which a thing exists, acts, or manifests itself; kind: *a form of animal life; a form of blackmail.*

As one digs deeply in the literature of the form recognition field, it quickly becomes apparent that the most often used term—*pattern*—is probably furthest from the intended meaning in this field of research. *Pattern* conveys the concept of a plan, a mold, or a model, in other words, of something that is to be imitated or compared with something else or something that dictates the form of something else. To me, this interpretation suggests that the use of the denotative term *pattern recognition* has itself tended to prejudge the theoretical issue. The word *pattern* carries the connotation, and thus the implicit theoretical construction, of a template matching process. One of the major premises put forward in this book is that this is not only a unsubstantiated prejudgment, but also that such a point of view must necessarily turn out to be ultimately incorrect. For this reason, I prefer not to use the word *pattern* in defining the perceptual task with which we are concerned. In spite of the fact that *pattern* is the term that has most often been used by computer scientists when they develop procedures that allow computer vision systems to classify images (and also increasingly so by psychologists when they build theories of recognition), this is certainly the least desirable term of any of those considered in this section.

The next two terms *configuration* and *Gestalt* are obviously extremely close in their denotation. However, *configuration* also suffers from some implicit theoretical prejudgments—some excess conceptual baggage. In this dictionary definition we can see that it has the handicap of the presumption that the parts are essential in that they must be "organized" or "configured" to be recognized. It thus gives a kind of reality to parts or features in a way that could lead us seriously astray.

Gestalt, on the other hand has exactly the opposite handicap. It suggests that arrangement or configuration is everything and ignores the role of the parts. This word, therefore, also has superfluous meaning. It not only assumes that the parts are inconsequential, but furthermore, that they, for some fundamental reason, are inaccessible. The term *Gestalt* is, therefore, basically a holistic or molar concept. It ignores the role for features in exactly the opposite sense that the term *configuration* is, at its most primitive roots, elementalist. Whereas, configuration instantiates the concept of parts and gives a kind of pre-empirical credibility and influence to them, *Gestalt* eschews parts in favor of some kind of a yet-to-be-defined global property or metric. Thus, both of these words also loaded with theoretical prejudices and biases. Until the scientific issues are resolved, therefore, both are inadequate as neutral definitions of what it is that we are studying. Nevertheless, my preference is for a more holistic theoretical approach to form recognition in spite of the current difficulty in formally specifying the global properties themselves.

Shape and *form* then remain. Zusne (1970), in his heroic cumulative review of the field of form perception, notes that most psychologists easily substitute the two words for each other. A close examination of the dictionary definition of the two words, however, suggests that there are also residual connotational differences between the two that may help us in choosing the most appropriate term. *Shape*, like *pattern*, is unfortunately also loaded with superfluous, a priori theoretical baggage. The dictionary definition of the term presented earlier, as we see, suggests that shape implies the outline or contour of an object. Many current theories of form recognition as well as computer vision programs, in particular, are based on contour extraction. Therefore, from the beginning, they are uncomfortably closely linked to the idea of a perimetric contour; they emphasize the edges, the boundaries, the outline of the object in both its representation and its recognition. Such an emphasis ignores other internal aspects of the object such as it texture and many other cues that help to define its form. Thus, the word *shape* also represents a potential prejudgment that is not supported by the scientific literature that has been devoted to understanding and explaining human form recognition. *Shape*, therefore, like most of the other alternatives is also too conceptually loaded a term and is not completely satisfactory. Like the others, it tends to impose or suggest a theoretical orientation that is probably incorrect.

We, therefore, are left with the word *form*. This term, at least, provides us with a definition that is open ended, albeit incomplete, and essentially uncommitted (in a theoretical sense) to any particular point of view. It is a word that is freer of any excess conceptual baggage than any of the others considered here. *Form*, although used only occasionally by researchers in this field, is from this point of view, clearly superior to the word *pattern*, the mainstay of most recent treatises. One of the very few to appreciate that this word was desirable just because of it lack of theoretical prejudgments was Zusne (1970). ALthough his book was aimed at a far broader range of topics than this one, it remains one of the most useful and insightful, as well as one of the most comprehensive, studies of the perception of form yet published. One of the most important reasons was his prescient realization that the choice of vocabulary is important in determining the very course of the scientific development of a field. Following his lead and the lexico-graphic discussion we have just presented, the word *form* is chosen as the preferred one.

However preferred, the word *form* still remains a complex and only par-tially defined one. There are other terms that overlap and are redundant in meaning with *form*. Philosophers speak of *categories* with a meaning that is very close to that intended by psychologists when they refer to a *form*. To the philosopher a *category* is more general than a *form* because it can de-note any group of items that fall within the rubric of a particular class or type and, thus, can be grouped together. Perceptual psychologists like my-self are more likely to restrict their interest to consideration of visual or geometrical forms or auditory forms such as melodies. However, to the de-gree that *category* includes form it would be careless not to consider this al-ternative philosophical concept.

It must be acknowledged, however, that the several dictionary defini-tions presented here are wildly incomplete and all, to a greater or lesser de-gree, are unsatisfactory. It would require considerably more precision in our language or in some yet-to-be-developed mathematical formulation to develop any degree of consensual agreement about a specific meaning for the term *form*. Just how difficult it is to arrive at that consensus can be ob-served in the following material that is abstracted and updated from one of my earlier books (Uttal, 1988). That work was concerned more generally with the perception of form than with the specific process of recognition. In seeking a variety of definitions for the word *form,* I found a large number of suggested alternatives.

1.4.2. Alternative Definitions of Form[7]

The word form has an enormously long history. Many attempts have been made to provide alternative technical definitions that may be useful to sci-entists beyond the simple ones provided in a dictionary. Some of these are poetic, some are fanciful, some are ponderous attempts by experimental psychologists or mathematicians to develop quantitative statements useful in their research. None is entirely satisfactory. But here are a few that have attracted some attention in recent years.

---

[7] The following section is abstracted and expanded from an earlier discussion of the meaning of the word *form* presented in an earlier book (Uttal, 1988).

Cherry (1957), for example, made an absolutely true, exquisitely elegant, but totally useless statement when he asserted:

> The concept of form is one of those rare bridges between science and art. It is a name we may give to the source of aesthetic delight we sometimes experience when we have found a "neat" mathematical solution or when we suddenly "see" broad relationships in what has hitherto been a mass of isolated facts. Form essentially emerges from the continual play of governing conditions or "laws." An artistic mode of expression, such as music, painting, sculpture, represents a "language"; through this means the artist instills ideas into us. His creation has form inasmuch as it represents a continuity of his past experience and that of others of his time, so long as it obeys some of the "rules." It has meaning for us if it represents a continuity and extension of our own experience. (p. 71)

Even when one reads those few books that are fully dedicated to the problem of form—some of the most notable among these are the pioneering biomathematical work by Thompson (1917) on growth and form, Whyte's (1951) edited collection, Zusne's (1970) comprehensive review of the field, Dodwell's (1970) fine analysis, and the extremely thoughtful collection of papers edited by Kubovy and Pomerantz (1981)—it becomes clear that we, as a scientific community, have not yet succeeded in precisely defining what it is that we mean by the word *form*. The great D'Arcy Thompson (1917), whose invention of modern morphology was one of the notable intellectual contributions of this century, equivocates (along with lesser savants) by analogizing spatial form with physical forces when he defines form in the following way:

> The form, then, of any portion of matter, whether it be living or dead, and the changes of form which are apparent in its movements and in its growth, may in all cases alike be described as due to the action of force. In short, the form of an object is a "diagram of forces," in this sense, at least, that from it we can judge of or deduce the forces that are acting or have acted on it: in this strict and particular sense, it is a diagram—in the case of a solid, of the forces which have been impressed on it when its conformation was produced, together with those which enable it to retain its conformation; in the case of a liquid (or of a gas) of the forces which are for the moment acting on it to restrain or balance its own inherent mobility. (p. 11)

As elegant as these statements are, there is no certainty that the "forces" to which Thompson alludes are of the same kind as those formularized by Newton or Kepler. Without knowing what the true nature of these forces are and what rules they follow, the natural geometry of form perception as the resultant of a system of applied forces remains equivocal.

Thompson (1917) also obviously appreciated the difficulty in defining form in words and predicted that it would ultimately be necessary to turn to mathematics for precision, to wit:

> The study of form may be descriptive merely, or it may become analytical. We begin by describing the shape of an object in the simple words of common speech; we end by defining it in the precise language of mathematics; and the one method tends to follow the other in strict scientific order and historical continuity. Thus, for instance, the form of the earth, of a raindrop or a rainbow, the shape of the hanging chain, or the path of a stone thrown up into the air, may all be described, however inadequately, in common words; but when we have learned to comprehend and to define the sphere, the catenary, or the parabola, we have made a wonderful and perhaps a manifold advance. The mathematical definition of a "form" has a quality of precision which was quite lacking in our earlier stage of mere description; it is expressed in few words or in still briefer symbols, and these words or symbols are so pregnant with meaning that thought itself is economized; we are brought by means of it in touch with Galileo's aphorism (as old as Plato, as old as Pythagoras, as old perhaps as the wisdom of the Egyptians) that "the Book of Nature is written in characters of Geometry." (p. 269)

Obviously, Thompson was consciously or unconsciously evading the specific issue in alluding only to the forces or the formulae defining and producing form as a genus, in spite of the fact (which he obviously realizes) that the word *form* is the essence of everything of which he writes. Equally obvious is the fact that this formal approach to a definition of form is inadequate: Many forms are not represented in a nontrivial way by mathematical formulas. Consider the form of a face, a cow, or a book. Even the new formality called the mathematics of fractals (Mandelbrot, 1983) is not able to represent the form of such highly structured objects. We do well with hyperbolic paraboloids and orderly trees; we do poorly with cats and spouses.

Duff (1969) suggested another pair of general definitions (using the word *pattern* in the way I use *form*):

1. A pattern [form] is any arbitrary ordered set of numbers, each representing particular values of a finite number of variables. . . . Each arbitrary set is given a label which thereby defines its class, with the result that two such sets might be associated within a particular class, although there may be no obvious similarity between the two sets.
2. A pattern [form] is an ordered set of numbers, each representing particular values of a finite number of variables, in which there are certain definable relationships between the numbers in the set, involving both the values of the numbers and their positions in the set. Two such sets

would only be given the same classifying label if they are observed to conform to the same definable relationships. (p. 134)

Duff goes on to break these two definitions up into five subclasses, the first of which is the same as his first definition, whereas the latter four further specify the second definition:

(a) Random Patterns [Forms], being patterns of the type described in the first definition.

(b) Point Patterns [Forms], in which the essential quality of the pattern could be represented by a set of points distributed with a particular relative orientation in the input field.

(c) Texture Patterns [Forms], in which there is a repetition of well-defined groups across the input field (although the group itself may be a random pattern; it is the presence of repetition which is significant here).

(d) Line Patterns [Forms], figures in which the essential quality of the pattern could be represented by a system of zero-width lines (connected points).

(e) Area Patterns (Forms), figures in which the essential quality of the pattern could be represented by a system of areas. (E.g., note that a circle is obviously a line pattern, as is, perhaps, an annulus of finite width, but a disc must be regarded as an area pattern if confusion with a circle is to be avoided.) (p. 135)

Although interesting and precise to a degree, such a set of definitions still does not help the psychologist to manipulate forms in a controlled manner. These definitions are in fact no better than such words as "dot pattern" or "texture" until further specified. If so particularized, however, they can help to clarify the formal distinctions between different properties or aspects of forms.

Whyte (1951), in a very interesting edited book, tabulated the following definitions of the word form that were suggested by himself and his other contributors.

The word "form" has many meanings, such as shape, configuration, structure, pattern, organization, and system of relations.... Common to the ideas of form, configuration, pattern, and stance, is the notion of an ordered complexity, a multiplicity which is governed by some unifying principle.... But "form" includes development and transformation. Indeed we can regard "matter" as that which persists, and "form" as that which changes, for no form is eternal. And form, like change itself, is in many fields still obscure. (p. 2)[8]

And

---

[8]All of these references are to be found in Whyte (1951) at the pages indicated.

The word "form" in this article will refer to the shapes of material objects, the arrangement in space of groups of them, and the arrangement in space of their component parts. (Humphreys-Owens, 1951, p. 8)[8]

And

If we understand by form something more than mere shape, if we mean by form all that can be known about the object with all the aids that science can provide, then it is to be expected that there will be systems of classification according to the various modes of apprehending the object. (Gregory, 1951, p. 23)[8]

And

In any definite situation offered by a real system, we have still the right to consider that its material and energetic elements can be combined in numerous ways (Power), but that a certain set of definite relations has been adopted (Form), resulting in the actual situation (Act). (Dalcq, 1951, p. 92)[8]

Peter Dodwell (1970), a psychologist, offers the following highly specialized and, to me, equally unsatisfactory definition of form (pattern):

By a visual pattern I shall mean a collection of contours or edges, which in turn are defined as region of sharp change in the level of a physical property of light (usually intensity impinging on the retina. (p. 2)

The problem with this definition, as noted earlier, is the linkage Dodwell makes between the aggregate organization (what he refers to as *pattern*) and the specialized contour attributes. Certainly forms or patterns could exist without lines or contours of any kind: A dot pattern is one obvious example. I believe this erroneous linkage of form and a particular kind of feature is a reflection of the selective attention that neurophysiologists gave to "line detectors" in the early 1970s. Such a misdirection illustrates the strong hold that the words of one scientific vocabulary can exert on theory development in another as well as on the contemporary scientific zeitgeist.

The psychologist of art, Rudolf Arnheim (1974), offered the following definition of *form*:

The words "shape" and "form" are often used as though they meant the same thing. Even in this book I am sometimes taking advantage of this opportunity to vary our language. Actually there is a useful difference of meaning between the two terms. The preceding chapter dealt with shape—that is, with the spatial aspects of appearance. But no visual pattern is only itself. It always represents something beyond its own individual existence—which is like saying that a shape is the form of some content. Content, of course, is not identical with subject matter, because in the arts subject matter itself serves only as form for some content. But the representation of objects by visual pattern is one of the form problems encountered by most artists. Representation involves a comparison between the model object and its image. (p. 82)

This discourse, although poetic, lucid, and interesting, is also totally useless in helping us manipulate form as an experimental variable.

In recent years there have been continued efforts to develop nomenclature systems that can specifically define a unique form. But the problem remains refractory. Zusne (1970), referred to the influence on psychophysical responses of "variables of the distal stimulus": He proposed the following interim definition:

[F]orm may be considered both a one-dimensional emergent of its physical dimensions and a multidimensional variable. (p. 175)

This kind of language merely hinted at a future definition, but does not constitute one. Zusne (1970) pressed on, however, and asserts elsewhere in his book that form can mean all of the following things to psychologists:

(a) the corporeal quality of an object in three dimensional space;

(b) the projection of such an object on a two dimensional surface;

(c) a flat, two dimensional pictorial representation;

(d) a nonrepresentational distribution of contours in a plane; or

(e) the values of coordinates in Euclidean space. (p. 1)

None of which satisfies the need for a general definition of the word.

Slice, Bookstein, Marcus, and Rohlf (1996) developed a glossary of the vocabulary used in a special field of form studies—Morphometrics (i.e., the "measurement" of "shape" from the Greek words "metron" and "morphe," respectively). Within the context of that special approach (of which I have more to say in subsequent chapters), they defined form as follows:

Form—In morphometrics, we represent the form of an object by a point in space of form variables, which are measurements of a geometric object that are unchanged by translations and rotations. If you allow for reflections, forms stand for all figures that have all of the same interlandmark distances. A form is usually represented by one of its figures a some specified location and in some specified orientation. When represented in this way, location and orientation are said to have been "removed." (p. 538)

Slice et al. (1996) introduced some new terms here that are important to understanding this definition. One was the term *landmark* which was defined as "a specific point on a biological form or image located according to some rule" (p. 540). Outlines, with and without landmarks, were also considered grist for morphometric analysis.

Precise definitions and specific quantitative measures of whatever it is that we mean by form thus seem to be continuously elusive to psychologists. Hochberg and McAlister's (1953) well known, but seriously mistitled paper ("A Quantitative Approach to Figural Goodness") is another example that makes this argument clear. Their "quantitative" measures of goodness (an aspect of form) are nothing more than counts of the numbers of line segments, angles, or points of intersection—properties that themselves in no way define the arrangement or the form of a visual stimulus, only the first-order statistics (numerosity) of its component parts.

Uhr (1966), one of the pioneers in the science of pattern recognition has attempted to clarify the meaning of the word *pattern* by stating:

> The study of patterns is the study of complexes—of structures, interactions, grammars, and syndromes. (p. 1)

But then goes on to note that:

> Almost all natural patterns are not even describable. Think of the particular examples of a pattern like **A** or **Table** as the exemplars or tokens, and the names **"A"** and **"table"** as types. We obviously do not have good complete descriptions of all of the token of "A" or of "Table." It would be an enormously tedious task to try to get and test such descriptions, and there is good reason to think that this is an impossible task *in principle*. (p. 3; italics added)

In summary, none of these definitions of what is meant by the word *form* come close to satisfying the needs of perceptual researchers to characterize, dimensionalize, or manipulate form in the same way that a monochromator satisfies the need for a tool for measuring and controlling wavelength. Perhaps because of its multidimensional nature, form is intrinsically difficult or even impossible to define, as suggested by Uhr, or to quantify in a useful manner. At best we manipulate something as simple as the height–width ratio of a rectangle and thus reduce the problem to a level at which the essence of a form is ignored; at worst we utilize complex stimulus scenes, so superloaded with symbolic meaning that they tap high-level cognitive and symbolic processes. Somewhere in between is the problematic use of analytic series such as the Fourier transform to represent in the frequency domain an object originally presented in the spatial domain.

All of this leads me back to The working definition of the word *form*, which I have come to use most often: Form, in some ill-defined manner, is at its most simplest and direct level—"global arrangement." The preceding paragraphs should help to clarify some of the vocabulary that present slightly different general meanings even though I, too, cannot produce anything more satisfactory than this simple capsule definition of the elusive word *form*. Chapter 2, on the other hand, discusses some of the formal representation methods that have been suggested in an effort to overcome this problem.

1.4.3. Recognize

Now that we have a word for the information (the substance) that is to be processed, it is worthwhile to look next at the process that is to be applied to this material. Again returning to our dictionary, we first find the following definition for the most frequent used process term *recognize*:

> **rec·og·nize** *v. tr.* **1.** To know to be something that has been perceived before: *recognize a face.* **2.** To know or identify from past experience or knowledge: *recognize hostility.* **3.** To perceive or show acceptance of the validity or reality of: *recognizes the concerns of the tenants.*

As often as the term *recognition* has been used, it has to be acknowledged that this word, like some of the near synonyms for *form*, also comes loaded with its own excess theoretical baggage in the form of implicit assumptions and prejudgments. The word *recognition* is sometimes considered to be synonymous with the words *recollection* and *remembrance*. All three terms implicitly suggest that the process is possible only with previously encountered stimuli. It, thus, impels our thinking toward comparisons with stimuli that have already been experienced. Furthermore, albeit somewhat less directly, the word *recognition* suggests that the naming process is critical to the recognition process. However, as we see later, there is ample evidence that we can recognize an object that has not been encountered previously, but which meets certain categorical criteria without naming it. A case is made here that the process of adding a tag or a name to the process is of secondary importance. Thus, the word *recognition*, as did some of the earlier words for form, provides an undesirable impetus toward theoretical thinking in a certain, and not necessarily correct, way. It would seem to be preferable to choose a word that is less theoretically loaded.

Some of the alternatives to *recognize* that have been used from time to time are *conceptualize, classify,* and *categorize*. Exercising our dictionary again we find:

> **con·cep·tu·al·ize** *v. tr.* **1.** To form a concept or concepts of, and especially to interpret in a conceptual way.

Concepts are defined as:

con·cept *n.* **1.** A general idea derived or inferred from specific instances or occurrences. **2.** Something formed in the mind; a thought or notion.

And, then:

clas·si·fy *v. tr.* **1.** To arrange or organize according to class or category.

And:

cat·e·go·rize *v. tr.* **1.** To put into a category or categories; classify.

Classify and categorize are, both obviously and unfortunately, circularly defined—one in terms of the other—and tautologies such as this are not useful scientific tools. These interlocking definitions also imply the existence of some kind of a system of classes or categories that also begin to suggest a pre-existing framework that may be superfluous to understanding the true nature of the process in which we are interested.

Conceptualize, on the other hand, is much closer in both its denotation and connotation to the process with which this book is concerned. This word conveys, to this author at least, the closest approximation to the meaning of what had hitherto been called *recognition.* All other factors, being equal, this is the word that would be preferable to use in the phrase "form conceptualization." This what I think is really happening when we "recognize a pattern"—a phrase in which both of the critical terms impel theoreticians in particular and quite probably incorrect directions—if our goal is to develop the most valid understanding of the manner in which form information is processed in a system like our brains. Unfortunately, such a neologism would make communication of some of these ideas even more difficult than it usually is and I revert to the rubric of *form recognition* in the remainder of this book.

The psychological process of recognition has been defined by a number of authors in ways that are closer to the needs of this book than these dictionary definitions. Uhr (1966), for example, referred to pattern recognition as "the naming of the appropriate class or the making of the appropriate response for the sensed data" (p. 3). He also pointed out that the "basic job" of a pattern recognizer "is to learn general concepts on the basis of specific examples—to perform inductions, and even to form the hypotheses that the inductive evidence is about." (p. 3)

However, it is appropriate to point out that explicit naming is not always essential. In many cases we can demonstrate that a form has been perceptually conceptualized by responding to it appropriately. The problem of course, given the inaccessibility of the perceptual experience itself, is how to indicate that something as been perceived in a particular manner. Verbal naming is one possible response, but so, too, can simple Class A responses serve the same purpose. Reversible figures are clear examples of this argument; they need not be known as Schroedinger's staircases or Necker's cubes to be designated by such simple discriminative responses as left or right or up or down. These simple responses indicate (within the limits of credulity that we wish to assign to our subjects) that they have been organized into one or the other of their alternative manifestations. We cannot know anything more about those perceptual experiences or their processes and mechanisms, simply that a reversal has occurred.

Another way of making clear what it is that we mean by form recognition is to particularize the specific questions that are asked and particular positions taken in pursuit of answers to this problem. The next section teases out those central theoretical and empirical issues in the process, some of which have already been alluded to and others of which are highlighted for the first time.

1.5. THE MAJOR THEORETICAL POSITIONS

In this section I highlight what I believe to be the great controversies or dichotomies that characterize form recognition science. These issues focus on the implicit assumptions made by contemporary artificial recognizers, students of organic recognition, and the theories that they generate. These controversies are often not explicit, but reflect implicit premises and assumptions that are prevalent in the field today. If progress is to be made toward an improved theory of form recognition, then these controversies must be made more explicit, particularly with regard to the consideration of plausible alternative assumptions that may be contradictory to the currently popular ones. The major issues are:

- Feature versus configuration assumptions—The local–global controversy.
- Comparison versus construction assumptions—The matching–reasoning controversy.
- The learning assumption—necessary or not? Is naming central or irrelevant?
- Description versus reduction—The behaviorist–cognitive neuroscience controversy.

1.5.1. Feature Versus Configuration Theories

Perhaps the major current theoretical dichotomy in the field of form recognition is represented by the schism between feature analytic modelers and those theoreticians that stress the primary importance of the global config-

uration of the stimulus. As noted earlier, the classic configuration or holistic theoretical approach was propounded by the Gestalt group in Germany
and is continued by a relatively small group of molar-oriented successors
among modern psychologists. However, the currently dominant elementalist, feature-oriented approach of most cognitive neuroscientists differs
substantially from this classic emphasis on the molar form of a stimulus.
Today's form recognition science is, thus, dominated by the component or
part oriented theories and programs developed by both psychologists and
computer scientists. From the point of view of a putative theoretical validity, it is unsatisfying to observe this trend because arguably most psychophysical evidence suggests that our visual system actually depends more
on the overall configuration of the stimulus rather than the aggregate of the
component features.

Why should this inconsistency between the psychophysical data and the
current reductionist theory exist? The answer to this rhetorical question is
straightforward and consists of three parts:

1. There have been notable successes in the cognate field of computer
science based on what is unarguably an elementalist, part oriented programming philosophy. These successes have uncritically been transferred from
the respective engineering development projects to explain organic form
recognition. This intellectual force has been enormously influential in direct-
ing our attention to the steps and modules that characterize the way computer programs are written.

2. There have been comparable successes in the cognate neurophysiological sciences based on the study of individual neurons. These successes
with the neuronal components have been equally uncritically transferred to
explaining processes better understood in terms of the huge networks of
neurons than in terms of the individual ones. This led to what has now become only a vestigial point of view—the idea that individual neurons can encode complex ideas, concepts, or images. Fortunately only a few old timers
hold to this simplistic assumption; most of my colleagues now agree that the
essence of cognition of all kinds is unlikely to be encoded by one or a few
cells. However, the problem of understanding such huge and complex networks has so far been, and promises to be in the future, intractable.

3. There has been a failure of mathematics to develop methods to represent global structure in a way that is relevant to the form recognition research question, or for that matter, any comparable one that deals directly
with configuration.

As a result of these influences, the molar, holistic, or configurational approach has lost favor in recent years. The more atomic or elementalist developments in computer modeling doted on the features of an image simply

because that is the way that computers must work. These machines operate at their most primitive level on the picture elements (pixels) of an image. They operate by executing relatively simple instructions that manipulate the bits and bytes of the pixels numerically representing the image. Therefore, they deal well with simple local structures and local interactions—if there are not too many of them. However, there are few comparable techniques available for processing the parameters and dimensions of global organization.

The enormous amount of effort put into computer modeling of form recognition in recent years sometimes obscures the fact that a general purpose form recognition system is still far from being achieved. All computer models suffer from what some authors have identified as a failure to generalize. Dreyfus (1992), especially, makes this point in his eloquent critique of artificial intelligence research carried out since the 1960s. A similar point made by Kovalevsky in 1980 has hardly been refuted by more recent progress—or lack thereof:

> We must accept the fact that it is impossible to make a universal machine which can learn an arbitrary classification of multidimensional signals. There the solution of the recognition problem must be based on a priori postulates (concerning the set of signals to be recognized) that will narrow the set of possible classifications. (p. v)

Of course, Kovalevsky is a computer scientist who was discussing the efficiency of computer methods and not the capabilities of the human visual system. This is not to say that the organic system is universally capable, but it clearly comes far closer to approximating such an ideal than does any known computer program.

Why should this be so? The main reason is that the brain operates by means of processes and mechanisms that are almost certainly different from those used by computer engineers or, for that matter, from those invoked by many of the theorists who are attempting to describe and explain the astonishing ability of the organic system to recognize forms. This assertion has to be qualified by the simple fact that we do not yet have even the barest glimmerings of an idea of what the logic used by the nervous system is like. What data we do have, however, suggests that there are fundamental differences between the brain and computers. Certainly the respective behaviors of computers and humans differ substantially.

One notable difficulty with any kind of form recognition, whether it be computer or neuron based, is that the stimulus representing a form is usually underdetermined. Three-dimensional objects, for example, are presented to a camera or to the eye as a two-dimensional image. Therefore, in most cases the stimulus does not even contain the information necessary to solve the problem it presents to a form recognizer. Such problems are said to be *ill-posed* and can only be solved by additional assumptions, hypotheses, and constraints. It is in this domain—adding constraining information—that the organic form recognizer excels.

Computer scientists achieve some degree of success in solving such ill-posed problems by tightly constraining their programs to deal with but a limited universe of possible forms presented in a very limited set of circumstances. They do so by adding assumptions about possible solutions, or by using approximation methods that can converge on a possible, if not unique, solution to the problem. For example, some computer programs are designed to categorize, recognize, or conceptualize items from such limited sets as specific fonts of alphabetic characters, bar codes, or other simple codes in which one character in one set stands in one-to-one correspondence with the members of another set. In many cases the problem is formulated solely in a particular context—picking out a particular form from a larger, but limited set of alternatives or recognizing the equivalence of a new input and a noisy version of some prototypical form. Rarely, if ever, does a computer program designed to work in one context succeed when confronted with another type of stimuli for which it had not been specifically prepared.

On the other hand, human form recognition (with the exception of some special situations) typically exceeds that of the computer, but for similar reasons. People also add constraints (e.g., rigidity or that mysterious and ill-defined *Pragnanz*) to a form recognition problem that sometimes permits them to do even better than a straightforward mathematical proof suggests an ideal observer should. (See, e.g., the work of Lappin, Doner, & Kottas, 1980; Braunstein, Hoffman, Shapiro, Andersen, & Bennett, 1986, in which the human observer exceed the performance of an ideal observer by using fewer then the predicted number of "views" and points to identify the form of a solid from a rotating projective image than was required by a computer program.)

Therefore, with few exceptions, computer models must be considered to be application specific, constrained by their limited technology, and, even more so, hindered by the absence of a theory that is comprehensive enough to deal with multiple tasks, much less the universal ideal that is approximated by the performance of the human visual system. There is no "general problem solver" worthy of the name.

The hope for future progress lies in the development of an alternative approach to the form recognition problem; I believe that this must come from a theory that ultimately eschews local features and concentrates on the organizational attributes of the whole form. Rather than the local and serial approach of a computer program, the brain more likely operates by parallel, simultaneous, and broadly distributed interactions of which we yet have the barest glimmerings.

In a similar vein, the conceptual forces generated by the microelectrode technique exerted a powerful influence on thinking about form recognition. The microelectrode, so useful in neurophysiology and so effective at defining the time course of activity at a single point in space, is terribly ineffective at correlating the activity of many different points in space. In place of global and organizational concepts and principles, it focuses the theoretical spotlight on the elemental neuron, the critical information-processing component of the nervous system, and its unquestioned specific sensitivity to specific temporal–spatial features of an incoming image. Lines, edges, and somewhat more complex, but still elemental, trigger shapes have been discovered in abundance. However, in making these important discoveries about individual neurons electrophysiologists have often submerged thinking about more complex neural nets and the essential role that the interaction among many neurons played in processing information about global form.

The compelling and, in many cases, revolutionary findings about single neurons were not just of interest to physiology. Just as computer technology did, these findings strongly influenced psychological theories and conceptual models of human visual recognition. The unfortunate effect was that the elegant findings from single cell research were overgeneralized from important descriptions of neural transmission codes to explanatory theories of central psychoneural equivalence—from the coding languages used to transmit information to the neural equivalents of perceived experience.

Finally, mathematics also failed us. Classical mathematics is highly analytic (see the later discussion of Fourier analysis on p. 78, in particular). Traditional mathematics emerged to meet the needs of the physical sciences dominated by simple (e.g., relatively uniform + or − electromagnetic valences and gravitational forces) interactions between point-like bodies, not the complex interactions of systems like the brain or, for that matter, even of a cluster of three or more mutually interacting objects. The neurons of the brain, however, are interconnected by means of complex, often multivalued, and intricately encoded multidimensional pathways that make the unsolvable three-body problem pale into insignificance.

Finally, there still is not even a good approximation to a completely satisfactory means of formalizing or representing what is meant by a form. There is no simple and pure mathematical expression that encodes a unique face or a picture of a man on horseback. Once one gets past the relatively simple forms described by quadratic or cubic equations, forms are represented by maps rather than by equations or by transformations into spatial frequency spectra that are as difficult to process as the original image or by using metrics that seem biologically unlikely. Chapter 2 expands on some of the suggested procedures for representing global form. As shown there, none is yet capable of representing a complex form such as a face in a manner that leads to a robust theory of form recognition.

The net effect of this triple-barreled influence on thinking about form recognition was the general acceptance of theories in which identifiable features were considered to be more important than the relationships among those features. Feature analysis became the accepted theoretical explanation of the psychological process of form recognition in spite of the substantial evidence that this was not how human perception operated. For example, the theories of Triesman (1986), Triesman and Gormican (1988), Julesz (1981, 1984), as well as many of the connectionist or neural net models all are based on the assumption that an analysis into features must occur as an initial step in the recognition process. The holistic, global, or configurational approach has languished under these intellectual pressures.

In spite of the ubiquitous support for the feature approach, it appears to some of us that this is not the way the human visual system operates. It seems as if computational and conceptual convenience has supplanted empirical fact and logical consistency. Therefore, a review of the theoretical arguments and psychological evidence on both sides of this very important question is a necessary part of any discussion of the psychology of form recognition.

1.5.2. Comparison Versus Construction Assumptions

Although the feature analysis premise is central to most of today's thinking about how an object might be recognized, there are two other issues that characterize most of the current work in this field. The connotative pressure of the term *re-cognition* strongly, but subtly, impelled research in this field toward various kinds of theory in which some kind of a comparison of the represented input image was carried out with a "library" or "list" of previously stored templates or prototypes. The central axiom of such an approach is that recognition requires an exhaustive effort to determine how well the properties or attributes of the input image, sometimes transformed in a set of features and sometimes dealt with in its entirety, compares with the prestored set of image prototypes. The library item with which the input image most closely correlates (in accord with a variety of different statistical or deterministic matching rules) then has its properties (including its name) attached to the image that is to be recognized.

This template or correlational approach is ubiquitous in the pattern recognition literature. One has to admit that in the absence of an alternative approach, this crude and inelegant attack on the problem probably could not have been avoided. However, the exhaustive nature of the comparison process raises serious questions about its validity as a theoretical model of human form recognition. Even a massively parallel system would be hard pressed to carry out all the necessary possible comparisons to identify a simple figure, given the huge number of possible templates against which it has to be compared. Furthermore, it is difficult to precisely state the number of templates one would have to have available or the time it would take to make the comparisons necessary to "recognize" even a simple image given the enormous number of possible stimulus forms that might be encountered. However, one can get a general impression of the magnitude of the problem by considering the number of combinations of even a small image. For example, suppose we consider something as simple as asking how many checkerboards combinations exist given only a zero or a one possibility in each square. This number is 2^{64}. This number is enormous, but it is a relatively simple exemplar of the enormity of the form recognition challenge—if one tries to solve it by the brute force method of exhaustive comparison. Imagine what an observer is confronted with if forced to deal not with binary values at each of 64 squares but, rather, a 24 bit value of a 256 × 256 pixel image. Yet, this 24 × 65,536 bit image represents a number of alternatives of enormously greater numerousness than even the great number involved in the 64 position binary checkerboard. Consider, also, that this huge number is not too dissimilar in magnitude to the standard RGB code used on contemporary computer displays![9]

Clearly the brute force approach to solving the recognition problem characterized by an exhaustive template lookup procedure is unlikely to work for exponentially increasing problems of this kind. The conclusion to which we are impelled is that techniques other than the exhaustive comparison of a sample image with a library of templates are required. One alternative in this case is the self-organizing classification of a form on the basis of its own, self-conveyed properties without recourse to comparisons. This approach may be classified as "constructive," "mediated," or even "reasoning" and sometimes "rational" (as opposed to "comparison" or "matching"). This alternative process depends on the idea that the input form itself contains whatever information is necessary for it to be recognized. This information, it is proposed, would be transformed from the input to a response by a logical process directly into a unique categorization.[10]

---

[9]Of course, humans do not use all of the information presented on a display. We do not discriminate between all of the colors that can be encoded and our acuity limits how much spatial information is a part of the recognition process. However, if one considers the vast number of different images that we can recognize, clearly the difficulty of this kind of information-processing challenge is of the same order of magnitude as the numbers presented in this Gedanken calculation.

[10]Such an approach worked well for the detection of dotted forms in dotted noise (Uttal, 1975). Human visual detection behavior was predicted by the autocorrelation function of the in-

It is in this regard that the question of whether or not a form must be named becomes salient. I propose that naming is a secondary aspect of the perception of a form and that a form can be recognized or conceptualized by virtue of its self-contained properties without being named. In this context it seems likely that such a preverbal recognition process can occur without the linguistic baggage with which it becomes encumbered when it is tagged with a particular name. Of course, being an inaccessible mental response, some means of communicating that it has occurred is necessary. A verbal response is one way in which this can be accomplished. However, it may be unnecessary. The task of identifying that some object has been recognized can also be done in a nonverbal manner; an animal's escape or avoidance behavior, an eye movement, or the choice of a correct button to push are all examples of nonverbal behavior that can signify successful recognition without naming.

Furthermore, verbal reports are not without their own disadvantages. One must keep in mind that mental events themselves are private and they are part of a complex system of interactive cognitive functions, any verbal report may well be obfuscated by other influences—for example, faulty memory, "logical" processing, prejudices and stereotypes, consistency with ad hoc personal theories, and so on. Thus, if we are able to bypass some of the irrelevant complexities introduced by language into the study of recognition, it may sometimes be desirable to avoid the use of language as a response mode altogether.

The point is that a human observer can perceptually respond to a stimulus form with perfectly appropriate and adaptive responses even if it is unnamable on the basis of our past experience. Naming, therefore, may be a convenience but not a necessary part of the recognition process. Indeed, in some cases its use may confuse both experimenters and theoreticians, and should be avoided wherever possible in favor of simple Class A responses (Brindley, 1960).

1.5.3. The Learning Assumption—Necessary or Not?

The third issue is not so much a controversy between two alternative positions as it is a corollary of the comparison versus construction dilemma. Let us assume for the sake of discussion that the exhaustive comparison (of an input image with a large library of possible alternatives) paradigm is the way that psychological form recognition actually occurs. If this assumption

---

put stimulus in a way that accounted for almost all of the variance in the results of several experiments. (For a fuller discussion of the autocorrelation hypothesis, see p. 213.) This is but a primitive example of the constructionist approach. However, a goal of our science should be to extend this kind of globally interactive and constructive process into future theories of form recognition.

is accepted then one is confronted with the need to create the library of comparison forms. How are the items in this list created? The need to answer this question has led to a substantial amount of activity among form recognition theorists aimed at solving the problem of how these templates can be taught to the recognition system. Learning algorithms of many different kinds, therefore, have been designed that range from the training of connectionist weights in neural networks to a more conventional adding of newly encountered forms to a library of prototype templates. The common feature of all of these approaches is that they seek to provide automatic or semiautomatic means of varying the state of a recognition system as a result of experience.

The issue in this case revolves around the relevance of both the nature of the library of templates or alternatives, on the one hand, and the training processes that must be used to fill that library, on the other. An argument can be made that both these issues are irrelevant, but rather are secondary issues that simply complicate the study of the fundamental nature of the recognition process. The search for the template library and its means of operating is based on the a priori assumption that the library exits and the comparison process is the one that accounts for form recognition. The modern version of this assumption also grew out of the available technology of computers and the means by which they could be made to imitate the organic recognition process.

The question remains—Was this approach a valid interpretation of the organic recognition process or merely a metaphor or analog that operated on vastly different principles? If the latter is true, then the search in the organic system for the template library and the means to fill it may be totally irrelevant, indeed a misdirection, away from an appreciation of the true nature of the process.

It is important to note that nothing I say here suggests that form recognition does not change (i.e., improve) with experience. The dynamics of this process over time and experience are extremely interesting in their own right. The point here is that learning may not be central to the recognition process and may, therefore, tell us very little, about how forms are recognized. The enormous attention played in the neurocomputing field, in particular, to learning algorithms may have been representative of the kind of displacement activity I alluded to earlier, obscuring the essence of the recognition problem.

1.5.4. Behaviorist Description Versus Mentalist Analysis

Finally, I return to the overarching issue with which this chapter began—the controversy between the behaviorist and the mentalist approaches to the study of psychological processes of which form recognition is only one example. I have previously argued (Uttal, 1998, 2000) that, in general, the molar, nonreductive, descriptive approach of the behaviorist school of thought (appropriately modified) provides a sounder foundation for scientific psychology than does the analytic, reductively explanatory, mentalist approach of the currently popular cognitive–neuroscientific–simulation tradition. A misinterpretation or exaggeration of what were the fundamental assumptions of behaviorism led to a diminishment of interest in perception, in general, and form recognition, in particular, throughout much of this century. I believe this rejection of perception studies to have been incorrect. Perception is as least as good a target for investigations as any other topic in scientific psychology—if we accept the limits and constraints that psychology faces in general. These are the barriers imposed on reductionism and mental accessibility.

It is my hope that the analysis presented in this book adds additional support to the argument that we can, at best, describe behavioral responses and the transforms from the stimulus that produce them, but not directly access or reductively explain the inner neural or cognitive processes that account for them. In a recent article, Luce (1999), although equitably presenting the advantages and disadvantages of the cognitive and behaviorist approaches respectively, pointed out the great weaknesses of the cognitive information-processing approach. His discussion of the disadvantages of the hypothetical mental architectures proposed by this form of mentalism are worth repeating here.

- The postulated mental architectures are very hypothetical, and a great deal of data are required to distinguish among various hypotheses about them. (p. 727)

This, of course, is another way of expressing the epistemological difficulty of dealing with complex systems. Luce suggested that progress is being made in spite of the "laborious" nature of the necessary experiments, but then makes a stronger, more theoretical and less pragmatic, argument.

- These models, especially when they go beyond the two stimuli/two response designs proliferate great numbers of free parameters whose empirical meanings are usually not very firm. What is worse, often they do not remain invariant when relatively small changes are made in the experimental design. For the most part, we, cannot, once and for all, estimate the relevant parameters from experiments designed to do just that, and then predict the outcome of other, usually more complex experiments. (p. 727)

Subsequently, he expressed (not too convincingly to me) the fact that progress is being made to overcome even this difficulty. From my point of view, however, Luce has raised two powerful and compelling arguments against conventional cognitive reductionism—one practical and one theoretical.

1.6. A SUMMARY OF THE CRITICAL QUESTIONS CONCERNING FORM RECOGNITION

The clarifying value of knowing what question is being asked when one tries to analyze or explain a process cannot be overestimated. As I indicated earlier, many times what has been identified as a study of the form recognition process turned out, in retrospect, to be actually a nonessential displacement activity. For example, many studies have been carried out to determine how forms are detected or discriminated or how we search for forms in an environment of distractors. The modeling of form recognition as a process that specifically intensifies edges is also often carried out with the implicit assumption that human form recognition, in some special way, depends on the contours or boundaries of a form rather than on some other aspect of its general organization. Computer and mathematical models are often driven not so much by the goal of explaining how organisms recognize forms as much as by some unarguably worthwhile practical goal of achieving successful categorization by electronic and optical systems. It typically does not matter to engineers what algorithm is used as long as it works. In fact, the usual criterion for a practical computer recognition system is how well it works, not what is going on inside the algorithm or how closely it corresponds to some organic recognition process. A program may be appreciated if it is mathematically elegant or inventive, but it is rare when someone in computer vision is concerned with the quest for psychobiological explication. Other studies that measure the sequence of eye movements that occurs when one attempts to recognize an object may also be indirectly of some interest but such studies also often direct our attention away from the critical issues and concentrate on behaviors that can be conveniently, if not relevantly, measured.

Most disconcerting to psychological theory studies of perceptual learning often use a form recognition paradigm simply as a metric of changes occurring during development or as a result of experience. Indeed, because of the strong emphasis on learning during the heyday of old fashioned behaviorism, the study of form processing was submerged into an environment that stressed learning almost to the exclusion of perception. Studies of the duration of various kinds of memory traces became the classic displacement activity substituting for investigations aimed specifically at the recognition process. As noted earlier, the choice of the word *recognition* subtly prejudged the theoretical issue by emphasizing previous learning as the essence of the recognition process. To "re-cognize" a previously presented image is one thing. To recognize a fresh image on the basis of its attributes and properties may be quite another. It is clear that the ways these difficult-to-define words are used can have a powerful effect on the theories that subsequently emerge.

Based on the summary of the discussion so far, the critical challenges faced in our efforts to understand the form recognition process can now be specifically stated. First, there is the perennial problem: *How do we formally define or represent a form in a way that allows it to be manipulated in a controlled fashion in empirical studies?* In other words, what mathematical or computational procedures can be used to represent or encode a form and into what space should those procedures transform the coded form? It is self-evident that the initial decision made in choosing a particular representation may also strongly influence the final theoretical outcome as well as the inferred meaning of the empirical data. For example, the availability of the Fourier analysis method led directly to what is now appreciated to be an incorrect explication of certain otherwise ambiguous neurophysiological data.

Second, there is a class of research questions that asks: *What are the critical attributes of a stimulus form that affect its recognizability?* This class of questions is simply and directly aimed at determining the properties or aspects or variables of the stimulus that can be shown to influence form recognition studies. Properties and attributes can be variously defined but it is essential to be able to ignore the nonessential ones and emphasize those that are relevant to the process. Most of all it should be remembered that attributes are not the same things as features. The term *attribute* is more general than the term *feature*. Some attributes may be features but it is also important to remember that configurational attributes, not incorporated within the feature rubric, may also be very, if not absolutely, important in determining the response to a form.

Third, there is a large set of empirical questions exemplified by: *How does manipulation (separately or in combination) of a previously defined critical attribute actually affect the recognition process?* Obviously the answers obtained in experimental studies to questions of this genre are going to interact strongly with those that seek to define the critical attributes themselves. It is equally obvious that without a clear-cut sense of what the critical attributes of a form may be, there is potentially an enormous waste of effort in the psychophysical laboratory.

Fourth, there is a class of inquiries that seeks to answer questions of a more critical nature: *What transformation from the stimulus to the response describes what happens when an organism conceptualizes a form?* Questions of this kind are central to a modern behaviorist study of form recognition. It is very important to appreciate that the goal in this case is to formally (i.e., mathematically or computationally) describe the nature of the informational changes that occur between stimuli and responses. The effort to produce reductive models of the mechanisms that produce those changes is likely to be futile for reasons that I have already discussed elsewhere (Uttal, 1998). The realistic behaviorist goal, on the other hand, is both to accept the fact and then to appreciate that these descriptive statements of the observed transformations remain neutral with regard to the exact nature of the internal, and therefore hidden and private, mechanisms. This is the essential difference between the goals of a cognitive mentalism and a descriptive behaviorism.

Fifth is the empirical question: *What data are available to us that can help to determine which of the alternative theories of form recognition is the most plausible?* Needless to say, answers to this question are often determined by the a priori theoretical proclivities of the investigator and validity may be very difficult to establish. Judgments concerning the saliency of findings are often heavily biased when data is recruited in support of one's own pet approach. It is sometimes very difficult to distinguish between a truly supportive empirical argument and an ephemeral one that is only weakly analogous to the inquiry at hand.

The question of empirical relevance, just stated, has subsidiary or corollary questions that deal with the main aspects of the currently accepted standard model in which features and comparisons play such a major role. The first subsidiary question is: *What empirical evidence can be invoked to distinguish between the two major alternative theoretical approaches—configuration and feature—to the form recognition problem?* The second subsidiary question is: *Can empirical evidence be found to distinguish between the template matching and the mediated, reasoning, or construction hypotheses, respectively?*

The sixth critical question asks: *What is the role of learning in the form recognition process? In other words, is learning essential? Can form recognition occur de novo without previous experience with a specific stimulus?* Restated—what are the limits of stimulus generalization?

An important corollary of the sixth question is: *What is the role of naming in the recognition process? Is it an essential part or is it irrelevant to the representation and recognition of the process?*

Seventh, there is a question about the internal structure of the recognition process: *Is form recognition a unitary process or does it have stages and subdivisions?* (I have already indicated my negative bias in answering this question.)

Eighth, there is the important technological question: *Do computer models and programs, or any other kinds of formal theories, no matter how successfully they may simulate human visually controlled behavior, represent any kind of truth about the psychobiology of the form recognition process?*

Ninth, the fundamental epistemological question must be answered: *Are there any insurmountable barriers to our ability to answer some of the all-too-*

easily posed questions that we ask concerning the mental process we call form
recognition?

This book considers some of these questions, some in greater detail than others. It should be obvious that the list of nine fundamental questions just posed are not going to be resolved within the covers of a single book. Rather, this is a program of research that is going to take many years and the efforts of many of us in this field to even begin to answer. In this book, I propose simply to continue the ongoing discussion.

I.7. A CAVEAT

As this expedition into the nature of form recognition begins, it is very important for me to reiterate several important points concerning the intended limits of this exercise. Arguments supporting the behavioral assumptions on which this present work is grounded have been extensively discussed in two of my earlier books (Uttal, 1998, 2000) so I do not consider them here in depth. Nevertheless, as we discuss the models and the psychology of form recognition, it is essential we keep in mind that part of my argument assumes there may well be boundaries that no scientific research can cross. I am not suggesting there is anything supernatural about the mind or any of the topics we discuss here. Rather, there are certain limits of complexity, numerousness, accessibility, and neutrality that may make conclusive solutions to the great conundrum of form recognition very difficult, if not impossible, to obtain. Some of the questions just posed may not be answerable!

The neutrality and complexity issues are best summed up in the following assertion: Both mathematics (including computational models) and behavioral observations are neutral with regard to the exact nature of underlying neural mechanisms and psychological processes. These methods are descriptive, rather than analytical processes, and there is no way that they can tease apart internal mechanisms. One way to describe this is that there is a "one to many" problem that must be faced. Any single behavior can be instantiated by a plethora of possible mechanisms. Engineers call this the black box constraint implying that a closed complex system can be decomposed into an innumerable number of alternative mechanisms. The converse—many quite different mechanisms can produce indistinguishable behaviors is, of course, also true. Thus, behavior alone cannot determine internal structures.

A further complication is, even if one could physically open the black box that the brain represents, surgically or electrophysiologically, the numerousness of the involved neurons and the complexity of the essential neural networks would not permit their analysis in a way that could possibly define the mechanisms. If this is true, then psychology had better be content with descriptive behaviorism!

Next, I point out that incredible and simplistic assumptions must be made concerning the nature of the so-called cognitive components to permit them to serve any serious role as the elements of an analytic, reductionist, valid statement of the structure of our minds. For example, the idea that cognitive modules of the type typically presented as theories of even such simple tasks as reaction times are fixed and operate in serial order is untenable. (See Pachella, 1974 and Uttal, 1998 for a complete discussion of this problem.)

The accessibility issue is a corollary of the neutrality issue and can be summed up by the following assertion: Just as the detailed nature of our psychological processes are not available to an external observer, so too are they unavailable to the introspecting individual. A substantial body of research (e.g., Bargh, 1997; Nisbett & Wilson, 1977; Wegner, 1994) also suggests that we, the "introspecting self-observer," have very poor insights into the motives, processes, and methods underlying our thoughts and decisions.

If this analysis is correct, then it means there can never be definitive proof that one particular method of form recognition is actually occurring in the brain. However, there is sufficient evidence, much of it ignored in the past, that can help us toward a "best fit," that is, the choice of a descriptive model or theory that is best able to order many of the findings forthcoming from this subfield of perceptual science. At the moment it seems that forces from other fields of science, most notably cellular physiology and computer programming, are misdirecting us toward a theory of form recognition that is not accurate in its formularization and is not germane to the problem of how we humans carry out these wonderful perceptual feats. The only way out of such a morass of conflicting, but unprovable, alternative hypothesis about internal mental processing is to turn to a revitalized and modified behaviorism.

With these caveats in mind and the essential questions concerning the nature of form recognition detailed in the preceding section, we are now ready to turn to more detailed discussions of some of the problems and challenges posed by them. The remainder of this book considers this field of scientific investigation from four different points of view.

Chapter 2 examines the various ways in which form itself has been dealt with in the literature. Specifically, it is concerned with the problem of representation, that is, what kinds of coded treatments of form are available and which of these may be useful in the specification of a form for subsequent processing.

Chapter 3 explores the empirical literature to see what has been learned in the psychophysical laboratory concerning form recognition. Operating within the confines just discussed, there is an enormous amount of information available that can be used to define the critical attributes and their effects if not to produce specific explanations. There are suggestions available in this domain that have often been ignored under the recent elementalist reign that may help to redirect our attention toward more plausible speculations and concepts in the field.

Chapter 4 organizes the major kinds of theory in this field. The rapidly developing history of explanations about the way in which organisms carry out form recognition is reviewed and then the main themes of modern theories are considered. Computer programming techniques that make no pretense of searching for or expecting to find biological or psychological explanation, but instead have been developed as useful tools to solve practical pattern recognition problems are briefly considered.

Chapter 5 summarizes this book, identifies emerging principles, and presents the components of a new behaviorist approach to solving the riddle of how we recognize forms.

2

On the Specification of Form
or How to Represent a Face
That It May Be Recognized

2.1. INTRODUCTION

This chapter reviews the history of efforts to define a form and to represent it in the form of a quantitative expression so that it can be used either in theory development or to manipulate stimuli in experiments. The absence of a universal means of representing broad classes of forms with a single formularization remains one of the most important impediments to progress in the scientific study of both human and computer form recognition. The development of a rigorous and unified representational system would permit progress to be made in answering many of the questions and overcome many of the obstacles encountered in Chapter 1.

It is obvious that there are innumerable distinguishable categories of form that can be constructed or sketched or generated either by a human or some computer algorithm. Familiar objects such as faces, animals, appliances, and flowers are now supplemented by exotic computer constructions that produce completely novel visual experiences. In Chapter 1, I pointed out that our theories of form recognition are still exceedingly primitive and, in general, have not been able to satisfy our desire to understand this wonderful human cognitive process. Many current theories are either loose extrapolations from some computer algorithm or remote metaphorical or verbal descriptions. Even the so-called "neural net" models are based on hypothetical networks that deviate more and more from what seem to be plausible explanations of actual neurophysiological function.

The challenge of "recognizing" the plethora of possible forms has not been solved by computer vision engineers in any way approximating the power of the human visual system. One has only to visit the assembly test and quality control rooms of even the most advanced semiconductor fabrication plants to be convinced of this assertion. The final examinations of the "chips" are still being carried out, in the main, by human observers in an activity that seems extraordinary tedious to the causal observer. It is in contexts like this that the clash between the powerful human ability to recognize forms and our inability to cope with tedium becomes most clearly manifest.

One of the main reasons for the failure of both biological form recognition theory and computer vision methodology is that our mathematics still does not provide us with a satisfactory means of dealing with global arrangement. We still do not know how to define a face, a rose, or a giraffe in a way that allows a computer to apply its powerful symbolic manipulative skills to the recognition process. The initial and quintessentially unsatisfactory solution to the challenging problem of representing a form is simply to reproduce it by taking a picture, drawing a map, or, in an equally isomorphic manner, to represent it as a mosaic of punctate pixels or voxels. The computational load created by this unencoded type of representation is enormous, often totally frustrating, and continues to be a major problem in the field. The *coding* of a form, in the sense of the production of a simpler or reduced characterization that still conveys the essentials of the original, is a major goal of any representation method.

Many of the representation methods described here revert to a kind of inherent elementalism. As I argued earlier, however, it is unsatisfactory (for the purposes of our science) to initially approach the problem from the point of view that a form is a list of independent features. Feature lists suffer from an enormous disadvantage from the start—the list of features used for one kind of form is typically not very useful for another. For example, we can define a set of rectangles by the lengths of its vertical and horizontal sides, but once we choose to move on to some other shape category, such as a face or a flower, the "features" of a rectangle are no longer germane to the new recognition task.

Similarly, some classes of geometric forms are easily represented by utilizing standard analytic geometry—a kind of mathematics that is specifically designed to represent forms in several dimensions. Unfortunately, as the form becomes more and more complex, so, too, do the expressions by which they are represented and eventually the analytic formulae begin to approach the complexity of the analog map or picture itself. Although it is easy to produce the standard linear, quadratic, or cubic forms using relatively simple expressions (e.g., $y = mx + b$; $r = ax^2 + by^2$; $z = ay^2 + b$; $y^2 = ax^3$), as the form of an object gets more complex or has major discontinuities, the expressions become either impossibly complex or intuitively meaningless infinite series. Imagine the traditional analytic geometry expression required to represent a face, for example. Something quite different has to be invoked and, as we see, several methods specific to faces have been proposed.

A major goal of all representation models described in this chapter is to simplify and normalize a form so it can be analyzed by algorithms and programs capable of carrying out the necessary classification or categorization. Representation is, therefore, considered in this chapter as a distinguishable process in the context of our theories that can and should be considered separately from the recognition process itself.

In its rawest form, even a simple image comprises a huge amount of data. Even the most powerful computers would explode under the pressure of the computational load imposed by a straightforward comparison (i.e., template matching) process. Thus the task of efficiently reducing, normalizing, or encoding the image for presentation to the later stages is critical to the success of such systems. This is the essence of the quest for an efficient encoding process—the search for informational minimization procedures able to capture the essence of an entire form with a very much reduced expression or set of data. This theme of information compression is ubiquitous throughout this chapter.

Beyond the ever present necessity to simplify and reduce for computational efficiency, however, lies another important goal for the effective representation of form. This is the need to quantify forms in a way that allows the psychological experimenter to carry out a controlled experiment. Without some way of ordering and measuring stimulus forms, it is very difficult to make sense of the results of even a well-designed experiment. A successful psychophysical study of form recognition requires that the physical parameters of the stimulus be quantified in a manner analogous to the way our system of measurement of wavelength has permitted such enormous progress in color vision. Without such a metric anchor, our ability to make progress in understanding how humans recognize forms will continue to be severely handicapped.

There is little or no *generalization* from one stimulus category to another. This, in a nutshell, is the source of the general problem confronted by all form recognition theorists. An algorithm or model that might work very well for cancer cells or hands or fingerprints is incapable of representing faces, or mammals, or crystals. Because it is widely appreciated that generalization from one set of forms to another is a very important unsolved problem, a number of authors have attempted to develop methods to accomplish just the kind of generalization that is missing from our current descriptive tools. Although, it has occasionally been possible to broaden the range of forms that could be represented, the general problem still largely remains unsolved. If such a universal or, at least near universal, means of fully representing a wide variety of forms in some other way than as analogs or pixel maps could be invented, it would be much easier to design experiments and to develop theories that were not confounded by the a priori commitment to a particular point of view. Few scientists argue that the initial assumptions and the theoretical base from which an investigator approaches an empirical study can have dominating influences on the way the data is interpreted (see, e.g., Hanson, 1958). The scientific study of organic form recognition could proceed with a minimum of such a priori constraints and misleading initial premises if our mathematics provided us with appropriate metrics of organization and form.

In the remainder of this chapter, I consider some of the most notable traditional approaches as well as some novel ways of representing forms.

2.2. ZUSNE'S TABULATION OF CONSTRUCTIVE GEOMETRIC APPROACHES

Zusne (1970), in what remains a very important review of the form perception experimental and theoretical literature, spent a considerable portion of his book in tabulating the methods for quantitatively generating geometrical forms for psychophysical research that had been developed up to that time. Each of these methods also can act as a means of representing form for psychological research. Zusne's approach was an eclectic one and he did not champion any particular point of view of the nature of human form recognition. However, he did deal with some of the most important aspects of the problem that motivated research in this field. For example, his approach to the holism–elementalism issue was a mixed one. Speaking of *form*, his pragmatic approach led him to say:

> It is usually perceived as a whole rather than in terms of its separate aspects or dimensions, so that it can be considered as a one-dimensional variable, along with color and movement. On the other hand, form does present, on closer examination, many different aspects or dimensions. When they change, form changes. . . . Thus, form may be considered both a one-dimensional emergent of its physical dimensions and a multidimensional variable. (p. 175)

In these remarks, Zusne considered form from the same perspective that I emphasize in this chapter—in terms of the multiple ways in which it can be represented. The more general issue—How does the human observer process form: as an one-dimensional entity or as a multidimensional attribute?—was not engaged by him.

If it had been, Zusne might have been deeply concerned with the conceptualization of "form detecting" neurons in the then current neurophysiological models of form perception. Although there is little doubt that the groundbreaking work of Hubel and Wiesel (1959, 1962) and Lettvin, Maturana, McCulloch, and Pitts (1959) revolutionized our thinking about the role played by single cortical neurons, even at the time of Zusne's (1970) book, doubts about the interpretation of these and subsequent results vis-à-vis their role in form recognition were being expressed. The history of the problem has seen the original ideas based on line sensitivities or movement detectors evolve into new concepts such as spatial frequency sensitive receptor systems or even more exotic ideas such as Hermite Eigenfunctions (Stewart & Pinkham, 1991, 1994). Nowadays, it seems clear that neurophysiological experiments like these pioneering ones are not likely to answer the question of the number of or kinds of dimensions that characterize a form.

We do have a clear appreciation, on the other hand, of how the geometry of a visual stimulus is represented in the earliest layers of the nervous system, through the work of a number of neurophysiologists. Although these low levels of visual processing are probably not the locus of the complex neural network processes that account for the cognitive act of form recognition, it appears that not only is there a separate channel for form up through the lateral geniculate body but, also, to the initial visual receiving area (V1) of the cerebral cortex (Livingstone & Hubel, 1988). Similarly, many neurons at various levels of the brain do individually display a specialized sensitivity to a relatively narrow range of spatiotemporal patterns.

The unavoidable fact, however, is that these individual cellular responses must be part of a much larger collection of interacting neurons required to implement the recognition process. Although some semblance of retinotopic (i.e., topologically constant) encoding is maintained through the lower levels of the nervous system, it is highly unlikely that such an isomorphic encoding geometry is maintained at the higher levels where neural activity becomes the psychoneural equivalent of the recognition process as it may be observed psychophysically. It is an equally inescapable fact that we have no better ideas of the coding mechanisms for these elevated levels of the brain than did any other vision scientists 30 years ago.

Zusne provided a thoughtful and detailed review of the methods that had been used from the 1950s to the 1970s to produce controlled sets of visual stimuli for the then current psychophysical studies of form perception. The idea of the controlled production of sets of forms was an important breakthrough. Prior to the 1950s, it had been a very arbitrary process. Pictures were mainly sketched or selected from natural contexts for use as visual stimuli. (An exception was the use of abstract forms by the Gestalt psychologists.) In some cases they were literally constructed as three-dimensional objects (Ames, 1955; Ittelson, 1952) Although some important discoveries were made (perhaps the most important was the appreciation of the ill-posed ambiguity of visual stimuli), there was still a great difference between stimulus control in the world of form perception and, for example, in the domain of color vision where wavelength anchored the experiments to a single physical dimension in a solid and sharply defined manner.

All of the methods that Zusne tabulated approached the problem of representing form from what can be designated as a *constructive* or *generative* approach. That is, virtually all of the pre 1970 methods he considered are actually means of generating stimulus forms in a "moderately" well-controlled manner. The generation process itself, therefore, became a prototypical means of representing forms. Until the seminal article by Attneave and Arnoult (1956), in which was proposed a specific method for generating forms, the arbitrary generation of a group of stimulus forms lacked any kind of order in the sense of any of the scales of measurement that Stevens (1951) suggested must be present on which to base a science. Ordinal, interval, and ratio scales were rare in the world of form perception. Without such scales for the stimuli, there was simply no hope of developing a mathematical model (or for that matter any coherent theory) of any kind of form perception; the literature of the time reflected this incoherency.

Attneave and Arnoult introduced a new idea—generating forms in accord with a specific set of rules so that the resulting stimuli were related to each other, at least in part, in a scalar manner. As much of a breakthrough as this idea was, it did not solve all of the problems that were created by the absence of a universally satisfactory way to quantify form. One continuing problem was that virtually all of the generating methods Zusne discussed could lead to the uncontrolled and unspecified emergence of perceptually salient properties during the generation process. That is, some very important attributes of a generated form could spuriously emerge that were not distinguished by the method or even explicit in the generating algorithms. Some of these emergent properties could and eventually were shown to have powerful effects on human discrimination and recognition.

The early 20th century Gestalt psychologists had forewarned about this problem by noting that the molar form of an object might display properties such as *Pragnanz, symmetry, collinearity*, or *goodness*, none of which were adequately defined or even anticipated by simple generating rules, but nevertheless could dominate the perceptual experience. Two forms could, therefore, be essentially "equivalent" in terms of the method, yet still have enormously different perceptual impacts. Symmetry, for example, could appear totally by chance in a form generated by any one of these generative procedures. Similarly, a random generating procedure could occasionally produce a straight line or some other regular form that could totally dominate the perceptual experience. Such unexpected global properties could make those particular "random" forms perceptually pop out from the other members of the set as strongly as if they had been printed in a different color. Another problem was that what were considered by the authors of these methods as random forms could actually take on an organizational quality that subtly linked them to some remembered object in a way that would make them more "recognizable" or "memorable" than other unrelated forms.

In the following paragraphs, I summarize the pre-1970 (which I designate as *first generation*) methods outlined by Zusne. His discussions of them were complete and my readers are referred there for consideration of the details of these interesting, but generally obsolescent and conceptually deeply flawed, methods. The most important of these constructive or generative methods include:

1. Attneave and Arnoult's (1956) original method was designed to produce two-dimensional forms by randomly selecting a set of points on a 100 × 100 matrix. The points were then connected according to rules so that the connecting lines defined the outline of a closed form. The selection of other sets of random numbers produced different forms. In this same article Attneave and Arnoult modified this original simple method to produce more complex objects by adopting three additional constraining rules:

a. No connecting line may be drawn twice.
b. No line may be drawn if it and other connecting lines enclose a point.
c. If a line is already a part of a shape, a new line may not cross it.

Although a wide variety of complex forms could be generated by this method, there still was no way to specify or prohibit the accidentally emerging global properties and attributes that were important for the process of recognition. Brown and Owen (1967) were probably the first to develop a computational algorithm to produce the Attneave and Arnoult (1956) stimuli automatically.

2. Fitts, Weinstein, Rappaport, Anderson, and Leonard (1956) and Fitts and Leonard (1957) proposed a somewhat simpler method to produce histogram-like stimuli and random checkerboard forms. They used 4 × 4 and 8 × 8 cell matrices and randomly selected a black (filled) or white (unfilled) value for each cell. Histogram like-stimuli were produced by filling in all of the cells in the column below the highest cell in each column. The random form stimuli simply used all of the cells that had been filled in by the random selection process. This latter method produced some very irregular forms, but again with unpredictable results concerning their perceptual saliency.

3. Thurmond (1966) modified the Fitts et al. (1956; Fitts & Leonard, 1957) method by using the values of a generated histogram to specify the amplitude of a set of equally spaced radii. He then connected these points to produce a closed contour of uneven radii. The Thurmond objects were very dif-

ferent than the Fitts and Leonard figures, but were produced by applying almost identical rules to a different substrate.

4. Curved segments could also be generated using a method also described by Attneave and Arnoult (1956). After deciding how many linear segments of a closed form were to be curved, points were selected on two segments that converged on a vertex. The two points were then connected by a regular curve defined by the equation of a circle.

The preceding material (summarized from Zusne, 1970) gives a general introduction to the methods for generating stimulus forms prior to the introduction of computers in the 1960s and 1970s. The general tactic was to act on a few simple rules and apply some kind of a random value generator to vary the properties of the members of the generated set. The outcome of such a process produced stimulus items that looked somewhat alike and that shared a common and partially determined origin. Nevertheless, the major difficulties still remain. First, the various methods produced forms that were visually quite distinct: there was no generality among them to permit them to be compared with each other in a robust manner. Second, control was lost over what turned out to be some of the critical global variables of form perception: the molar organizational attributes. Because of this latter failing, these stimuli could only be used in a shotgun manner not too dissimilar to the arbitrary drawings of an even earlier time.

2.3.   THE SECOND GENERATION

In the years following the publication of articles described in Zusne's (1970) review, a number of new developments were suggested that were sufficiently different in concept and implementation to be considered a second generation of image representation. This second generation was characterized by methods that were more definitive in defining forms. Typically, some ambiguity remained and there was often a need for an extended set of special rules, exceptions, and conditions. A more serious problem with these improved methods, however, was the same lack of generality observed in some of the methods mentioned in the previous section. As with so many other theories, systems, and methods in computer science and psychology, the universes in which they operated were severely constrained. The following section provides a partial review of several of the most important of these second generation coding schemes.

2.3.1.   Leeuwenberg's Coding Scheme

Leeuwenberg (1971, 1978) proposed a coding system for two- and three-dimensional visual forms that had many attractive features. His goal was to set up a quasi-algebraic system of expressions that could be evaluated to generate geometrical structures. Within a limited context of repetitive forms and regular structures, he was able to accomplish exactly that. It is interesting to note, however, that Leeuwenberg was not actually interested in developing an algebra of visual stimuli that could be used in experiments. Instead, his theory was aimed at developing a model of how forms were encoded in memory. In other words, his intent was actually to propose a cognitive model of the internal representation of perceptual experiences that was coded in an economical manner rather than a representation system for stimulus forms. Leeuwenberg (1978) specifically stated that his system was a representation of the "memory code" and not of any "perceptual process," to wit:

> The theory does not in fact deal with the perceptual process, though the suggestion may be otherwise, but with the result of this process, which is the memory code. (p. 278)

In actuality, however, such an association with the internal memory code must be considered to be highly speculative. Given the inaccessibility of these internal "codes," Leeuwenberg's work might well have been ignored as simply another unprovable "hypothetical construct." However, this would overlook the incontrovertible value of his model as a procedure for specifying and generating forms that could have been used as stimuli in psychophysical experiments or processed by computers.

Leeuwenberg (1978) was entirely correct, on the other hand, when he said that the proposed coding system "is only applicable to the structures of patterns in as far as these are not loaded with associations and meanings" (p. 279). His method of encoding two- and three-dimensional forms is one that deals purely with the geometrical structure of the stimuli and is not intended to assert or represent anything about the semantic content. Indeed, it is by itself neutral with regard to the influence of any of the attributes of any of the forms it represents on visual perception. Nothing in the representational code, therefore, says anything about human perception, per se. To establish the influence of the various dimensions and properties of specific constructions would require that these data be linked with the outcome of psychophysical experiments.

The Leeuwenberg form coding system is based on the organization of primitive elemental units (denoted by him as *grains*), and the rules that govern the spatial relations among successive grains. Figure 2.1, for example, shows a simple case in which the most primitive "code" for an arc is reduced through a succession of progressively simpler codes to a highly condensed formula, the sequential evaluation of which acts to reproduce the form. Slight modifications of the final condensed formula allows the researcher to manipulate various attributes of the form. The object (i.e., the

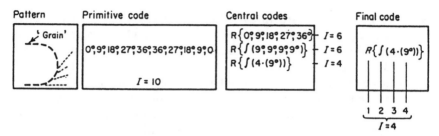

FIG. 2.1. A demonstration of the Leeuwenberg system for representing a global form (left-most box) and progressively converting it into the final quantitative representation shown in the right-most box. Although this method is not universally applicable to all forms, it was an interesting attempt to represent complex forms in an algebraic representation. From Leeuwenberg (1978). Reproduced with permission from Wiley.

"pattern") shown in Fig. 2.1 is a particularly simple form composed of a sequence of the small line segments—the segments being the grains in this particular case. The key to this particular application of Leeuwenberg's coding theory as well as it general utility is that the relation between the segments can be completely defined by the successive angles between them. Thus, the most "primitive" code is nothing more than a serial listing of the constituent angles and an equally precise statement of the nature of the grains.

The box in Fig. 2.1 labeled "central codes" shows the succession of steps of formula condensation; first a difference table is generated and the differences listed. This difference table is then condensed further by noting that there are four equal differences. Finally, by taking advantage of the symmetry of the object, the already condensed code is operated on by R{ } to repeat and mirror the portion of the sequence that has already been specified by the expression with the { } brackets. The symbol R{ } had a very specific meaning in the Leeuwenberg coding scheme: It directs the scientist to decode the sequence in the { } and then repeat it in reverse order.

In addition to R, the Leeuwenberg coding scheme coding scheme required that a large number of specialized operators be explicitly defined. Indeed, Leeuwenberg produced an entirely new and extensive set of operators for his coding scheme, a few of which are shown in Table 2.1. The integral sign ∫, in this case, takes on a nonstandard meaning (sequential addition) as also shown in Table 2.1. The complexity of this system is compounded by the fact that the meaning of the operators in Table 2.1 had to be clarified by a set of additional rules. For example, one of Leeuwenberg's rules (Number 4) provides the following supplemental direction be applied to the specific definition of operator 1. "The symbols enclosed in the brackets are run through cyclically and alternating until an identical period is about to follow" (Leeuwenberg, 1978, p. 280).

TABLE 2.1
A Sample of Form Operators

---

1. reversal: $R \{a, b\} = a, b, b, a$
2. integration: $\int (1, 3, 2) = 0, 1, 4, 6$
3. iteration: $3 \cdot \{a, b\} = a, b, a, b, a, b$
4. alternation: $(a, b)(c, d, e) = a, c, b, d, a, e, b, c, a, d, b, e$
5. chunking: $(a, b)(\{e, d\}, e) = a, c, d, b, e$
6. enlarging: $2 \cdot (a, b) = a, a, b, b$
7. left-right: $\pm (a, b, c) = +a, -b, +c, -a, +b, -c$

Note. From Leeuwenberg (1978).

Like the Fourier analysis approach discussed later in this chapter, the Leeuwenberg system can, within limits, be used both to represent a simple form and to reconstruct it. Furthermore, it also shares with the Fourier method some advantages and disadvantages. The major disadvantage of the Leeuwenberg method is the system of operators and their subsidiary rules are virtually unlimited and may not be generalizable from one category of form to another. Unlike arithmetic with its four basic operators, in principle capable of representing all of mathematics, or the Fourier system with its single set of orthogonal functions, a full blown Leeuwenberg representation system would require the expression of a huge system of rules and operators to handle a variety of different kinds of forms. Even then, it is not universal—it works only on a set of forms that can be constructed from simple repetitive operations. Irregular forms, with nonrepetitive grains and angles, would be extremely difficult to encode with such simple expressions.

On the other hand, a system such as the one proposed by Leeuwenberg does have some clear advantages, particularly if compared to some of the methods described by Zusne (1970). It provides a means for both encoding existing forms and creating new ones that are specific and do not fortuitously vary with the vagaries of a random number generator. It, thus, provides a form "algebra" that can be used to add images together or subtract properties from an image in a way that may predict the appearance of the resulting image. If it had been proposed after the general availability of modern graphic computers, the system might have had a much greater impact on stimulus generation than it ultimately did.

2.3.2. Julesz' Statistical Forms[1]

Another notable attempt to generate a coding system for visual stimuli was developed for the study of texture discrimination by Julesz (1962, 1975,

---

[1]Some of the material in this section has been abstracted and updated from my earlier work (Uttal, 1988).

1978). His idea was to use statistical constraints to generate repetitive patterns and to study the ability of human observers to distinguish between textures with different statistical properties. I have discussed his method previously (Uttal, 1988) and, therefore, only briefly recount the method Julesz used here.

The first two orders of statistical complexity proposed by Julesz are comparable to the moments (e.g., mean and variance) of descriptive statistics. The significance of each of the orders can best be understood if described in terms of dot patterns. The first statistical order of texture defined by Julesz (1975) is closely associated with the mean number of dots in the stimulus, that is, its mean density. Because dot densities are related to the energy being emitted by a surface, whether there are black dots on a white background or vice versa, first-order texture is also linearly related to the overall luminance of a dotted stimulus form. This is a straightforward extrapolation of a simple statistical idea, and it is intuitively obvious just what this first-order statistical measure signifies.

Julesz' second statistical order of texture is not quite so obvious, but it is still possible to achieve a relatively direct appreciation of what it means. The second-order statistic describes an aspect of a dotted form that is most closely related to the average spacing between dots—a textural property perceived by an observer as the "clumpiness" or "laciness" of the dots. It is analogous to the variance in ordinary descriptive statistics. Thus, two textures might have identical first-order statistics (equal numbers of dots distributed in equal sized areas) but may differ in their second-order statistics (as reflected in the degree to which the dots are bunched and separated) in a way that makes them appear very different. It is also important to appreciate that the second-order statistic describes much the same information described by the autocorrelation function or the spatial frequency spectrum. All three of these measures are sensitive to the regularity and periodicity of the stimulus material.

Third-order textural statistics are much less easily described in a simple intuitive way. Julesz described a statistical test in which a sample triangle of three dots are "thrown" onto a pair of dotted patterns.[2] If, on the average, the triangle's corners fall onto three dots the same number of times on the two different dotted forms, then the forms are said to possess the same third-order statistics.

Another way to conceptualize the idea of the third-order statistics of dot pattern more intuitively is to consider it as a common property of the ele-

---

[2]Surprisingly, as pointed out by Girvan (1999), Julesz' technique was a rediscovery of an 18th century technique attributed to the mathematician G. L. de Buffon (1707–1788). Buffon's "needle" technique, had itself been antedated by a "stick scattering" procedure developed by Udo of Aachen, a Benedictine monk who lived in the 13th century (Schipke & Eberhardt, 1999).

ments that make up the pattern, as opposed to the more global measures of density or clustering that were described by the first two orders. For example, Julesz has shown that if a texture is made up of U-shaped objects a third-order statistical difference is produced between two subregions when the objects are rotated (180°) even though this rotation maintains the same lengths of horizontal and vertical line components in the two parts of the scene. (Such a third-order difference is not discriminable.) However, if the U-shaped elements are rotated 90°, the respective lengths of the horizontal and vertical components in the figure changes. This produces a difference in the third-order statistics and this difference is immediately obvious to the observer.

Julesz notes another important general property of textured forms with regard to their statistical rather than their perceptual role. First, if two forms have identical statistics at one order, then all lower orders must also be identical, However, as we have seen, the converse rule is not true: Higher order statistics are independent of those of lower order. One can straightforwardly produce forms that are identical in their first order yet differ in their second- and third-order statistics as easily as forms that are identical in their second-order statistics (and thus necessarily in their first-order statistics), yet differ in their third-order statistics.

By applying the statistical generating rules, Julesz was able to both encode some simple forms and to generate some more complex ones. Over the years, he and other authors have carried out studies in which the human ability to discriminate these statistically defined textures was examined. The first-order statistic, as we have seen, is closely comparable to brightness or density measurements and, although constrained by some kind of differential threshold limits, it is obvious that human observers have a considerable ability to discriminate stimuli varying only in their first-order statistics. Barlow (1978) provided the definitive experimental result for first-order statistics. Pollack (1971) had shown earlier that subjects could rank order stimuli varying in their laciness or clumpiness, thus clearly demonstrating that humans are sensitive to the second-order statistics of repetitive forms.

The issue is not so clear cut when one considers the effect of third-order statistics on visual form discrimination. Originally, Julesz, Gilbert, Shepp, and Frisch (1973) reported that subjects could not distinguish between stimuli that differed in their third-order statistics but not in their first- and second-order statistics. However, later work (Caelli, Julesz, & Gilbert, 1978) led to the conclusion that there were some forms in which differences in third-order statistics could be discriminated. These special cases occurred when the statistical generating rule "accidentally" produced some special forms. These special forms included near linear arrays, corners, and closed figures of dots as well as some other special conditions in their statistical properties.

On the basis of these special forms Julesz and his colleagues were led back to a kind of feature sensitive model of the human visual system based on what he called *Textons*. Textons were supposed to be attributes of forms to which the perceptual system was specially sensitive. This special sensitivity was capable of overwhelming the perceptual power of the statistical orders. Textons were also one of the earliest coding methods that promised to incorporate some of the Gestalt principles of perception. Linear arrays and closed figures were analogous to the good continuity and closure principles suggested years earlier by the Gestalt psychologists.

Julesz' statistical analysis system is another example of an ingenious and useful system, albeit one that has many of the same kind of limits as others with which we have dealt. It works relatively well in a very limited domain of stimulus types to generate new forms in a precise way. It is also useful in the encoding of narrow classes of existing forms. As with so many other of the representation schemes discussed in this chapter, it does not generalize and, therefore, does not provide us with a universal means of quantifying the variety of other kinds of stimuli with which students of perception must be concerned.

2.3.3. Zero Crossings

The late David Marr published a book (Marr, 1982) that had enormous impact on the field of vision in general and recognition in particular. In that book he expanded on the value a system of representing images based on *zero crossings* that had been developed a few years earlier by Marr and Hildreth (1980). A zero crossing is the point on a three-dimensional curve where the value of the vertical coordinate $z = f(x,y)$ (corresponding to the amplitude of the two-dimensional image) passes through zero. Marr and Hildreth (1980) noted that an operator called the *Laplacian of The Gaussian* designated the zero crossings of an image. The Laplacian operator in rectangular coordinates is defined as

$$\nabla^2 = \frac{\delta}{\delta x^2} + \frac{\delta}{\delta y^2} \tag{2.1}$$

and the two-dimensional Gaussian function is defined as

$$G(x,y) = \frac{x^2 + y^2}{e2\pi\sigma^2} \tag{2.2}$$

where σ is the standard deviation of the Gaussian function. The Laplacian of the Gaussian is then defined by the following expression when the coordinates are transformed into a radial coordinate system:

$$\nabla^2 G(r) = \frac{-1}{\pi\sigma^4}\left(1 - \frac{r^2}{2\sigma^2}\right)\frac{-r^2}{e2\sigma^2} \tag{2.3}$$

The radial coordinate system was thought to be especially useful in this case because $\nabla^2 G(r)$ in such a format approximates the Mexican Hat shape long known to be the prototypical receptive field shape of low level visual neurons.

A system of such operators of various sizes (produced by varying r) can thus serve as a representational system for a form. $\nabla^2 G(r)$ is an excellent edge detector and can, therefore, be used to transform an image whose intensity is varying over wide ranges into edge-only types of images. In this way information is reduced in accord with the goal of efficient encoding but the essential information—the boundaries—is preserved. An additional advantage is that $\nabla^2 G(r)$ preserves the direction of the function from which it approaches the zero value (i.e., from − to + or from + to −). The advantage of the Marr and Hildreth method is that it does work on a wide variety of two-dimensional forms. Its main disadvantage is that it produces a representation of edges, boundaries, and contours. The emphasis on this particular attribute of a form prejudices any theories of form recognition based on it.

2.4. SHANNON'S INFORMATION THEORY

We have seen in the preceding section how the first and second generation's[3] efforts to quantify and represent forms for theory generation and experimental manipulation were constrained to the generation of narrow classes of geometrical objects. Other efforts to develop efficient coding schemes approached the problem from a different direction; rather then attempting to generate narrow classes of forms, the main goal was to represent forms by developing mathematical descriptions of them. Some (e.g., Leeuwenberg's method) can be designated as synthetic): They are designed to create new forms. Others (e.g., Marr and Hildreth's method) are better defined as analytic: They are designed to process an existing form into some simpler representation. We now describe another analytic method that has had enormous impact on perceptual science.

Since the 1960s, one of the often used words in scientific psychology has been *information*, or more specifically, the *amount of information*. The concept was brought to psychological attention shortly after its modern devel-

---

[3]Although information theory antedates the previously described methods, it is quite different and more modern in concept than are they. I place it here for conceptual clarity rather than historical continuity.

opment by two remarkable theoreticians—Norbert Wiener (1948) and Claude Shannon (1948). Weaver (1949), in describing the history of the development of the idea of information, noted this was one of those curious cases in which the two major contributing authors both went out of their way (unlike Newton and Leibniz, for example) to acknowledge their interaction, their respective contributions, and the important role that a number of other people played in creating what was clearly one of the most important developments in 20th-century science. Wiener, for example, noted the contributions of others such as R. A. Fisher and V. A. Kolmogoroff to the development of his and Shannon's methods for measuring information quantity. Both Wiener and Shannon (see, e.g., Shannon & Weaver, 1949, p. 85) were courteous and appreciative of the contribution to their thinking that had been made by the other.

Their interests, however, did differ; Wiener in his 1948 book, was one of the first to suggest the contribution of information theory and his special brand of control mathematics—Cybernetics—to the psychological and biological sciences. Shannon, an employee of Bell Laboratories, was influenced by his environment to concentrate on the applications that were relevant to hardware communication systems.

The history of information theory does not, however, start with Wiener and Shannon or their contemporaries such as Fisher and Kolmogoroff. For example, Schmidt (1941) published on the problem of regulating machines in what many consider to be from a truly cybernetic point of view. Given the long-term issue of regulation, many others, unacknowledged and now forgotten, must have also contributed to this important set of developments. Weaver also pointed out that this extraordinary intellectual development was based, in large part, on work done much earlier by such luminaries in physics as Boltzmann (1894), Szilard (1925), von Neumann (1932) as well as Shannon's predecessors at Bell Laboratories, Nyquist (1924), and Hartley (1928). All these mathematicians and physicists were interested in finding some way to measure and describe the information transmitted through communication systems. Needless to say, they too stood on the shoulders of the practical engineers who invented telegraphy (S. F. B. Morse between 1832 and 1835), telephony (A. G. Bell in 1876), wireless radio transmission (G. Marconi in 1896), and the subsequent development of television technologies (attributable to a surprisingly large number of contributors *from the late 19th century on!*)

Although most histories of television start with Baird's mechanical scanner in 1923 and Zworkin's invention of the iconoscope in the same year, TV's history is actually far older. Systems were proposed by Carey as far back as 1875 and by Nipkow in 1884. By 1897 Braun had developed the cathode ray tube and it was applied in an early wired TV system by Rosing in 1907. In 1908 Campbell-Swinton described a system that was in all possible ways conceptually modern. Broadcasting actually occurred in Germany as early as 1923.[4] The development of these practical technologies stimulated enormous interest in formal theories of communication.

Nevertheless, Shannon and Weiner's respective contributions are still considered among the milestones of the field. Shannon's (1948) unique contribution was to provide a specific formula for the amount of information in a message. It has now become a classic measure for engineers and mathematicians as well as psychologists; in its most familiar form it is usually represented as:

$$I = \sum_{1}^{a} p_i \log_2 p_i \qquad (2.4)$$

were I (also known as H in recent terminology) is the amount of information in a message, p_i is the probability that any one of a possible alternative messages is sent. With the logarithm taken to the base 2, the unit of information measurement is the familiar "bit."

The concept of information entered into psychological thinking very quickly. By the early 1950s, psychologists expected that the idea of information processing could be a major reorganizing principle in psychological science. Only a few years after Shannon's seminal work, Miller (1951) and Licklider and Miller (1951) were using the latter's formula for the amount of information in discussing the content of speech messages in Stevens' (1951) monumental *Handbook Of Experimental Psychology*. Not long after that, information measures were in active use as a variable in experimental reports to measure the information content of absolute judgments by Garner and Hake (1951) and Hake and Garner (1951), auditory stimuli by Pollack (1952, 1953), reaction times by Hick (1952) and Hyman (1953), and visually presented dot patterns by Klemmer and Frick (1953).

The impact of information theory continued to grow and interest in it immediately expanded. Miller (1954) published an early tutorial paper discussing the nature of information theory and its possible uses in psychology. A major meeting had already been held by 1954 on the topic of "The Estimation of Information Flow" that involved more than 40 of America's most distinguished experimental psychologists. Quastler (1955) edited the proceedings of the meeting and the resulting book was specifically titled *Information Theory in Psychology*. By the early 1960s, the information measure was a well accepted and fundamental theoretical concept in psychological research. Garner's (1962) classic and still informative theoretical book on *Uncertainty and Structure in Psychological Concepts* used the information idea

---

[4]The full history of television is available from the Encyclopedia Britannica [On Line]—article on Television Systems. The material discussed here is derived from that source.

as the foundation of what was to become an entirely new approach to psychological science.

The idea that the human was an information communicator and processor made up of functional units, much like those of which a computer was constructed, became the thematic metaphor of modern cognitive psychology. Unfortunately, the ultimate role played by the computer metaphor will probably turn out to be less than had been hoped for by its early proponents; many psychologists now feel that it is too confining and may, in fact, be based on some unsupportable assumptions. The supposed analogies between human cognitive processes and computer programs have not proven to be sufficiently robust to support a continuing commitment to this compelling metaphor. Nowadays, most psychologists agree that, although it was useful in organizing our theories, the processes used by computers are likely to be completely different than those used by an organic information processor.

The information measure, however, continues to play a very useful role in studies of human motor performance. Based on this measure, reliable laws of human psychomotor information processing capabilities have been repeatedly demonstrated. Among the most important of these are the well known Hick–Hyman law (Hick, 1952; Hyman, 1953) relating reaction time to the number of alternative stimuli that might be presented:

$$RT = a + bLog_2 N \qquad (2.5)$$

where RT is the reaction time, N is the number of alternatives, and a and b are constants.

Our concern with information theory and measurements is not with speech or psychomotor responses, however, but rather with the specification of the form of a two-dimensional stimulus. As with the other research areas, it is also possible to measure the "information content" of images with the Shannon measure. It is simply a matter of knowing how many possible conditions there are at each cell on the picture matrix and how many cells are on the matrix. For example, a small square 4×4 matrix can be defined and the probabilities specified such that each square could be either black (0) or white (1). If all combinations of black or white are equally probable, then the information content of the matrix is the same—16 bits. However, this is the maximum amount of information that can be sent by such a matrix when any particular combination of black and white cells is specified—*if each cell's state is totally independent of its neighbors*. If, on the other hand, the individual cells are related to each other, as they would be in any natural form, then the image is said to be redundant and much less information is transmitted in the same length message. If, for example, each matrix element is independent of its neighbors, then the amount of information is the same regardless of the particular image—there are literally 2^{16} different random alternatives that can exhibit this same measure of information and yet be different from each other. To the degree that this independence is not present, the amount of information is reduced. Thus, although the information measure can tell the observer *how much* information is present in an image, the information measure can not be used to tell us what image has been transmitted. What it can do is to provide some guidelines for the compression of the image so that redundant information (e.g., the values of identical adjacent cells) does not have to be transmitted.

For example, if dependencies between the various cells in the matrix do exist, then the amount of information is reduced because the probability of each cell is not completely independent of its neighbors. Thus, the amount of information in an 4 × 4 matrix that is all black (and this fact is encompassed within the probability tables) is essentially 1 bit, not 16 bits, as it was in the random condition. This measure of the amount of information may be used in some situations to define the perceptual complexity of an image up to the limits of the observer's ability to discriminate the fine detail.

2.5. MANDELBROT'S FRACTALS

In 1983, a remarkable and beautiful book was published by Mandelbrot.[5] In this work, he described a new approach to geometry to help represent certain types of geometrical forms. Like many other novel mathematical ideas, the concepts of fractal geometry became grist for a lot of nonsense concerning the metaphysical nature of the human mind and psychopathologies as well as a useful engineering tool. Fractals became cult objects for musicians and artists, all of whom were stimulated by the beauty of the geometries produced by the mathematical expressions. In a more scientifically productive vein, however, Mandelbrot's new geometry was also appreciated by psychologists; it seemed to be an interesting alternative way to represent and produce controlled stimulus forms for psychophysical studies of form perception.

In his book, Mandelbrot (1983) discussed the history that led him to postulate a mathematical system that is capable of representing an enormous variety of forms. The sources of his ideas were manifold. He was influenced by theories that had been invented to account for Brownian motion, for the probability distribution of words in written languages, and for the distribution of galaxies—among many others curiosities of scientific observation and arcane mathematical excursions in the past. A key idea was the contri-

---

[5]The 1983 book was an elaboration and updating of an earlier version (Mandelbrot, 1977). The present discussion is based on the 1983 volume.

bution of concept of the fractional dimension, an idea that was probably (although, according to Mandelbrot, there were so many other influences that this is not entirely certain) originally suggested by a German mathematician—Hausdorf (1919). Hausdorf's suggestion was that even though we are used to dealing with the three dimensions of space as being integers, there remain other possible dimensions that are not integer.

Dimensions in general are denoted by D. Mandelbrot was concerned with two different kinds of dimensions: The Hausdorf dimension D_H and the topological dimension D_T. A fractal (an object or a form) is defined as any object in which $D_H > D_T$. Specifically, D_H is the dimension of an object determined by the expression:

$$D_H = \frac{\log N}{\log n} \qquad (2.6)$$

where N is equal to the number of unit lengths along an irregular path between two points and n is the number of unit lengths along a direct linear path between the two objects. If D_H is not an integer, then the dimension is fractal.

The basic reason for both the utility of and the beautiful artifacts produced by the fractal notation lies in the fact that the equations used to generate irregular fractal paths are recursive. That is, the same equation may be applied over and over again to each of the unit length segments in the original figure to produce miniature, but self-similar, replications of the larger form. This recursive replication of the original form is endless and many fractals keep on replicating themselves up to the limits of computational precision to ever more microscopic versions.

The value of the fractal notation for representing forms is that it can encode an enormous number of forms, some of which are familiar and appear to be natural objects. The shape of the brain, alveolar and vascular treelike structures, mountainous landscapes, bubbles, galaxies, flowers can all be produced from relatively simple expressions, recursively evaluated. Equally well, beautiful and mysterious objects that are totally unfamiliar can also be generated by this precise mathematical language. As such, the fractal representation method became useful to researchers who sought methods of controlling the attributes of a set of forms in perceptual experiments. Among the earliest psychophysical studies in which fractal were used as stimuli were two carried out by Pentland (1984, 1986). In these studies he asked his subjects to rank the "roughness" of fractal stimuli that were plotted in two- and three-dimensional space. The first type of stimulus consisted of irregular paths comparable to the path of a molecule in Brownian motion. The second, an apparently three-dimensional object, was also to be judged for roughness. Subjects judgments of roughness generally corresponded with the fractal measures.

Shortly thereafter, Cutting and Garvin (1987) published a report in which they generated a series of fractal stimuli and asked their observers to judge the "complexity" of the figures using a 1–10 rating scale. In their experiments they manipulated the fractal dimension, the number of segments and the depth to which they the recursive generating rules were evaluated. Of these three, the recursion depth was the one that correlated best with the rating scales.

Cutting and Garvin (1987) then compared the correlations between the fractal measures of complexity and several other measures of complexity. Three in particular (a) the logarithm of the number of sides, (b) the perimeter squared divided by the area, and (c) the Leeuwenberg codes (discussed earlier in this chapter) correlated very well with the number of recursions, the fractal dimension, and the number of segments respectively. Thus all six measures were indicators of the otherwise subtle attribute that could be summed up by the term *complexity*. Each had its own advantages, but each was also encumbered with the generic weakness that so many of these generative protocols for representing forms share—an inability to generalize to forms other than the ones whose specific attributes they originally measured.

In the few years that followed, other investigators (e.g., Butler, 1991; Miyashita, Higuchi, Sakai, & Masui, 1991) suggested advanced methods for producing fractal images for psychological experiments. Subsequently, experiments were reported that used fractal stimuli to study various aspects of perceptual function. Some of these simply used the human to estimate the fractal dimension of stimuli (e.g., Kumar, Zhou, & Glaser, 1993). Others, however, went further and used this notation system for studying aspects of human visual perception, sometimes with only limited success in linking the measurable fractal characteristics with human perceptual sensitivities. Gilden, Schmuckler, and Clayton (1993), for example, studied the sensitivity of subjects to the statistical properties of fractal stimuli. They concluded that many of the mathematical properties of fractal stimuli had little or no influence and that contour perception could be better understood in terms of signal and noise measures.

Fractal generated stimuli were also used by Passmore and Johnston (1995) to study slant in depth perception experiments. They found that their subjects were able to do better when the field of view was enlarged. However, when they compared texture cues and fractal stimuli that had been low-pass spatial frequency filtered (blurred), subjects were relatively less sensitive to the fractal stimuli than they were to textured ones. The implication of their work, like that of Gilden, Schmuckler, and Clayton (1993), was that fractal stimuli did not seem to assay any special sensitivity in human perception. Similarly, when Rainville and Kingdom (1999) studied mirror symmetry using fractal noise, they discovered the noise had to be of the same scale as the stimulus patterns to have a substantial effect.

The overall conclusion drawn from all these studies is that the human visual system is relatively insensitive to one of the most important properties of fractal geometry—its recursive reduction to ever smaller self-similar components. However beautiful the pictures produced by fractal generating rules may be and however useful they may be in creating and encoding some kinds of images, the organic visual system does not seem especially sensitive to the aspects of a form measured by fractal geometry.

Notwithstanding this apparent irrelevancy to human vision, the value of Mandelbrot's contribution to psychology, as a mathematical tool and even as a means of generating new classes of experimental stimuli, should not be minimized. Indeed, it has already shown itself to be useful in theoretically describing many other physical and organic systems. It is in this latter context that it may further contribute to the psychology of visual perception. Kriz (1996), for example, suggested that fractal coding may be used to describe stimuli in a more holistic manner that certainly has much appeal to psychologists oriented toward the molar and Gestalt assumptions of a nonelementalist form recognition theory. Globus (1992) has also suggested that the fractal properties of the brain (as opposed to perceptual responses) may provide the basis for a noncomputational theory of brain function. It is yet to be seen how these recent psychobiological speculations will ultimately play out; there is no question that the mathematical tool has already played an important role in mathematics and other fields of science and the arts.

2.6. FOURIER'S ANALYSIS THEOREM

One of the most popular means of representing images is to apply a two-dimensional Fourier analysis. Throughout the 17th century, mathematicians such as Taylor (1685–1731) and Bernoulli (1667–1748) had shown that even very complex functions could be represented by adding up a series of simple *basis* functions. Bernouli, in particular, proposed the following functional relationship between a function and one of the most common sets of basis functions—a sinusoidal series.[6]

---

[6]Sinusoids are not the only possible set of basis functions that can be added together to reproduce an original form. Virtually any other set of "orthogonal" functions (i.e., a set in which no member can be derived from a combination of other members) can be used including square waves, checkerboards, Gabor functions, and even sets of Gaussian functions.

$$f(x) = \sum_{n=1}^{\infty} A_n \sin\left(\frac{n\pi x}{l}\right) \text{ for } 0 \le x \le l \qquad (2.7)$$

The important point inherent in this equation is that virtually any function $f(x)$ could be reproduced by adding together a set of sinusoidal basis elements.

From these seminal ideas, came one of the most important developments in mathematical thinking of the millennium—Fourier analysis—the development of Fourier (1768–1830). Fourier was another of the great polymaths of scientific history. He was also well known as an Egyptologist who had accompanied the Napoleonic army in its conquest of Egypt and then contributed to the encyclopedic 21-volume report on the archeological discoveries of the French expeditions.

As well as being an exceptionally talented and gifted theoretical mathematician, Fourier was specifically concerned with the practical problem of specifying the spread of heat on a surface. This work led him to enunciate the theory of what have come to be called both Fourier series and Fourier integrals in a classic mathematical document—The Analytic Theory of Heat (Fourier, 1822/1878). The impact of Fourier analysis went far beyond the study of heat, however. The widespread acceptance and enormous influence of the idea was based on Bernoulli's assumption that the sum of an infinite series of sinusoidal functions can be used to perfectly recreate *any function* as long as it met certain conditions of convergence, continuity, and, most of all, linear superimposition. (Superimposition means that the various components of the series must be capable of being added together in a simple, that is, linear, arithmetic way.) Almost all real images meet all of these qualifications. Indeed, one needn't add all the terms in what was an infinitely long series; even truncated sums of only a relatively few terms of a series could adequately approximate a function for most practical applications. This effect was enhanced by the fact that as the frequency of the sinusoidal components in a long additive series increased, their respective exponents tended toward zero, and therefore, their influence and effect diminished.

Fourier's immense contribution went one step beyond Bernoulli's suggesting it was possible not only to add together a number of selected sinusoids to represent a function, but to solve the inverse problem—to let the function specify which sinusoidal (understood to include both sine and cosine components) functions had to be summed to carry out that representation. In other words, Fourier's theorem specified which components at which phase angles had to be added together to reproduce the original function. This analytic task was more difficult than the synthetic one of adding together an arbitrary set of sinusoids; it required that the amplitudes (i.e., the coefficients) and the respective phase angles of an unknown set of sinusoids of varying frequencies had to be determined *from the properties of the original function*. As Fourier showed, this amazing process could be carried out in a systematic and formal manner. This idea had a powerful influence on many areas of modern science.

Fourier proposed the following expression, a modification of the Bernouli formula for a sum of a series of sinusoids, to represent a function $f(x)$:

$$f(x) = \frac{1}{2}a_0 + \sum_{n=1}^{\infty}(a_n \cos nx + b_n \sin nx) \qquad (2.8)$$

The task of the analyst was now to determine the coefficients a_n and b_n from the properties of $f(x)$ itself. Fourier's solution to this problem generated the following two equations:

$$a_n = \frac{1}{\pi}\int_{-\pi}^{\pi} f(x)\cos nx dx \qquad (2.9)$$

and

$$b_n = \frac{1}{\pi}\int_{-\pi}^{\pi} f(x)\sin nx dx \qquad (2.10)$$

By evaluating these two integrals, the coefficients needed to evaluate equation 2.8 could be determined and a close approximation to any function obtained in the form of a series of a select set of sinusoids. How close was simply determined by the size of n; economy of computation time and precision always being balanced against each other.

So far I have only discussed the one-dimensional form of Fourier analysis. Obviously this is incomplete if one is interested, as we are here, in the representation of two-dimensional forms. In the one-dimensional space, the function is represented by a sum of sinusoidal functions of different amplitudes, frequencies, and phase angles. However, these components vary in only one dimension—along the frequency axis. In the two-dimensional frequency space in which an image was transformed by a Fourier analysis, the family of sinusoidal basis functions is far more complex. First, the spatial sinusoids that are the basis functions are represented by two-dimensional grids. However, rather than simply being variations along a unidimensional horizontal axis, they may vary along an unlimited number or orientations.

Thus, the Fourier spectrum (the set of component spatial sinusoids) of an image is itself a two-dimensional array of what appear to be points in the *frequency space* defined by vertical and horizontal axes representing spatial frequencies. In fact, there are two such functions defined when one carries out a two-dimensional Fourier analysis: one specifying the amplitude of each of the component frequencies and the other defining the phase angle of each of these component spatial frequencies. Furthermore, as just noted, not only are there spatial sinusoids oriented vertically and horizontally to be dealt with, but also the space in the quadrants between the axes must represent a much larger collection of oblique functions.

Because of the increased complexity of applying the Fourier analysis technique in two dimensions, the mathematics implementing the *Fourier transform* is designed to go directly from $f(x,y)$ (the original image) space to two functions in the (ω_1, ω_2) spatial frequency space.[7] These two functions represent the amplitudes and phase angles of the component spatial sinusoids, respectively.[8] Equation 2.11 describes the Fourier transform of $f(x,y)$:

$$F(\omega_1,\omega_2) = \int\int_{-\infty}^{\infty} f(x,y)\{\exp - i(\omega_1 x + \omega_2 y)\}dxdy \qquad (2.11)$$

Sometimes it is useful to use both the Cartesian space (x,y) and the frequency space (ω_1,ω_2) simultaneously. Jacobson and Wechsler (1988) developed such a scheme. The main advantage of representing a form in both domains is that separation of the components of an image can be best accomplished in this manner. Some elements are best distinguished by the usual x,y space representation and some by the spatial frequency representation. The letters of which this paragraph are composed, are an example of the former, On the other hand, a plaid pattern approximating a particular set of spatial frequencies exemplifies an element of the pattern that is better represented by the latter representation: the frequency space. As usual, it is the particular task and the particular object(s) or form(s) to be recognized that determine the choice of the most appropriate representation scheme.

The Fourier representation of an image is not encumbered by the limitations of some of the methods we have described already: the geometrical generation and the information measures. Each Fourier transformed representation can be reversed back into the original image by a process called (not surprisingly), *Inverse Fourier Transformation*. Thus, the representation of an image in terms of a sum of a series of terms is mathematically precise and unique as well as being nearly universal. The challenge now faced is to

---

[7] ω_1, ω_2 represent the horizontal and vertical axes of a new space within which measurements are made in terms of the spatial frequencies of the sinusoidal spatial functions rather than the distance measures used in the more familiar x,y space.

[8] Although perfect reconstruction of a form requires both amplitude and phase information, an imperfect, but sometimes useful, approximation to the original image can be obtained from the phase information alone in some cases. I am grateful to Dr. Dana Sinno of the MIT Lincoln Laboratories for bringing this little known point to my attention.

determine whether this powerful mathematical method is biologically or psychologically relevant.

Any answer to the question of the relevancy of the Fourier representation method to psychobiological theory has to prefaced with an acknowledgment of its great strength. Fourier analysis meets many of the specifications of an ideal representational system: (a) It is driven by the nature of the original image; (b) it is encoded in a manner that is reversible to the original image; and (c) it is applicable to virtually all real images.

Unfortunately, its great mathematical power is, at the same time, its great weakness as a psychobiological theory. In fact, it is so general that its suitability as an explanatory theoretical model of vision should have been questioned from the beginning. *This is so because it works (mathematically) regardless of whether or not the underlying processes or neural machinery are composed of frequency sensitive mechanisms.* In other words, it is, from some points of view, too general and too powerful or, in another terminology, it is neutral with regard to the actual underlying mechanisms.

Nevertheless, many psychobiological models of vision (for summaries see De Valois & De Valois, 1988; Graham, 1989; Olzak & Thomas, 1986) are based on the assumption that this type of transform is not only a good means of mathematically representing images but also the means by which the nervous system is physiologically organized. Following the work[9] of Kabrisky (1966) and Campbell and Robson (1968), the idea that this analysis method was physiologically and anatomically instantiated in the form of spatial frequency channels gained wide popularity. This physiological theory, however, is not of concern at this stage in our discussion.

Rather, the problem confronted here as just noted, is that the descriptive and representational powers of the Fourier mathematics are so general and so powerful that they would work to describe physiological and perceptual functions regardless of whether or not such spatial frequency tuned components were actually present in the nervous system. Furthermore, however satisfactory and convenient the sinusoid function-based Fourier transform may be as a means of uniquely representing an image, it is not the only analytic method or set of hypothetical basis functions capable of doing so. Stewart and Pinkham (1991, 1994), for example, have shown that all mathematical procedures (including the sinusoid-based Fourier analysis) proposed as "explanations" of visual processing are actually

---

[9]I take some pleasure in noting that in Uttal (1958) I was one of the first to apply Fourier analysis to a psychophysical problem. The application was not in the field of vision, but in the arena of somatosensory perception. Because it was known that the impedance of the skin varied with the frequency of alternating currents, I suspected that the Fourier components of square pulses of current might be differentially affected as a function of the duration of the pulse. In fact, calculating the current in terms of its frequency components led to a close approximation to a psychophysical reciprocity law for the skin in the range of 10 μsec to 10 msec.

equivalent to (i.e., duals of) each other and can be shown to be special cases of a more general form of mathematical representation called Hermitic Eigenfunctions. Each, however, is based on distinctly different physiological assumptions that are, in turn, quite separable from the mathematical ones. Any of the mathematical models is capable of modeling the actual biology of the nervous system equally well (Stewart and Pinkham's point) and none, therefore, is capable of discriminating between any of the biological assumptions.

The point is that whatever the mathematical formulation and however successfully it may describe a form, any method such as Fourier analysis, Hermitic Eigenfunctions, or Gaussian modulated sinusoids (Gabor functions) is actually, fundamentally, and "in principle" neutral with regard to the specific underlying mechanisms. These methods may perfectly describe any form in terms of sinusoids (or any other set of basis functions) and yet there may be nothing like the spatial components actually encoded in real neural networks. Similarly, if there is any sensitivity to the Fourier components evident in the psychophysical data, so too should one be able to demonstrate sensitivity to any of the components developed by any of the other methods. The problem, to recapitulate, is that the method is too powerful! It works (mathematically) independently of the internal mechanisms; that is, the hypothetical frequency components of the system are generated regardless of their actual physical existence.

The fallible Fourier anatomical–physiological–perceptual hypothesis (as opposed to the indisputably robust Fourier analytic procedure) has evolved over the years. The classic sinusoids have been replaced with other basis functions such as Gabor functions, square waves, or even sets of normal curves. Although each new theoretical development may have produced a more convenient physiological analog, it is still impossible to assert that the brain is a Fourier or any other specific kind of physiological "engine."

There have been other criticisms raised concerning the Fourier-based psychobiological theory of human vision. Poggio (1982), for example, noted the following discrepancies:

> The main points against a Fourier interpretation are: (1) The bandwidth of the channels is not very narrow. It is impossible to represent "Fourier coefficients" by means of cells with spatially localized receptive fields. (2) As Campbell and Robson found, early visual information processing is not linear (e.g., probability summation [Wilson & Geize, 1977] and a failure of superimposition). (3) No convincing demonstration has yet been made that phase information is coded. (p. 88)

Other arguments against the Fourier physiological–anatomical theory have been raised from time to time, some of which are corollaries of the ar-

guments presented by Poggio (1982). These include (1) The putative channels do, in fact, interact and are not independent as required by Fourier Theory. (2) The theory of physiological channels seems to work only for stimuli
that are presented in the form of spatial frequency patterns. (3) There do not
seem to be enough channels; and so on. As of this date, fortunately, there
does seem to be some amelioration of the extreme and uncritical acceptance
of the Fourier approach to the psychobiology of visual perception.

Wenger and Townsend (2000, 2001) also concerned themselves with the
problem of the relevancy of the Fourier model to psychological studies.
Their particular concern was with the popular idea that low-frequency information encoded the configurational attributes of faces. They raised
three specific caveats concerning this hypothesis:

- First, and possibly most important for present purposes, the validity and
  coherence of the mapping between ranges of spatial frequencies and
  those aspects of the stimulus that support performance indicative of
  configural, holistic, featural, and so on, processing is compromised by a
  lack of definitional precision with respect to the latter constructs....
- Second, the heuristic [of low spatial frequencies coding configurations]
  oversimplifies the distinction between global and local processing....
- Third, in some applications it overlooks the degree to which various
  spatial frequency ranges might function to support performance in task-
  specific ways. (p. 126)

Wenger and Townsend (2000, 2001) thus concluded that their work cannot "answer the question of whether there exists *any* critical spatial frequency band for faces" (p. 138). Nor did they provide any support for either
the low-frequency hypotheses or high-frequency precedence hypothesis in
face processing. Rather they argued for a task-dependency hypothesis (i.e.,
that those aspects of a stimulus used by the nervous system depended on
the task at hand). Without so categorizing their point of view, Wenger and
Townsend clearly are expressing a kind of prototypical nonreductive behaviorism here. Such a behaviorist viewpoint would logically suggest that
the ability of any mathematical description or psychophysical outcome to
uniquely define the internal anatomy and physiology of a closed system is
always going to be questionable.

There are, however, many uses of the Fourier analysis approach that are
quite uncontroversial and quite useful. The powerful and elegant Fourier
analytic method provides an effective means of manipulating images, both
as stimuli in psychological experiments and for computer image processing
and communication. Changing the analog image into a set of numerical values opens the door to the processes of filtering (selectively subtracting
information by removing certain bands of spatial frequencies) or superim-

posing (selectively adding information by adding certain bands of spatial frequencies) images. Processing images by filtering permits the experimenter to enhance certain image attributes and to produce images that are, for example, blurred (low pass filtering) or edge enhanced (high pass filtering) in specific ways. Superimposition permits the experimenter to carry out such procedures as image averaging, an extremely useful means of reducing the effect of spurious noise. It is also possible, of course, to add additional noise information by superimposing a relatively noise free image and selected kinds of noise. Such a controlled means of image degradation has been used frequently throughout psychophysics as a means of varying the visual properties of an image.

The analysis methods proposed by Fourier, therefore, adds an enormous amount of precision and quantification to anyone interested in studying or manipulating images. It raises the study of form out of the muck of arbitrariness and vague nebulosity in which it was mired prior to its application. What had been an arcane mathematical technique, useful only to engineers and physicists, became in the latter half of the 20th century a mainstay of both form perception and computer vision scientists. However, the practical utility and the indisputable power of the method also meant that it could be misused in a theoretical context. The psychobiological theory that spatial frequency channels existed as anatomical or physiological entities in the nervous system was one extreme overgeneralization of the analytic method. Let us consider why this happened and what are the true limitations of the frequency analytic methods in general once one goes beyond their unarguable utility to represent stimuli in a quantitative manner.

The most obvious source of spatial frequency thinking in theories of visual perception, of course, is the fact I have already alluded to several times; namely that the Fourier theorem is, in a certain sense, too powerful to be theoretically definitive—in spite of its extreme value in many other contexts. That is, it works regardless of the actual underlying physical mechanism. Fourier's contribution was to state a general procedure for describing functions in a standard way, not to provide a means of peering into a closed system to determine its inner workings. This is often misunderstood by those who apply the method. Hopefully not to overstate the point, this descriptive mathematical procedure, like all others, is actually completely neutral with regard to the psychobiology of perceptual experience.

A second problem that arises when one uses the Fourier analytic method to describe a form is that it transfers the analog image in the usual x,y space into a set of numbers in the ω_1,ω_2 (spatial frequency) space which can, itself be extremely difficult to interpret. Certainly, the visual system makes no sense of the Fourier transformed image. Although it is completely unknown what transformational space is used by the nervous system to represent images, there is (arguably, I appreciate) no special reason beyond the existence of this particular formularization to assume that the brain uses a Fourier transform, rather than some other not yet formularized transform, to represent and encode images. Indeed, because there are well-known discrepancies between predictions made by the Fourier method and the psychophysical data, there is at least some suggestion that this model is incomplete, at best. At worst, it has propelled us willy-nilly toward an interpretation of how organic form recognition works that is very likely to be quite inaccurate.

Third, Fourier analysis and any other coding system that depends entirely on the characteristics of a given stimulus ignores another major aspect of the nature of visual perception. As Klemmer and Loftus (1958) demonstrated and Garner (1962) emphasized in his very important book, discrimination of visual forms is dependent not only on the characteristics of the individual stimulus but also those of the domain of similar forms from which it was selected. Our own work on task-dependence (Uttal, Baruch, & Allen, 1995a; 1995b; 1997) also shows that the nervous system may be far more adaptable than can be encompassed in any simple Fourier theory of perception. Thus, the incompleteness of Fourier analysis as a coding scheme for the human perception of forms is once again highlighted. Indeed, incompleteness is a property of virtually all the coding schemes we discussed so far. None comes close to imitating the extraordinary and special property of human form perception—generalization from one stimulus domain to another.

Another important general point is that many of these theories that may at first glance seem to be very different are actually based on very similar fundamentals. Neurophysiological theories of form perception actually share some common assumptions with the Fourier mathematical approach. Both encode forms by combining elements (spatial frequencies in the former case and the output of spatiotemporally sensitive neural mechanisms in the latter) into a single composite entity. The details are different, but the general concepts are the same. Fourier synthesis is achieved by superimposing or adding the basis functions together. Neural combination is accomplished by a less tangible and more mysterious process currently referred to as binding. Unfortunately, this latter word hides the fact that neural combination (and interaction) is accomplished by very complex and, perhaps, inexplicable processes.

2.7. THOMPSON AND BOOKSTEIN'S MORPHOMETRICS

Morphometrics, briefly introduced in Chapter 1, is a explicitly quantitative geometrical approach to the representation and study of shape and form. From its inception practitioners of this approach were particularly inter-

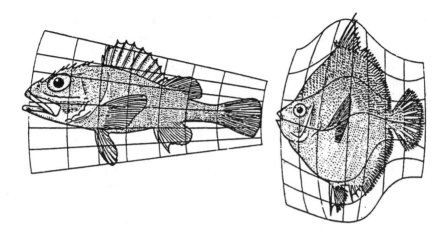

FIG. 2.2. Thompson's graphical demonstration of how a simple topological distortion can account for the shapes of many different kinds of fish. From Thompson (1917).

ested in developing a means of not only representing forms but also of comparing them. The precursor of modern morphometrics clearly was the graphic approach taken by Thompson (1917), although historians of the topic trace influences on him as far back as the medieval mathematician and artist Albrecht Durer (1478–1528). Thompson certainly must also have been influenced by Descartes' invention of analytic geometry and by the 19th-century naturalists who were enchanted by the beauty of the huge variety of natural forms their explorations were discovering. Although these early naturalists did not emphasize the link between the objects of interest to them and mathematical elegance, clearly such objects as the chambered nautilus stimulated ideas of regularity and symmetry that were to have important repercussion in the years that followed. An insightful, albeit brief, history of the origins of morphometrics can be found in Reyment (1996).

Thompson's great contribution was to graphically combine the analog representation of geometrical images and the idea of a deformable coordinate system. Figure 2.2 clearly makes the point that different species (of fish, in this particular case) are actually "topologically" very similar to each other when compared on such an elastic grid. That is, although the proportions may differ greatly from one species to another, all fish (and, presumably, this held for all other closely related classes of animals and plants) were actually evolutionarily stretched and distorted versions of each other.

Thompson was fully aware of the relevance and need for mathematics to carry out his vision of a science of form; however, his interpretations and manipulations were almost entirely graphical (i.e., pictorial) rather than mathematical. That is, all of his demonstrations are presented in the form of drawings, probably made by hand, rather than expressed in the notation of formulae and variables. In this regard, his work had not progressed much beyond that of Dürer[10] who had used many of the same graphical techniques in drafting his art. In fact in some respects, Dürer (who has also been considered to be one of the founders of modern geometry) was actually well ahead of Thompson in applying mathematics to geometry. As Bookstein (1978), speaking of the qualitative nature of the work of Thompson and others who followed him, pointed out:

> The problem here is fundamental. It seems impossible to extract quantity, as Thompson formulated it, in any straightforward way. Even after a decade during which the brightest graduate students all have had access to computing power adequate for large multivariate data sets, there is no hint in the literature of a line of attack on quantification since one has painstakingly drawn out the Cartesian grid. (p. 76)

And later:

> At the conclusion of my survey to 1977 of the literature on Cartesian transformation, I find no improvement from within morphometrics or without, no methodological advance for particular styles of data, that is comparable in stature with Thompson's original method. Six decades after its publication the method still resists quantification except in special cases. . . . Any one trying to make new headway must begin to build, as I do, exactly where Thompson left off. (p. 89)

Although some may dispute the point, it seems that the modern emergence of morphometrics is attributable to the work of this same Fred L. Bookstein, then a graduate student at the University of Michigan. His dissertation was one of those unexpected treatises of innovative genius (Bookstein, 1978) that was to have an enormous effect on the representation and comparison of forms and the modern development of the field of morphometrics. In his dissertation, Bookstein proposed a novel method for quantifying the grid-like representations of forms so eloquently championed by Thompson. The essential aspect of Bookstein's contribution was that any form drawn on a rectangular grid such as the one shown in Fig. 2.2 could be transformed by a specialized geometry[11] into another set in which

---

[10]Nowhere is Dürer's fascination and commitment to mathematics more clearly illustrated than in his great engraving *Melancholia* in which the tools, concepts, and objects of arithmetic and geometry are depicted together. Dürer must have been a remarkable person. His self-portrait (1500) is almost photographic and his engravings are still among the most treasured of renaissance art. His role as a mathematician is much less well known, but is appreciated by historians of mathematics. Clearly, he should rank with Leonardo and Michelangelo among the most remarkable intellects of all time.

[11]Bookstein used a non-affine geometry in his method. That is, transformed lines do not remain parallel in the transformed image. Instead, lines can become curves and polygons may

the intersections were also at 90° (i.e., thus defining the new set of coordinates as *biorthogonal*, if not affine) but the connecting grid lines themselves might be curved. This new set of transformed axes looks much like the one Thompson drew, which was shown in Fig. 2.2. The process of going from a rectangular grid to a biorthogonal one was defined by Bookstein as *differential stretch*—the mathematical equivalent of growth.

The computation of the new curved interconnecting grid lines requires the evaluation of partial derivatives and is not considered in detail here. However, once the formula for the component arcs of the curves connecting the points of intersections are computed, it is also possible to interpolate between the intersections to produce a full reconstruction of the image in the newly transformed biorthogonal coordinate system. In other words, it is now possible to go from the first to the second representation in Fig. 2.2 in a formal, mathematical, and rigorous manner, rather than in the graphical procedure used by Thompson (1917).

The essence of Bookstein's contribution can be interpreted in another context. He was able to link Thompson's (1917) graphical morphometrics with the concept of splines of the kind used by structural engineers in finite element analysis (his specific methods are described more fully in later works; see Bookstein, 1987, 1989, 1991). *Splines* are functions which can approximate the course of a curve, but only within a small range, say between a pair of points on the curve. The key goal in deriving splines of any kind (including those joining points of intersection or "landmarks" along the biorthogonal curves) is to have the trajectories of the endpoints be identical to the splines to which they connect. A set of relatively simple curvilinear splines can thus be joined together to represent a curve whose overall form is too complex to be represented in its entirety by any single function. The idea that a set of structural elements, comparable to those used in engineering bridges, can be used to represent fish or faces or any of a wide variety of other forms of biological relevance was an important intellectual step forward. Indeed, it was a quantum leap; one that offered a novel and creative way to transform and represent forms. For a good review of these and other historical developments in this field, see Marcus, Corti, Loy, Naylor, and Slice (1996).

2.8. THE REPRESENTATION OF THE HUMAN FACE

Perhaps the most difficult of all forms for which to establish a reasonable coding scheme is the human face. Yet, face recognition is carried out with

---

have curved sides. This is in accord with the growth criterion that was such an important part of the biological problems to which his work was mainly intended to be applied.

such power and versatility and with a virtually instantaneous response by the human observer. A familiar face can be picked out of a huge crowd; distorted or caricaturized faces identified from what may seem initially to be totally inadequate cues; and faces can be recognized even after such substantial changes as the removal of a mustache or beard or a complete change of hairstyle. Indeed, accurate recognition may occur even though the observer might not recognize what particular change had occurred. On the other hand, even one's spouse could go unrecognized if encountered in a totally unexpected and unusual context.

Obviously, face recognition by humans is an extraordinarily complex process involving many levels of cognitive processing. Most of these levels still retain many mysterious and unexplained aspects for students of form recognition. In a subsequent chapter I consider what we have learned about the process of face recognition in particular. For the present, however, attention is directed to the special problem of how one might represent or encode a face for analysis and research.

Face recognition has become a very difficult problem for several reasons. One reason, of course, is that there is no single and simple metric along which to measure faces. Therefore, it has been extremely difficult to program into a computer the ability to adjust to such nonnormative presentations as those obtained from different perspectives as a face is turned or tilted from the canonical "face-on" (i.e., frontoparallel) view. Furthermore, the face is a very elastic object itself. Changes in expression can seriously hinder even the fastest computer from solving the recognition problem so easily handled by the human observer. To overcome this seemingly intractable obstacle a number of different specialized methods particularly designed to represent faces has been proposed. Both two- and three-dimensional systems have been suggested, all in the hopes that a particularly sensitive scheme will allow the next stage of the recognition process—recognition itself—to be more easily handled. Whatever comparison system is used, it is certain that the initial way a face is represented is ultimately critical to later stages of the recognition process. A modern review of the field of face recognition can be found in Wechsler, Phillips, Bruce, Soulie, and Huang (1998).

First, a comment is appropriate that applies to face recognition in particular and form recognition in general. This theme has already been introduced and I return to it in later chapters but its importance is so great that it bears reiteration now. Although the least likely of those proposed, the usual theory of human form recognition entails the comparison or correlation of a probe face with a collection of prestored faces to see which matches best. This is the standard way that computer models of the process are currently being programmed. Why this should be so is reasonably obvious: Few alternative models have been proposed that would permit simple computer logic to be applied to the recognition problem with all of its high level (i.e., cognitive) ramifications. Inasmuch as successful computer recognition of faces would have enormous scientific, legal, and commercial value, computer scientists continue to do what can be done, and will probably continue to do so until a more realistic and holistic theory of recognition evolves. Even so, the comparison, matching, or correlation process must be distinguished from the representation process that is the major concern in this chapter. The hope is that some new representation method will eventually permit an alternative recognition strategy to emerge.

Scientists interested in face representation have drawn on the world of theoretical physics for the concept of a face space. Valentine (1991, 2001) is among those who have developed the concept that a face can be represented in a special multidimensional space in which the dimensions are defined by measures of the features of which it is composed. Each face, therefore, is objectified as a point in this multidimensional space. O'Toole, Wenger, and Townsend (2001) distinguish among three different kinds of face spaces:

- Abstract Face Spaces: An abstract face space is defined independently of the geometry of the face. The space may contain no remnant of the overall form of the original space but essentially codes it as an abstract collection of numerical measures. The relationships among different faces in such an abstract space are independent of their role in perception or in tests of their similarity. The dimensions in this case are more or less arbitrary.

- Psychological Face Spaces: Psychological face spaces, on the other hand, are defined by their role in perception. Faces are presented for comparison to determine their recognizability or confusion. Multidimensional scaling procedures are then invoked to define a space whose dimensions are based on these perceptual similarities.

- Physical Face Spaces: Physical face spaces are defined by physical (i.e., computational) evaluations of their similarity. For example, if a correlational analysis is carried out among a large number of faces represented either in their raw pixel form or in some transformed version of it, some faces will be shown to be more similar to others and others to be less similar. The metrics of similarity establish the dimensions of a physical space by means of such methods as principle components analyses. (Abstracted from O'Toole, Wenger, and Townsend, 2001)

As we see in the next sections, the classification of any proposed system into one of these three categories is not always unique. As with so many other aspects of the form recognition problem, ingenious combinations of the different approaches are ubiquitous. This fact, by itself, is an important aspect of the problems confronted in this book. So many different methods have been applied and so many of them have been at least marginally successful, at least partially, that it is unlikely any single one provides a unique answer to how we perceptually process faces. Rather, the enormous adaptability and the existence of the very large number of possible interacting strategies may represent a profoundly important ultimate "truth" about form recognition in general.

2.8.1. Eigenfaces

Given the amount of interest in face recognition, it is not surprising that numerous alternative coding schemes have been proposed and implemented. It is difficult to review all of them, but some have become increasingly important in recent years. For example, consider the concept of the *Eigenface*. The Eigenface space concept was originally proposed by Kohonen, Oja, and Lehtio (1981) as a means of storing information in distributed memory systems. In recent years, Turk and Pentland (1991) have continued the development of the concept of the Eigenface[12] specifically as an algorithm for use in face recognition programs. In this case the Eigenfaces represent a condensed representation of the set of faces that are to be compared with the unknown face.

Specifically, an Eigenface is a vector (of values) in a standardized and reduced subspace. It is a computed reduction of the total data set of pixels in which the set of comparison faces were initially represented to a set of characteristic values that are defined by the comparison set of faces. It represents the key information associated with each face in the comparison set in the form of a unique "solution" to the problem posed by the superset of all possible faces. The "Eigen–" component idea may be further specialized to *Eigeneyes* and *Eigenmouths* (see, e.g., Cottrell, Daily, Padgett, & Adolphs, 2001).

The problem with which the Eigenface concept is supposed to deal is the huge number of values in the original images. If each pixel must participate in any suggested analysis or comparison process, the computational load is enormous; it is not even certain that such an unreduced form is the way that the nervous system functions. Indeed, doting on all of the pixels in a face-form seems antithetical to the way the human is likely to actually processes face information. The easy recognizability of caricatures and our sensitivity to the configurational attributes of a face are strong evidence that the total amount of raw information in a face is not key to its recognition.

---

[12]The *Eigenface* is a mathematical analog of the more familiar formal mathematical *Eigenfunction* which is the solution of an integral equation or matrix for a particular value (the *Eigenvalue*). Several different means to reduce the original equation or matrix to the eigenfunction are available including Principle Component Analyses.

Somehow, we abstract from the total stimulus, a reduced amount of critical information.

To imitate this human property and to reduce the data set, a new space of Eigenfaces is computed from the set of faces with which the probe or unknown face is to be compared, typically by carrying out a Principle Component Analysis. The resulting vectors representing each face in the new face space represents a much smaller data set than was contained in the original set of library images. Therefore, the comparison process can be carried out faster and with more attention given to key aspects of the faces than to the individual pixels of the original picture space. In this regard, calculation of the two-dimensional face space is comparable to image compression in one-dimensional communication systems. Interestingly, such subtleties as the inability of observers of one racial group to distinguish between members of another, is modeled fairly well by the Eigenface approach to generating the reduced subspace.

Craw, Costen, Kato, and Akamatsu (1999) studied the efficacy of the Eigenface and face space approach in a novel way. Rather than using all information in the original pictures to compute their Eigenfaces and Eigenspace, they used only a limited set of landmarks. In this way the actual shape of the face became unimportant at the same time that the spatial relationships among the landmarks became more significant. The lines connecting these landmarks were connected by a linear interpolation, similar in concept to the thin spline technique used by Bookstein (1991). According to Craw and his colleagues, this is a more effective means of producing a correct recognition. The use of connecting lines and landmarks is also prevalent, as we see later when we discuss morphing and dynamic link architectures, throughout the entire effort to represent forms. It is another means of reducing the amount of information that must be processed. It is also a strategy that seems to be unlikely to be instantiated in the organic recognizer.

Craw and his colleagues (Craw et al., 1999) joined many others when they pointed out that their methods and, by inference, all formal methods, are severely limited. If the computed Eigenfaces and face space were applied to an object that is not a face, then the model failed completely, that is, "such a manipulation is not useful" (p. 735). Like all other such methods it worked only for a narrowly defined set of objects. Once again we see evidence of the general difficulty identified by Dreyfus (1972, 1992) that virtually all artificial intelligence systems are severely limited in the ability to generalize to other data sets.

Furthermore, there are some special problems with this approach. In achieving its goal of reduction in the dimensionality of the face space, all pixels and regions in the original image must be evaluated. However, not all parts of a face image are equally important; the nose, eyes, and mouth (and, perhaps even more important, their relationship to each other) are particularly salient. Nevertheless, degrees of saliency are not figured into the usual way that Eigenfaces are computed.

2.8.2. Dynamic Link Architectures

Many representation methods thus far take advantage of some kind of a elastic grid superimposed on a face. The general morphometrics approach initialized by Thompson (1917) and revitalized by Bookstein (1978) as well as the Eigenface idea (Turk & Pentland, 1991) are based on such an idea. In each case, either a Cartesian rectangular grid or a specialized grid anchored to particular landmarks provides the foundation for a system of face representation. The grid may then be processed by either a Principle Components Analysis (typically used by proponents of the Eigenface method) or by what has come to be generically designated as a *Dynamic Link Architecture* (DLA). In general, DLAs (e.g., as generally used by the proponents of the morphometrics method) depend on a comparison of the grids that are constructed from different faces.

Modified DLA approaches have been further developed by Bigun, Duc, Smeraldi, Fischer, and Makarov (1998) and by Okada, Steffens, Maurer, Hong, Elagin, Neven, and Malsburg (1998). In both these studies the deformations in the grid are analyzed by means of *Gabor-based wavelets*, another set of basis functions playing a role comparable to the sinusoids of a traditional Fourier analysis. The wavelets are spatial sinusoids which are constrained to a Gaussian function to produce a novel set of localized basis functions. Each wavelet is convolved with the face image to produce a correspondence value at a particular point on the image in much the same way that a set of spatially unconstrained sinusoids can be used to represent an image. Okada et al. (1998) used 40 wavelets of differing frequency and orientation to map faces. The set of 40 wavelet functions measured at each point constitute a vector they call a *jet* and it is these jets that actually encode a form. The reduced data sets represented by these jets were evaluated by subsequent comparison processes to determine the similarity between two faces.

Although the wavelet and jet method differs from the standard Fourier sinusoidal method and may have some computational advantages, in principle all of these methods are very much alike. A set of basis functions (either the spatial sinusoids or the Gabor-based wavelets) are used to represent a form by linear superimposition. The sinusoids extend over the whole image; the wavelets are localized by the constraining Gaussian functions. The respective transformations or representations of the image are then compared. In the case of the elastic graphs, the key nodes or landmarks, as metricized by the jets, by a set of orthogonal sinusoids, by a system of splines, or by any one of a number of other methods, are then used to make an estimate of correlation or similarity.

Closely related to the dynamic link models are methods based on "morphing." Morphing techniques were originally designed to transform one form into another. The morphing technology has become famous for the special effects that it produces in movies and television. A face can be "morphed" into another or a pattern on a floor can be morphed into a human form, a trick made famous in the 1991 movie, *Terminator II: Judgment Day*.

Morphing methods are also based on a superimposed grid, often linked at particular intersections or landmarks. The grids are then stretched to determine how much and what kind of controlled distortion or "morphing" is required to change one form into the other. The complexity of the transformation (i.e., its trajectory) correlates with the similarity of the forms being compared. O'Toole, Wenger and Townsend (2001) distinguished between *pre-morph* and *completely corresponded pre-morph* codes. The former require manual specification of landmarks or "fiducial points" required to establish the morphing grid; the latter carries out the process automatically.

Dynamic link models and morphing codes for representing objects require that the grids of forms to be compared be reasonably similar to each other and share common landmarks. Forms with totally different landmark patterns can sometimes produce nonsensical transformations. Similarly, two objects to be morphed must be arranged so they are presented in a more or less canonical orientation. As Fig. 2.2 shows, very different fish shapes can be transformed into each other with great ease. It would be very difficult however to transform a fish's body into a human face with a smooth transformation using this method.

Although the comparison process is not the main topic of this chapter, it should be noted that any of the methods that use the transformation from one represented form to another as the method of choice for recognition is confronted with many different alternative methods to determine correspondences. Some are quite complex, but others are quite simple. For example, if one simply added up the length of the lines connecting the set of landmark or fiducial points to their corresponding landmarks, this would be an useful measure of their "similarity." Recognition could be accomplished by choosing the smallest value of this sum as the criterion. Again, it is unlikely that this is the way the process occurs in human perception.

2.9. ROGERS AND TROFANENKO'S HEXAGONS

Efforts to represent shapes in a quantified manner have continued over the years. As usual, the problem of generalizing from the particular application to a broader universe of shapes has never been completely solved. However, any progress, no matter how small, in developing measures of form would be an important contribution. Rogers and Torfanenko (1979) proposed a novel method in which a prototype congruent hexagon was used to provide a metric for more complex forms. These prototype hexagons were laid edge to edge to produce forms that not only approximated a wide variety of "beehive cell-like" configurations but provided a basis for assigning a measure of the resulting shapes.

Figure 2.3 shows a part (55 of 82 possibilities) of the noncongruent set of complex shapes that can be produced by combining six of the prototype hexagons. The number of possible shapes goes up rapidly as the number of hexagons increases. Whereas 6 hexagons can specify 82 different shapes, 10 hexagons permit 30,490 different shapes to be constructed according to Rogers and Trofanenko (1979). Obviously, this can become cumbersome very quickly. Nevertheless, the important thing these authors contribute is a set of measures that characterize each of the compound shapes produced by combing "n" hexagons. Thus, as shapes are constructed (e.g., to provide a set of stimuli for psychophysical experiments) measures can be calculated that define the geometrical properties of the generated forms. Some of the most useful measures proposed by Rogers and Trofanenko include:

1. Bounding area: The number of hexagons in the smallest convex hull that can be drawn around the shape. In general, the bounding area will be larger than the shape itself since additional hexagons will have to be added to make concavities into convexities.

2. Connectivity: The number of edge to edge contacts between the hexagons that make up a shape.

3. Interfacial perimeter: The number of hexagon edges that are not in contact with other edges.

4. Spatial entropy: Defined for a six hexagon shape as $\sum_{i=1}^{6} p(i) \ln p(i)$ where $p(i)$ is the proportion of the hexagons with a particular number of "nearest neighbors." For the six hexagon set, therefore, one will have sum up the six proportions for nearest neighbor counts varying from 1 to 6. This measure is indicated for each of the shapes shown in Fig. 2.3. (Abstracted from Rogers and Trofanenko, 1979, p. 289)

The entropy measure, in particular, is interesting because it does provide a measure of an important property of the hexagon generated shapes. However, like all other information and statistical measures, it does not define a unique shape. As seen in Fig. 2.3, as many as 15 shapes can have the same entropy measure. Furthermore, in the absence of supportive evidence, there is nothing at this point to suggest the visual system is selectively sensitive to the entropy measure. A "seat of the pants" examination of the shapes in Fig.

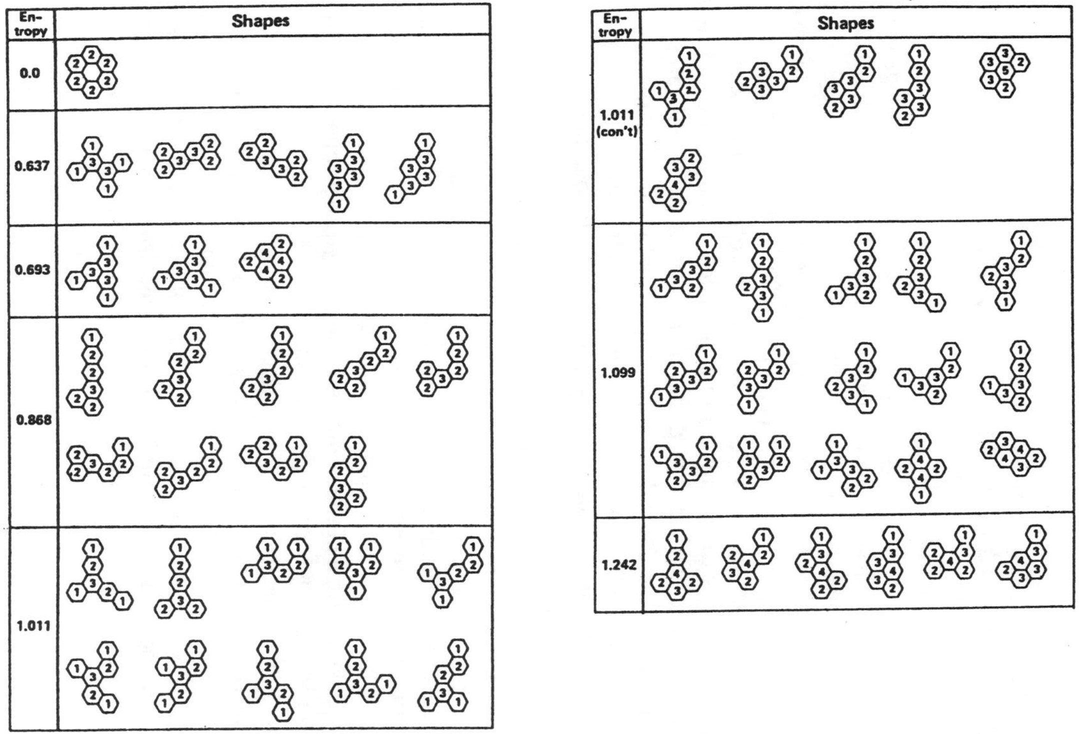

FIG. 2.3. Another system for representing a wide variety of geometrical forms using a standard hexagon as the prototypical element. From Rogers and Trofanenko (1979).

2.3 suggests, to the contrary, that a human observer might be better able to distinguish between some forms that have the same entropy measure than between others that differ substantially along this dimension.

2.10. SOME ADDITIONAL METHODS FOR REPRESENTING FORMS IN COMPUTERS

Psychologists and mathematicians have worked collaboratively for more than a half century with the proponents of a new tradition in engineering and science—*computer image processing* or, as it is more popularly known, *computer vision*. Achieving the goal of *simulating* form recognition (as distinguished from the goal of *explaining* it) became possible only with the development of computers in the latter half of the 20th century. The reason for the delay is obvious. Images or forms typically involve vast amounts of information and only with the advent of high speed computers could these enormous databases be processed and manipulated in a reasonable time and with a reasonable expenditure of energy. The task was further complicated by the fact that many algorithms were sequentially interactive; that is, they required many iterations of the functional relations between many different spatial locations on the image.

Many, if not most, of the algorithms developed by computer vision scientists are not intended to recapitulate or even to speculate about the *mechanisms* of organic vision but, rather, are ad hoc procedures intended to imitate the organic recognition *processes* by any means, biologically plausible or not. Although we do not know the exact nature of the representation codes used by humans, computer vision scientists always have detailed and specific knowledge of the coding schemes they programmed into their computers to carry out the targeted tasks.

The metaphorical question—How does a computer *know* a form?—is more realistically phrased as—How does a computer *encode* or *represent* a form? Just as we know little of the conscious or unconscious nature of human perception, the metaphor of computer self-awareness is a useless excursion into speculation and futile extrapolation from what can be measured and understood functionally or behaviorally. The term *know* is an anthropomorphic holdover from older forms of human theology and philosophy that contaminates engineering dialogs just as vacuous discussions of consciousness corrupt discussions of human psychological function.

2.10.1. Anzai's Taxonomy of Computer Representation Methods

There are several taxonomies of available computer representational systems; one of the most comprehensive and useful was prepared by Anzai (1992). Anzai, a computer scientist, was exclusively interested in describing the ways in which a form or other complex data sets could be represented inside a computer memory. Not all of his methods deal directly with visually presented forms, but most have a analogous relationship to visual forms. Indeed, inasmuch as *representation* of visual forms is typically intended to mean the symbolic encoding or reduction in the information content of the original form, there is no need to demand some kind of an isomorphic similarity between the encoded representation and the original form. Thus, although some entries in Anzai's taxonomy may seem distant and unsuitable and although some are more efficient than others for the representation of visual form, virtually all possess at least some value in computer vision applications.

The types of computer representation methods proposed by Anzai, include the following categories, some of which I have renamed to be more consistent with the vocabulary used throughout this book. My comments on his categorical scheme of representation methods highlight those aspects that might be of psychological relevance.

Bit and Pixel Arrays. This category is the most direct way to enter form information into a computer. There is minimum encoding, simply an isomorphic depiction of the original form itself, transformed to the resolution limits of the computer, and stored as an exhaustive array of numerical values for each pixel. Each pixel may consist of one or more bits of information. If only one bit is used, then a "binary" or black–white rendition is all that is possible. If eight (nominally) bits are used, a gray scale representing 256 (2^8) different intensities at each pixel may be encoded; 24 bits permits an enormous number (2^{24}) of different colors to be encoded at each pixel location. The array of pixel values may be displayed or processed in many ways but without further processing the displayed image of the original form such a representation is limited to the capabilities of the hardware to store a particular number of pixels (the *sampling density*) and the number of bits at each pixel (specifying the number of *quantification levels*). The ideas underlying this essentially isomorphic two-dimensional mapping techniques translate directly to three- and higher dimensional formats (in which a two-dimensional "pixel" becomes a three-dimensional "voxel").

Geometry. Simple geometrical relations as well as plane and solid geometry can also be used to encode forms. For example, the amount of information in the unencoded pixel array described in Anzai's first category can be reduced for objects that can be defined in terms of vertices. A supplementary and often arbitrary rule is required, however, such as: To reproduce the form, connect the list of vertices with straight lines, arcs of a circle of diameter D, or any one of a large number of different splines.

Graphs. Many different forms are well represented by a graph, a means of encoding that loses much of the metric geometry of the original form but still preserves the essential topological relations. For example, the exact metric form (i.e., specific distance between stations) of the subway system of a large city is not essential to using it successfully. A topologically consistent representation that is based, alternatively, on the times it takes to get from one point to another, may be more useful. A full discussion of the advantages and uses of graph theory may be found in Harary (1972). Graphs may also be used to encode forms that are not naturally graph like (as is a subway system). By the use of such relationships as *above, behind, part of,* and *within*, a graph-like representation may even be constructed of a street scene. Of course, additional reconstruction rules or a list of prototypical components may be necessary to establish a good representation of such a complex scene with a graph.

Trees. Tree representations are really subsets of the graph approach. A graph can be "factored into a spanning forest," a collection of tree-like structures (see Harary, 1972, p. 92). Family trees, taxonomies themselves, and many other kinds of nongeometric families, as well as visual objects, can be represented by tree structures. Tree representations were particularly important for programming massively parallel computers during their heyday because the arrangement of the many processors in such a system was naturally a "tree." Other subsets of graphs including "butterflies" and "strings" have also been developed by computer scientists in their efforts to find efficient means of representing data of all kinds, not just spatial forms.

Lists. One of the most popular approaches to encoding forms and relationships of all kinds in the 1960s and 1970s involved the use of list processing languages. The computer programs dealt with objects on the basis of their propinquity to each other in predetermined lists. Lists, however, can also serve as a simple medium for the representation of forms. For example, a set of similar objects can be listed in the following form: Object N ((Rectangle) (Large) (Height to Width Ratio) (Color)). By filling in the options for a set of such forms, an encoded representation of a particular member may be identified. A single trigger number given to items in the list may allow one to quickly and accurately reconstruct the original form by evaluating the list. This is exactly the procedure originally used by the Asian telegraph systems to transmit Chinese calligraphic characters. Each character had its own particular number. The number of the character was transmitted telegraphically and the number translated back into the character at the receiving end of the line. The problem, with such list structures, however, is that the lists had to be complete and sufficiently comprehensive to transmit all possible information. Unexpected new information (e.g., a new character) that did not possess a code number at both the transmitting and receiving stations could not be represented and subsequently decoded.

Predicate Logic. Anzai suggested that predicate logic is a more formal elaboration of the idea of lists and shares many of the same advantages and disadvantages. However, predicate and other related forms of "logical" representation have a huge advantage over the simple list. That advantage is they can be manipulated in much the same way that algebraic expressions can. Thus, whereas a simple list must be exhaustive and its computational utility limited to simple propinquity in a list, a logical approach may permit many other kinds of relations to be defined and complex structures represented with formulae that, when evaluated, can reproduce or represent forms. Predicates are comparable to attributes or dimensions. For example, "Size" may be considered to be a predicate of a sample rectangle. The predicate "Size" is characterized further by adding terms such as (Object1, large) telling us that it is "True" that Object 1 is an object whose size is large. In conjunction with several other predicates (e.g., shape, color, etc.) numerous objects can be defined. Furthermore, relationships among several objects can be determined by carrying out familiar logical operations such as AND or asserting statements such as *If Shape(Object1, rectangle) and Size(Object1, large) then there exists Length (Object1, long) and Width (Object1, long)*. A list of predicates, therefore, can be manipulated by means of well-defined syntactical rules to infer other relationships among and properties of objects that can either be used to represent an object or form or to determine such factors as similarity. This manipulative power goes far beyond the capabilities of a simple list.

Semantic Networks. Closely related to graphs, lists, and predicate logic is the concept of the *semantic network*. The basic requirement for developing such a means of representing objects or form is the preliminary preparation of a sizable base of common sense knowledge, also a *sine qua non* of the predicate logic or list methods. Once having established that knowledge base (no mean task in itself) the relationships between attributes of the objects can be used to relate or depict objects by the application of logical and associative rules. Special purpose computer programming languages exist for most of these approaches. For example, a semantic processing language called NETL has been designed by Fahlman (1979) and list processing languages have been developed by Gerlernter, Hansen, and Gerberich (1960).

Procedures. Anzai (1992) also noted other kinds of procedures or constructive algorithms that can be used to represent objects. The basic idea in this case is to utilize some formula or set of procedural rules that generate an object when evaluated. Leeuwenberg's (1971) method for generating certain types of forms is obviously an example of such a procedural method. A simpler example would be the following set of rules for generating a square.

- Start at Point a.
- Draw a line to the west one unit in length.
- Draw a line to the south one unit in length.
- Draw a line to the east one unit in length.
- Draw a line to the north one unit in length.

To the extent that figures are simple enough to be generated by such a procedural or constructive sequence of actions, this too may be used as a means of representing objects in a computer memory.

　　Unfortunately, the nearly universal problem with many, if not all, of these methods is that they are unable to cope with proliferation. That is, a tree or a predicate logic system may work for small universes of discourse, but they will collapse as the database of relationships grows simply due to the unfulfillable computational load. In this sense nearly all these models represent theoretical "toys" that are incapable of dealing with the complexity of the real world.

2.10.2. Barr and Feigenbaum's Taxonomy of Artificial Intelligence Representation Methods

Anzai's (1992) tabulation of representation methods that are available to computer programmers is, for the most part, innocent of any relevance to psychological theory. The main exception to this generalization are the list and predicate logic methods that have been transformed into artificial intelligence theories and, thus, putative models of how minds might work. For example, the predicate logic is an exemplar of logical representation schemes that have been popular in this field for many years. This category has been discussed in detail in Barr and Feigenbaum's (1981) first volume of the still important *Handbook of Artificial Intelligence*. In addition, this volume makes its own tabulation of representation schemes, most of which have already been described in the discussion of Anzai's more recent taxonomy. Nevertheless, it may also be useful to present a brief outline of their list at this point.[13] An explanatory comment is added if one of these items has not already been discussed.

---

[13]Because of the way the handbook was put together, it is difficult to determine the exact authorship of the taxonomy of representation procedures. The list of contributors to this section include Barr, Davidson, Filman, Appelt, Gardner, Bennett, and Teflik (p. xiii).

1. Logic:

   a. Propositional Calculus—in which the logic is based on the truth or falsity of the propositions comparable to
   b. Boolean Algebra.
   c. Predicate Calculus (Logic).
   d. First-Order Logic—Predicate calculus supplemented by operators or functions and by the notion of predicate equality between cases.

2. Procedures:
3. Semantic Networks:
4. Production Systems:
5. Direct (Analogical) Representations:
6. Semantic Primitives:
7. Frames and Scripts:
   Frame and scripts are methods for organizing or representing information in terms of expectancies or predetermined knowledge bases. The main goal of anyone using this approach is to carefully define the universe of discourse so as to limit the range of possible responses.

2.10.3. Zhu's List of Representation Methods

In an article discussed later in this chapter, Zhu (1999) reviewed a completely different set of representation methods than those already proposed. All items in his list are based on some kind of a statistical criterion of shape. The statistical representation methods proposed by Zhu included:

Statistical Models of Shape. Kendall (1989) proposed a method for the representation of shape based on a matrix of k points in m dimensions. The space of all possible shapes was visualized as a sphere in $m \times (k - 1)$ dimensions. Each particular shape was a particular point in this spherical space. A statistical analysis was then be carried out to determine if a particular shape was an accidental form or had a high probability of being real.

Deformable Templates. Quite closely linked to the morphometric model described earlier was Grenander's (1993) use of the elastic transformations of a form to define its shape. This technique is also a statistical one that is organized according to a pyramid ranging from the most global organization to the most local components.

Accidental and Nonaccidental Shapes. Lowe (1985) suggested that good forms could be represented on the basis of their probability of occurrence given the nature of the form. Collinear arrangements of line segments, for example, were considered to be likely and broken segments were considered to be unlikely. Rigidity is also a determinant of the probability of a particular form being real.

Active Contour Models. This approach was also a statistical model of form based on the first and second derivatives of a curve. The probability of a particular curve is dependent, therefore, on such properties of a curve as its elasticity. (Abstracted from Zhu, 1999)

2.10.4. Representation by Geometrical Components

Most of the methods described so far carry out their functions by encoding some kind of a logical relation or by literally imaging the entire form in an array. Another geometrical approach that has only been alluded to in passing is to store an image as a list of geometrical subcomponents or parts. For example, a rectangle could be encoded as a set of four lines (literally) with additional information describing where they were located and how they were spatially related to each other. This approach can also be followed for three-dimensional objects[14] —a modular representation method using solid shapes was originally suggested by Binford (1971) and Marr and Nishihara (1978). The idea behind their component approach was to create a small library of basic shapes, most often simple cylinders in which the diameter and length could be adjusted as necessary to serve a particular role as a part of the object being represented.

Several of these basic cylinders could be concatenated into a slightly larger subcomponent of the form. In each case these concatenated components were organized by having the coordinates of each of its subcomponents associated with those of the other parts. Each of these more complex parts could then be concatenated with other intermediate level components to represent the entire form. Other authors (e.g., Requicha, 1980) suggested the use of more complex sets of primitives adding cubes and slabs to the prototypical cylinder.

The hoped for advantage of such a system was that a relatively small set of fundamental geometrical components—perhaps even limited to a single prototypical cylinder—could be used as a simple geometrical "alphabet" to represent any other solid object in the same way that letters can represent a less tangible idea. The disadvantage is that as the object to be represented gets more and more complex, the list of components and their relationships becomes impracticably large.

---

[14]The idea of solid components as features has also been the basis of some theories of form recognition. This topic is discussed on page 204.

It is interesting to note the analogy between this method and those of the more formal Fourier-type models. Both function by either analyzing a form into or synthesizing a form from components. The advantage of the geometrical component approach is that the parts are chosen from the same domain or space as the whole object. The transformation of a form into its Fourier components introduces new dimensions and domains that are from a practical point of view quite remote from the original form.

2.10.5. Neural Net Representation[15]

Among the most currently popular, if not the most productive means of representing forms, objects, and even intangible configurations within a computer is the *neural net*. Early speculations, (e.g., by J. Hughlings Jackson in the 19th century) that thoughts were accounted for by the interaction of many different regions in the brain (as opposed to some of the highly localized ideas epitomized by the phrenologists; e.g., Gall & Spurzheim, 1808) planted the seeds of the idea of *distribution* and *parallelicity*. The "neural" network leapt into engineering as well as psychological consciousness by virtue of the early stimulation provided by the works of McCulloch and Pitts (1943), Pitts and McCulloch (1947), Hebb (1949), Rosenblatt (1958), Selfridge (1958), and Grossberg (1970). A new and more recent impetus to neural network ideas was the influence of the two volumes by Rumelhart, McClelland and the PDP Research group (1986) and McClelland, Rumelhart, and the PDP Research Group (1986), respectively. Based on the assumed similarity between brain mechanisms and the neural network or connectionist representations, this field has exploded in activity and influence in recent years.

There, however, is a vast difference between Jackson's primitive ideas and the modern ones expressed in the post-World War II writings. Jackson's concern was with the "nodes" or chunks of the brain that were comparable to the modern idea of centers and nuclei which themselves consist of very large numbers of neurons. The more modern idea, although it has gone through a partial transformation from the original idea of the individual neuron cum node to larger functional units as nodes, is still essentially based on the idea of interacting nets of individual components in much the same sense that McCulloch and Pitts (1943) originally conceived. Nevertheless, distribution means something quite different to each generation. The concept of the modern distributed "network" is a far more localized idea than the classic Jacksonian view of widespread cortical distribution. Indeed, the modern network is quite local with interconnections simulating synaptic connections operating only between nearby neuron-like nodes.

---

[15]Once again, a neural net may be considered as either a representation means or as a free standing theory in its own right. Neural net *theories* are discussed extensively in Chapter 4.

The current neural network model of representation has the distinct conceptual advantage of being more or less isomorphic to the actual biological neural representation. The retina encodes visual information as a two-dimensional spatial pattern based on an optical image projected by the cornea and lens system. Ignoring for the moment details such as the different limits of chromatic sensitivity and the actual physical extent of this optical image, the projected spatial map is initially represented at each point by the neural activity induced in an array of receptors. In general, neural net theories are also based on such a sampled image with the sampling carried out by an analogous first stage or level of receptor processing. At this level, the spatial geometry and the intensity of the image at each point is encoded by a corresponding amount of activity in each receptor. Although there may be some immediate interaction among the components of this first layer of receptors, the earliest representation is punctate, sampled, and isomorphic to the projected image; in other words the lowest level coding is *retinotopic.*

One of the significant events in the history of the neural net approach was the enunciation by Hebb (1949) of what has come to be the basic learning rule. Hebb (1949), a psychologist, not a mathematician or computer engineer, was an insightful psychobiologist and student of neural system organization. He asserted:

> When an axon of cell A is near enough to excite a cell B and repeatedly or persistently takes part in firing it, some growth process or metabolic change takes place in one or both cells such that A's efficiency, as one of the cells firing B, is increased. (p. 50)

To put it directly, *use produces synaptic efficiency.* This statement has come to be known as *Hebb's Rule* and served as an operational description of the *Hebb Synapse.* It has been the basis of most neural net theories ever developed. Interestingly, there is still little direct experimental evidence[16] that changes in synaptic efficiency lead to dynamic behavioral changes we call learning or that memory of previous events is stored in state of the synapse. However, the logic, the physiology, the anatomy, and the absence of plausible alternatives are so compelling that this rule and the corresponding hypothesis of changes in synaptic state being equivalent to "learning" are now nearly universally accepted. In artificial neural nets, the analogous rule that use, perhaps associated with reinforcement (i.e., validation), produces efficiency is also ubiquitous.

---

[16]It is appropriate to note once again for emphasis, that it is possible, perhaps even likely that such information is unobtainable. The demonstration of synaptic plasticity in model preparations like Aplysia (Kandel & Tauc, 1965) is not tantamount to explaining the processes in vertebrates, especially mammals, as Kandel, himself, has repeatedly pointed out.

The general characteristics that a neural net model should display were tabulated by Rumelhart, Hinton, and McClelland (1986). These characteristics include:

1. A set of processing units.
2. A state of activation.
3. An output function for each unit.
4. A propagation rule for propagating patterns of activities through the network of connectivities.
5. An activation rule for combining the inputs on a unit with the current state of that unit to produce a new level of activation for the unit.
6. A learning rule whereby patterns of connectivity are modified by experience.
7. An environment within which the system must operate. (p. 46)

Neural net theory was originally strongly influenced by both previously demonstrated and plausible hypotheses concerning the biology of the nervous system. The brain's general characteristics helped to instantiate a particular kind of logic from the beginning. It was characterized by distributed networks, synapse based learning, and the hierarchical organization of the central nervous system. These basic concepts have persisted.

As the years went by, however, there was a subtle change in the activities of practitioners in this field. What had been *neural* net theory has gradually become *neurocomputing*. That is, activities, in large part, began to deviate from the seminal biological or psychological interests and principles to computer engineering studies in which the constraints of hardware and mathematics were more effective in driving developments in this field. Neurocomputing these days has many vestiges of its biological roots, but these vestiges are mainly those of the terminology of the science from which it evolved—the neurosciences. Neurocomputing, born neural net theory, has grown more on the basis of mathematical insights and computer capabilities rather than on a foundation of new neurophysiological or neuroanatomical observations.

What happened, of course, was that study of real neural parallel processing systems ran up against the barriers of complexity and numerousness, of combinatorics, and of chaotic uncertainty. Furthermore, there always lurked in the wings the specter of high-level symbolic processing that is not well described by the local interaction–parallel processing metaphor and its essential representational isomorphism. It became increasingly clear that observation of networks of sufficient complexity to be of even presumptive psychological significance would be infeasible. As a result, neurocomputing has become its own identifiable field of engineering, preserving a vocabulary from its past, but not capable of dealing with anything other than the simplest real neural nets and certainly not capable of answering such profound questions such as: How is mental activity produced by neural activity? In large part, thus constrained by the technology and logic of computers rather than of the nervous or behavioral systems, neural net models are often restricted to a domain that almost is exclusive of psychological relevance. Despite the claims of some of its proponents, most neural net models of mental activity are still "toy" simulations or remote analogies in this sense.

Some investigators (e.g., Gutta & Wechsler, 1998) have stepped beyond the simple neural net models to include categorical classification by means of decision trees once the image has been processed by the neural net. Whether this strategy overcomes any of the difficulties and limitations one encounters in the form recognition process is yet to be determined. Others (e.g., Cottrell, Dailey, Padgett, & Adolphs, 2001) have combined the neural net idea with the Eigenface idea. Many other variants of the neural net idea have been presented in recent years. Nevertheless, it is still not clear whether or not we will ever be able to unravel enough of the tangled web of organic neural nets to make neurocomputing relevant to human psychology and physiology in the future.

The original neural net approach did have another contribution to make. The ideas remerged in the form of theoretical models of cognitive processes. It is in this context that the synonym "connectionist" is most often used. In this regard there has been considerable interest and many exciting new developments. The approach, however, is not based on actual neural nets per se but rather on the mathematical models of imagined or invented systems that are able to reproduce some inferred aspects of cognition as they are expressed in behavior. Like all other mathematical models of cognitive processing, however, such a formularization is, in principle, neutral with regard to the actual physiological instantiation. *It may describe, represent, or model, but not reduce!* Neural net models are highly sophisticated computational or mathematical algorithms that in many cases effectively describe systems. However, in some curious sense, these models are disarticulated from the neuronal mechanisms from which they originally sprang.

Of course, computer models of neural nets have some powerful advantages. Their formal structure puts firm constraints on impossible theories and speculative hand waving. The extreme precision of the calculations provided by a computer is often cited as an advantage, however, such precision may be irrelevant to the soft kind of logic used by the brain.

Whatever the limitations and caveats, the idea of a distributed, parallel processing network of nodes with input weights that vary with experience is one of the most interesting theoretical approaches to modeling cognition and its associated explicit behaviors. The reason for this preeminence is the closeness of the original metaphor: The fact is that the real nervous system must be organized in a way that is similar in basic principle to the characteristics listed by Rumelhart, Hinton, and McClelland (1986, p. 46). Of course, the great discrepancy between the level of complexity and numerousness of the components in real neural networks and the simulated ones always raises questions about the salience of such models. The capabilities of a multibillion component neural net may be very different than one made up of a dozen or so, of several thousand, or even several million. These differences may not be just quantitative, but may actually emerge in ways that become qualitative.

Another factor that mitigates against our considering neural net models in their current form to be "the" ultimate answer in the search for an adequate method of representing cognitive or behavioral processes is that the concept of the node in the models has undergone a progressive change over the years. Where nodes were originally considered to be neurons, they are now referred to as much larger processing units, composed of many interacting neurons or functional units that are no longer capable of being considered as individual neurons. Instead, the nodes in many current modules are functional units that themselves have properties not found in a single neuron.

Another issue, often raised, is how much of the recognition process occurs within the relatively restricted geometry of the neural net itself and how much is accounted for by higher order symbolic processes for which we have no corresponding structural explanation. At those levels, the whole idea of a neural net becomes epistemologically intractable, however ontologically correct it may be.

I return to consider neural net theories of form recognition later. For the moment, it is obvious that they represent a useful means of showing how a form can be represented in a distributed network and how this representation can be transformed within the confines of the network. But, for many of us, they remain incomplete models of either the physiology of real neural nets or the psychology of cognitive processes.

2.10.6. First Order (Raw) Pixel Arrays

So far in this part of the discussion, I have surveyed some ingenious and elaborate methods for representing forms for computer manipulation. Only briefly mentioned among these esoteric and sometimes mathematically complex transformation methods lies another representation scheme that is used much more frequently in computer vision research. It is none other than the original pixel encoded image that contains the huge amounts of information that other methods seek to minimize. A substantial amount of computer image processing can be carried out, however, on this raw image.

Among the most popular and familiar processing method for these raw images is simple template matching or convolution. The image is scanned with a prototype, mask, or template that is equal in size to a portion of the original image that depends on the task. If the task is to locate a relatively small object in the image space, then a small mask is chosen. If the task is to recognize an object that fills the entire image space then a mask the size of the original image is correlated with that image.

A measure of the correlation between the mask and the image can be computed in many ways. However, one of the most common is simply to convolve the mask with the picture. If the goal is to locate a small part of the depicted scene, then the convolution mask is scanned across the entire image and the convolution integral computed at many different locations. The convolution integral $C(x,y)$ is defined by the following equation:

$$C(x,y) = \int\int_{-\infty}^{+\infty} f_1(\xi,\eta)\, f_2(x-\xi, y-\eta)\, d\xi d\eta \qquad (2.12)$$

where $f_1(\xi,\eta)$ is the equation of the mask located at (ξ,η) in the x,y plane of the image and $f_2(x-\xi,y-\eta)$ is the equation of the image minus the coordinates of the shifted position of the mask. $C(x,y)$ is then evaluated for all (ξ,η). When Eqn. 2.12 is evaluated, one part of the image (i.e., one particular position (ξ,η) or one image of a set) may produce the highest numeric value for $C(x,y)$ and this highest correlation signals the best match, otherwise known as recognition.

There are many other convolution type processes available for form processing. A single impulse function may be used as the "kernel" (rather than a structured mask) to determine how an image is blurred, for example, when it is passed through an aberrant lens. The image itself may be used as the kernel to compute the autocorrelation function—a splendid way to extract periodic information from an image; and a set of sinusoidal kernels may be used to extract the component frequencies of an image. The latter, not too surprisingly, is exactly equivalent to a Fourier analysis.

Because of the general nature of this unreduced form (i.e., the raw, pixel map), the universe of objects to which this relatively unencoded version can be applied is unrestricted. The processing algorithms that can be applied to a raw image are, therefore, unlimited. However, any transformations that are used are applied willy-nilly. Without some a priori categorization of the image, there is no natural way to choose which transformation will be most effective if applied to a raw image. No distinctions are made among the letters of a font or a set of faces or of a set of objects like chairs. All are processed independently of their nature; subsequent transforms must be used to carry out some simulated perceptual process. O'Toole,

Wenger, and Townsend (2001) considered such codes and point out that when higher level processes (e.g., recognition) rather than lower level (e.g., edge enhancement) are required, the raw image representation is usually inadequate. One major problem is the lack of standardized or normalized landmarks, orientations, sizes, and localizations on which many recognition algorithms depend. Subsequent processing to achieve this kind of normalization quickly becomes indistinguishable in complexity, if not in detail, from the higher level coding methods previously described.

2.11. CAN GESTALT PROPERTIES BE INCORPORATED INTO A REPRESENTATION MODEL?

Since the beginning of this book I have repeatedly asserted that the global qualities of an image seem to be very difficult to incorporate into any of the representation schemes so far uncovered. As a result these highly salient molar form attributes (psychologically speaking) typically have played only a minimal role in formal theories of the recognition process. Psychologists, on the other hand, have been very concerned about the molar or holistic aspects of a stimulus form for many years. Mathematical formulations, so often based on elementalist assertions and discretely programmed computer algorithms, usually eschew or finesse this important issue. The question inevitably arises: Is the absence of global properties from the formal models the result of some "in principle" barrier that cannot be overcome or is it possible to introduce metrics of the Gestalt properties into methods for representing a form?

That the Gestalt properties are important in determining the human visual response is no longer questioned. Since the work of the Gestalt psychologists (e.g., Kohler, Koffka, and Wertheimer) during the first half of the 20th century, it has been impossible to deny that global aspects of visual form dictate in large part what we see. (I deal with the psychophysical data supporting this assertion in detail in Chapter 3.) Many psychologists have gone beyond the early Gestalt descriptions and demonstrations to study the details of *grouping* (e.g., Hochberg & Hardy, 1960; Kubovy & Holcombe, 1998; Oyama, 1961) or *common fate* (e.g., Newsome, Britten, & Movshon, 1989; Uttal, Spillman, Sturzel, & Sekuler, 2000) and a few others, most notably Garner (1974), have considered the even more abstract problem of *Figural Goodness.*

For more than half a century there has been continued discussion of how various processes, analogized from physical principles, might explain some of the organizational aspects of human perception. The methods of *relaxation* or *potential hill climbing* used to solve complex mathematical equations by iterative methods, the *minimal* and the *least energy* principles concepts in theoretical physics, and the *annealing* idea, so popular in contemporary connectionist theory, are all based on the idea that a kind of natural tendency toward simplicity and energy minimization operates in nature. Nature, it is contended, not only tries to reduce its costs, but also has a tendency to evolve simple and efficient solutions to the perceptual problems by which organisms are challenged. As we see in Chapter 4, this is the context in which the best modern theories are placed.

That a number of authors have approached the problem of the perceptual pressures intrinsic in the Gestalt laws are examples of these forces toward simplification. Both Attneave (1972) and Perkins (1982) have described qualitative models in which our brains "converge" on a perceptual solution to the problems posed by a stimulus. Perkins (1982), for example, concluded:

> All of the theories outlined so far belong to a general family. All might be called "convergence theories." That is, whatever, the details, in each case the visual system arrives at a partial or total interpretation through a series of intermediate interpretations that converge on one possessing the target regularities. (p. 89)

Perkins then pointed out that the essence of this approach is tantamount to "relaxation theory," but it should also be noted that it is not inconsistent with any of the other earlier mentioned methods that by iteration or any other method attempts to reduce the "forces," "energies," or "stresses" to a minimum. Perkins specifically linked this relaxation approach to some of the well-known Gestalt laws. In Chapter 4, we see how some of the most (and, arguably, best) modern theories of form recognition are based on such minimization principles.

In spite of this widespread kind of enthusiasm for incorporating global principles into psychological theories, Gestalt properties, however, still remain mainly outside the realm of mainstream formal modeling. Even those who are aware of the importance of introducing global properties into their theories often end up approaching the problem from an elementalist point of view. For example, Ullman (1996), although well aware of the importance of the configurational properties of a stimulus, sought to extract the "salient" and "figure-like" attributes of a form. He attacks the problem ". . . by computing a measure of saliency at each point in the image" (p. 245). He further explained his approach by noting, "For simplicity, the input image is assumed to be composed of contours" (p. 245). To Ullman, component saliency (the primitive) was a measure that increases with the length and smoothness of a contour. Salient contours must then be combined by computational processes that fill and combine in order to define what he calls "overall salience." Whatever the final outcome, it is clear this approach is fundamentally elemental and directed by the nature of the components rather than the global properties of the stimulus.

Notable counterexamples of this elemental approach have been presented by Palmer (1982), Hoffman (1994), and Zhu (1999). Each made a concerted effort to use the global Gestalt properties of a form as the primitives of a formal representation system.

Palmer (1982) specifically acknowledged the importance of Garner's (1974) pioneering work on "goodness" as he, too, championed a holistic approach to form recognition. Palmer stated:

> Garner's formulation is important to the present paper for several reasons. First, it is the only theory of figural goodness that is specifically related the transformational structure. . . . Second, it is the only theory that does not require perceptual analysis to proceed by first breaking down a whole figure into local component parts and then recognizing relations among the parts. The size of the R & R [rotation and reflection] subset is determined simply by operations on whole figures; transforming wholes and comparing them to each other for identity. In this sense Garner's theory is closest in spirit to the Gestalt tradition. . . . (p. 98)

What Garner had done was to emphasize that *self-similarity under rotation* was one key to figural goodness. That is, if one rotated a circle it still remained a circle at all angles of rotation. A circle, therefore, was, according to his metric, the figure with the highest degree of that elusive measure "goodness." Figures that generated different figures at different angles of rotation generated less "good" figures to the degree that perceptually different forms were created at various angle of rotation.

The approach that Garner suggested was an example of a more general mathematical approach—transformations as described by *group theory*. Palmer's (1982) contribution was to generalize this concept to a more complete theory of visual form. He was among those who linked group theory to the properties of *perceptual grouping* as well as to *goodness*. Another important figure with a similar goal was Hoffman (1966, 1985, 1994). Both were aiming in the same direction—to find a way to express or represent the global properties of a visual form.

Although both Palmer and Hoffman attempted to link their theoretical model to the then current excitement about the cortical neuronal shape detectors (an elementalist idea) and much of the specifics of their respective models were based on the interaction of subcomponents of the form, this was, from my point of view, not an essential aspect of their work. The more important point was to show that the mathematics of group theoretical transformations could be used to describe global or "Gestalt" attributes. The key idea is that when transformed according to certain rules, some forms maintain their original geometry. This may be in the form of topological transformations but, more particularly, Palmer was interested in the *automorphisms* (originally described by Weyl, 1952) which returned the original form both topologically and metrically. The set of transformations that produced automorphic transformations defined a *group* in that mathematics. Hoffman's mathematics (Lie algebra) was distinctly different from Palmer's, however the intent was the same, i.e., to concentrate on transformations of the entire form rather than on its component details. The form would guide and constrain the transformations, but the nature of the transformation was the key element in both group theories.

Both Palmer (1982) and Hoffman (1994) argued that their group mathematical theories generated the various properties discovered by the Gestalt psychologists. *Symmetry, common fate, continuity, similarity,* and *proximity,* even the elusive *Pragnanz* were all, they felt, represented by the group transformation approach to form perception. Thus, they individually argued that this was the best way to represent forms for both psychological and mathematical inquiries.

For reasons that are not too obscure, the Palmer and Hoffman approaches have not gained much application in recent years. Perhaps they are too complex mathematically for most perceptual scientists, but I think there is a more fundamental reason, namely that their intrinsic holism ran counter to the then prevailing elementalism. Although both these scholars actually developed neuronal instantiations of their work (e.g., Hoffman, 1994, refers to neurons as the "Lie group germs," p. 24), this not-too-subtle play to neuronal componentry was not able to overcome the reluctance of most in the field to abandon the essential elementalism of the then (and still) dominant Zeitgeist.

Recently another attempt (Zhu, 1999) to represent the Gestalt properties of visual forms in quite a different manner has been proposed. Rather than being based on the group theory, Zhu suggested that a statistical approach may be more useful. The key aspect of his model is that ordered forms are more likely than are irregular arrays. For example, two line segments that are aligned are more likely to be parts of the same form than are two randomly aligned segments. In other words, a good form is one with a large *nonaccidental statistic.*

Zhu's model of Gestalt properties is based on the ideas inherent in the *Markov random field* (MRF) as described by Gemen and Gemen (1984), a method they proposed for restoring blurred and noisy images by describing the statistics of similarity of nearby pixels in an image. Zhu collected a sample of outline shapes of animate objects and computed histograms of the occurrence of arcs with particular curvatures along the outlines of the shapes. This histogram was then modeled by applying a measure of the MRF called the Gibbs Distribution $p(x,e)$ which is equal to:

$$p(x,e) = \frac{1}{z} e^{-U(x,e)/T} \tag{2.13}$$

where x is the image matrix of pixels, e is the set of edges in that images, $U(x,e)$ is an expression for the differences in adjacent images, and T and Z are constants. With the Gibbs distribution available for his sample of outline shapes, Zhu provided a means of measuring the differences between random and nonrandom shapes. These differences were then shown to be equivalent to some of the Gestalt laws (i.e., perceptual tendencies) that people exhibit when presented with ambiguous shapes.

Zhu's linkage of the MRF with the Gestalt laws seems like a promising approach, but as we have seen, the ultimate acceptance of many promising theories seems to dependent on many other criteria than the conventional scientific ones.

Collectively, all the Gestalt type theories discussed in this section emphasize the compelling power of the overall stimulus form to force our perceptions in a particular direction. The forces so demonstrated are modeled in a number of ways including:

- Simplicity
- Relaxation processes
- Increased probabilities
- Transformational constancies
- Regularities
- Markov Random Fields

among many other possibilities.

This is an interesting mix; some externalize the forces (e.g., simplicity); some internalize them (e.g., relaxation processes). The actual state of affairs, and the most likely one, may be alternatively construed as an interaction between the forces exerted by the form and the constraining processing rules that operate in the human brain: The form interacts with the rules to produce only a limited set of perceptual responses. The more ambiguity, the more freedom for the rules to dominate; the less, the more the form dominates. Once again, the enormous adaptive power of the perceptual system is characterized. Once again, it seems, there may be many plausible answers to some of the most basic questions we ask about how we recognize forms.

The items in this list constitute a completely different vocabulary and concept of the nature of form recognition than do those in most contemporary theory. Rather than emphasizing parts, elements, and features, they speak a language of configurations and wholes. In Chapter 4, I discuss how such a new point of view may be instantiated. Nevertheless, it must be remembered that we must satisfy ourselves with a description of the transformations that occur between the stimulus form and the perceptual response and eschew any effort to "explain" in detail, the exact mechanisms at work. It may be, therefore, that the question asked in this section can only be answered in a very restricted context. It seems extremely important, however, if one is concerned at all that one's theories map onto the empirical data, that every effort be made to emphasize the global and configural aspects when deciding what representational technique to select. That emphasis on globality, as we see in Chapter 3, is where the psychophysical data points.

2.12. SUMMARY

In this chapter, I reviewed the many ways that forms can be represented independent of whatever subsequent processing is to be performed on them. This is the essential first step and the choice of a representation method often predetermines the recognition, or detection, or discrimination theory of choice that follows.

Several other important general conclusions can be drawn from this review.

1. The main motivating force for the representation of forms in some other way than as a complete raw image is the need for reduction, simplification, and normalization. However the nervous systems goes about processing forms, it is clear that none of our formal quantitative models are capable of dealing with the totality of the data involved in even a simple form. If progress is to be made, it is essential we have a means of abstracting the essential attributes and, in terms of human perception, this almost certainly means the global, holistic, Gestalt properties. Humans, almost certainly, respond to some abstracted or reduced version of the information provided to them in the original retinal projection. For reasons that transcend the practical and not insignificant matter of computational overload, it is necessary to determine which aspects of the stimulus can be ignored as we specify the nature of the salient stimulus.

2. Virtually all methods of form representation presented in this chapter are capable of dealing with only a limited domain of stimulus types. As Dreyfus (1972, 1992) so eloquently pointed out, the absence of generalization is perhaps the greatest detriment to progress in both the field of artificial intelligence and psychological theory.

3. Many of the methods of representation, although framed in different terminologies, are actually mathematical duals of each other. That is, they can be derived from each other through what may sometimes be indirect

pathways. From this perspective, the morphometric, DLA, and several of the face representation algorithms are obviously closely related formally, if not historically. Other methods, which may seem initially to be quite different, also eventually turn out to be near duals when examined more closely. Given that each is attempting to provide a solution to the same problem, this is not surprising. However, the fact that the apparent diversity of methods may not, in some mathematical sense, be real should not be overlooked.

4. Each of the different classes of representation methods may display its own particular set of limitations. Any model that uses a random generating process as a seed is likely to produce forms that may accidentally produce powerful, but unanticipated, perceptual attributes. This was especially true of some of the older methods summarized by Zusne (1970). Others may suffer, as noted, from a very limited universe of forms to which they may be applied and be unable to generalize from one universe to another.

5. If there is anything else that is made clear by this survey, no conclusion stands out more than the fact that most current representation methods (and the theories that follow from them) are elementalist. That is, the global attributes of a form are still recalcitrant to quantification and representation. With only a few exceptions have investigators even attempted to incorporate such holistic or Gestalt measures as Pragnanz or goodness or propinquity into their formularizations. Only in the final sections of this chapter were a few examples of holistic representations encountered. This is certainly one of the most important current challenges faced by any student for form recognition. Future success in providing a means of representing the holistic aspects of stimuli will go a long way to providing the necessary foundation for a theory that realistically describes human cognitive processes. The alternatives are a continued series of mathematical artifices that bear little relation to human behavior.

For years if not centuries, psychologists, as the primary students of human perception have been more concerned about the molar properties of visual perception and the stimuli that generate these responses than any other group studying form recognition. The conflict between what we do know about human perception and the available means of theorizing about it has become one of the main issues in the study of cognition. Chapter 3 considers this issue among the others that motivate perceptual science by reviewing the psychophysical data relating to form recognition.

3

The Psychophysical Data

3.1. INTRODUCTION

The purpose of this chapter is to review and evaluate a selected sample the empirical psychophysical literature relevant to the form recognition task. My goal is not only to determine what these articles are purported to say but also to continue to explore the conceptual and factual limits of what these findings *can* say. Some of the issues raised here are fundamental to understanding the limits of psychological experimentation to assay mental processes. Therefore, it is not possible to overemphasize the importance of such an inquiry throughout psychological science. Even a cursory adherence to behaviorism suggests that, all-too-often, well-established limits of inference and hypothesis have been violated in an exuberant and overenthusiastic search for answers to the unanswerable. Perception in general, and form recognition, in particular, must face these issues if the long-term viability of the science is to be assured.

By psychophysical data, I specifically refer to the corpus of studies that seeks to relate controlled changes in physically defined stimuli (*independent variables*) with behavioral measurements of the responses (*dependent variables*) to those stimuli. The physical stimuli that are used in such studies are limited by a very simple criterion: psychological efficacy. That is, a physical energy is grist for the psychophysical mill if it can produce some kind of a behavioral response. It would make no sense to psychophysically explore such a variable as x-rays; no one to this date has determined that humans are directly able to sense this particular band of the electromagnetic spectrum. On the other hand, visible light, another band of the "same kind" of energy (but composed of different electromagnetic wavelengths) is responded to with great sensitivity and sharply differential perceptual effects as the wavelength is varied.

Over the history of the science, a wide variety of behavioral responses have been chosen for use in psychophysical experiments. One reason for this diversity has been the enormous difficulty of defining the mental processes assumed to be occurring. Because we have not produced a satisfactory mental taxonomy (for a full discussion of this topic see Uttal, 2001), the variety of dependent psychophysical variables that can be used is bounded by the behaviors that can be evoked. For all practical purposes, given the huge informational capacity of the spoken language, this repertoire of responses is virtually unlimited. This does not mean, however, that "all will be revealed in due course" (in the words of a famous fictional detective). Unfortunately for the wistful dreams of some reductively oriented psychologists, the world is much more complicated than that: Behavior is not transparent to the underlying cognitive processes and may not reveal anything about the mechanisms that account for recognition behaviors.

Responses may be indirect or may be very direct. Indirect measures may be used to compile graphs that designate some attribute of the psychological responses. For example, the threshold for photic stimuli of different wavelengths may be determined by compiling the results of a series of choices between visibility and invisibility of a set of stimuli of different radiances. Another example of an indirect measure is the time it takes to respond (e.g., *reaction time* or *sorting time*) to determine both how "difficult" a recognition is or the effect of a particular variable on the perceived response. Differences in reaction times are therefore considered to reflect some attribute of the cognitive processing of the stimuli. In other instance even more indirect measures such as "rank order" can be used but such measures are subject to even more severe constraints and subjective influences and are terribly polluted by what we call "cognitive penetration."

On the other hand, very "direct" measures such as subjective reports of some aspect of the appearance of the form are often used to explore something about visual form (e.g., a statement that a reversible form is perceived to be oriented to the left or right, or up or down). In this case the verbally *reported* perceptual state is taken at face value. If the subject reports that a stimulus is perceived in some way, it assumed that this is, indeed, the way it is seen. To compensate for the myriad possibilities of erroneous reports, intentional, accidental, or even ironic, data of this kind are usually obtained from large groups of subjects. Many visual perception studies of this genre consist of demonstrations; in these cases the collective report concerning the nature of the perceptual experience is the database and the aggregate of the introspective reports is assumed, a priori, to be veridical with the "typical" or "normal" perceptual experience. Whether this is an acceptable strategy or not is a topic of intense debate and is encrusted with many ramifications and complications.

In other experimental protocols, particularly those used in the recognition task, the subject may be asked to directly name the presented stimulus from a list of names, either provided to the subject prior to the experiment or of such an obvious and familiar nature that common names satisfy the experimenter's needs. The percentage of trials in which a stimulus is correctly identified (i.e., *percent correct*) is one of the most familiar dependent variables in this kind of psychological research. Subsequently, confusion matrices (tables of failures to discriminate) may be used to metricize similarity more precisely. It is even possible to extract the parameters of concealed or occult (i.e., undefined by the experimenter) dimensions on the basis of which subjects are supposedly controlling and evaluating stimuli. Such methods as multidimensional scaling, factor analysis, and principle component analysis are available to process form recognition data and, on the basis of that data, to suggest plausible and possible dimensions along which subjects may be encoding the stimuli.

Experimental protocols of even more complicated design are often used to process the data to extract more detailed information than is available from the simple metrics just described. For example, the psychophysical method called *Signal Detection Theory* (SDT) is often invoked. New measures have been created (e.g., d', a measure of raw sensory discriminability) to help distinguish between sensory capabilities and criterion level or judgmental effects (usually represented by β) that vary with the subject's acceptance of a level of risk. This is an important aspect of psychophysics because there is a constant problem with "*top down*" influences on the results of an experiment that reflect powerful *cognitive penetration* of sensory or perceptual responses by what should be considered to be high level interpretive "*noise.*"[1]

If nothing else, our current awareness of the effects of subjective criteria should alert us to the necessity for controlling these judgmental factors. One of the best ways to do this is to use multialternative, forced-choice procedures. These methods do not permit the subject to say "I don't know," or to choose between a *yes* or a *no*, and thus minimize the effect of varying criteria on the results of an experiment. After many years of working with such methods, I am now convinced that any experiment that uses a *yes–no* procedure without controlling for criteria shifts in some way produces findings that are virtually worthless. The slightest change in the procedure or a new sample of observers can produce totally discrepant results unless these criterion effects are managed.

---

[1]Noise is defined here as any mitigating or degrading information that distorts the raw response to a stimulus. Of course, one scientist's noise is another's substance. Students of learning look at what a perceptionist calls "noise" as a primary measure of the decay of memory.

Measures of statistical variability can also be used to discriminate between alternative hypotheses. The entire edifice of descriptive and inferential statistics thus also stands available to manipulate, process, reduce, and constrain psychophysical data. In short, the technology for the psychophysical study of form recognition, as well as many other kinds of perceptual research, has been highly developed and is available for what has historically been an enormous variety of experimental designs.

However, this brings us to one of the most, if not the most, fundamental issues in the world of psychological science. We may phrase this generic question in the following way: *Is it possible to use these highly developed and precise psychophysical methods to answer the main questions posed in the study of form recognition?*

This is an extremely complex question and it sits on a foundation of one of the most fundamental issues in psychological science—the one inquiring into the *accessibility* of mental processes and mechanisms. There are some facts we can assert with great certainty as we begin to consider this issue. One of the most obvious is that there is no guarantee that any verbal response is valid. Actors, liars, the self-deluded, as well as perfectly normal and well-intentioned observers, misperceive, misremember, or misreport their subjective states. Verbal reports are cluttered, obscured, and transformed for a host of reasons, some of which are consciously or unconsciously self-serving and others of which are degraded by the dynamics of time and distortions of perceptual space. From the initial presentation of a stimulus (which may be misperceived for illusory and geometrical reasons or because of misdirected attention), to the interpretive stages (where stress, preceding conditions, prejudices, and stereotypes may lead to misreading even unambiguous stimuli), to the recall and retrieval stage (where fading traces and logical consistency may deform stored memories), to the reporting stage (where criterion thresholds and sequence effects as well as simple misspeaking may perturb validity), there are innumerable opportunities for the perceptual effect of a stimulus to be transformed and distorted.[2]

Even if one accepts the fact that we can reduce much of this uncertainty by well-designed experimental protocols (e.g., by demanding simple "Class A" responses, Brindley, 1960), there still remain barriers of a very fundamental kind to any assertion that psychophysics can assay mental processes. To understand and evaluate these barriers, it is necessary to be specific about which questions are being asked. Analyzing the problems in terms of the questions being asked is one way to seek clarification. Reconsideration of the questions asked on pages 51–54 in Chapter 1 and the addi-

---

[2]I appreciate that I have violated my own argument against cognitive reducibility in constructing the previous sentence by hypothesizing a series of component activities. Rest assured that I consider this to be a literary device and a convenience, not serious science.

tion of some new ones suggest that there are actually three distinctly different classes for which different answers to the generic question just posed might or might not be appropriate.

The first class consists of simple technical challenges. As important as it is and as complete as the discussion of it was in Chapter 2, the question of how a form might be represented in a way that allows it to be used in psychophysical experiment, is really characteristic of this class. A wide variety of representation methods were considered there and almost all of them could and have been used in studying form recognition. Some, of course, were inadequate for one reason or another. For example, some simply did not control what were eventually determined to be perceptually important variables of the stimulus. Others were shown to be formally equivalent and, thus, were not unique. Some were associated with what were eventually shown to be implausible psychobiological or cognitive mechanisms. In fact, none of these caveats really matters. As repeatedly pointed out, the assumptions of the formal mathematics of the representation can be separated from the associated, but independent, assumptions of the nature of the internal mechanisms; this first class of questions deals only with the formal mathematical assumptions and issues of experimental convenience.

Next, there is a second class of question that approaches the problem from a very reductive and ontologically explanatory point of view. Questions of this class are concerned with the mental architecture of the internal "mechanisms" that are responsible for the observed behavior. For example:

1. Is the internal processing underlying form recognition based on a global or local processing mechanism?
2. Is the internal processing underlying form recognition due to as comparison or a reasoning process?
3. What processes take place inside the brain that are the equivalent of form recognition?
4. Is form recognition a unitary process or an aggregate of semi-independent cognitive functions or operators?
5. If so, should we parse form recognition into component processes?
6. Is form recognition based on serial or parallel internal processing?
7. What are the cognitive and neural mechanisms of stimulus generalization?
8. Does form recognition depend on internal symbolic or isomorphic representation?
9. Is form recognition analytic or synthetic?
10. Are recognition, discrimination, and detection separate processes?
11. Are representation and correspondence separate processes?

The prototypical question of all of these exemplars of this second class is:

What are the modular internal physiological or cognitive processing mechanisms that account for the observable behavior?

All members of this class of questions are based on the assumptions that the internal mechanisms are both accessible and analyzable. In fact, however, these internal mechanisms are not directly observable and, at best, can only be indirectly and inconclusively inferred from the directly observable behavior.

Finally, there is third class of question that deals with the identification and perceptual efficacy of the stimuli and their dimensions that are manipulated in the psychophysical experiments. This category involves many of the issues raised in the second category but from a behavioral, functional, and descriptive point of view rather than a reductive one. Questions of this third type include:

1. Does parameter x affect perception?

2. What are the attributes of a stimulus that affect its recognition?

3. How do these attributes affect recognition? In other words, how do we describe the transformations of the dimensions of the stimulus into those of the response? For example, a question of the second class might ask: "What are the mechanisms of recognition?" A related question of this third class asks: "What is the functional relationship between the stimulus and the response? Thus, many of the intractable reductive questions of the second class may be transformed into tractable questions of the third class including:

- How does manipulation of the global dimensions affect recognition behavior?
- How does manipulation of the local dimensions affect recognition behavior?
- How does the nature of the task affect recognition?
- What effects occur as a result of organizing the stimuli so they *must* be processed in serial or parallel order or according to some other experimenter induced restraint?
- What are the limits of form generalization?

4. How do experience, learning, and memory affect form recognition?

Questions like these concern efficacy, process, and transformation, but do not deal with internal physiological or cognitive mechanisms.

With regard to the first class of question, I believe the choice of the particular mathematics of representation and description that should be used can be resolved relatively easily. Whatever model fits the data best with the smallest number of assumptions is the model of choice—*as the most appropriate formal description of the behavior under observation.* Remembering the caveat that no mathematical or computational theory can uniquely define internal mechanisms and the fundamental fact that formal models or theories of any kind are fundamentally neutral with regard to internal structure, the choice between alternative models must depend solely on descriptive accuracy as well as the convenience and simplicity of the respective formulations in situations where the descriptions are comparable. (However, even this is not an absolute, one should also consider the problems concerning the "simplicity" criterion discussed on page 132.)

At this juncture the point of view of form recognition expressed here diverges drastically from the currently most popular forms of psychological theory: cognitively reductive mentalism and neuroreductionism. I argue here that the second class of question cannot be answered for reasons of fundamental principle. Answering any of them would depend on a level of accessibility of mental activity that is not obtainable in principle or practice. This argument was spelled out in detail in two earlier works (Uttal, 1998, 2000) and has been briefly recapitulated in Chapter 1. Needless to say, this is not the standard model of the relationship between neurons and percepts. Spillman (1999) summed up the antithetical neuroreductionistic approach to perception in an astute and eloquent article. In particular, he argued for an association of the results of psychophysical experiments and single cell recordings. Readers interested in his alternative point of view would do well to read his article.

Spillman and I disagree on several important points. For example, it seems to me that the new neurophysiological evidence he cites concerning wide-ranging collaterals and feedback circuits, if nothing else, makes it clear that the nervous system is much more complex than we had thought and that the possibility of computational or neurophysiologically untangling its circuits has diminished rather than been enhanced. What we do agree on, however is that if scientists paid more attention to some of the epistemological issues (including the assumptions on which our empirical work is based) before they collected their empirical measures, this might help clarify the entire scene.

Stebbins (1995), among others, raised the same issue when he reconsidered his long and fruitful career in the field of animal psychophysics and perception. He highlighted the barriers inhibiting the acquisition of structural knowledge when he said:

> Our methods are unable to yield precise and exact measurement of these [complex perceptual] phenomena, and in fact, these methods may interfere with what they purport to measure. For this reason our [psychophysical] results are uncertain and even indeterminate. (p. 331)

This then brings me to the third class of questions. It is here, and only here, that psychophysics can begin to provide understanding in the form of transformations and efficacies. This class includes questions that are not the implausible and unobtainable reductive queries of the second class (which I believe are intractable for fundamental reasons) but questions that ask nothing more than if and how a stimulus affects an observable response. Questions of this sort are tractable, instantiate the goals and capabilities of the behavioral approach, and delimit the boundaries and constraints of the scientific study of form recognition.

The prototypes of this third, scientifically tractable, class of questions are:

What variables of the physical stimulus affect form recognition?

And

What is the functional (i.e., transformational) relationship between the parameters of the stimulus and the parameters of the response?

These questions, from the point of view of what is the most defensible form of psychological theory—behaviorism, define the boundary on one side of which sits attainable psychophysical answers and on the other side sits unsupportable speculation, fragile hypothetical constructs, and imaginative invention, but not any approximation to scientific certainty or observable reality. Of course, many would argue that science is incapable of certainty or of determining reality. Nevertheless, whatever the boundaries of science are and however our search for wisdom may be constrained, the important point is that beyond these limits lies a potential for misdirection and error that exceeds the potential for progress of a science characterized by more modest and realistic expectations.

Therefore, it should not be assumed that the tripartite taxonomy of question types proposed here is a debilitating constraint on our science or a reflection of an unnecessarily pessimistic point of view. It is, quite to the contrary, a realistic expression of what psychophysics can and cannot do and an optimism that our science will, in the long run, avoid false theories and conceptual pitfalls. Furthermore, expressing the epistemological fact that none of our measurements can directly access cognition certainly does not place any practical limits on the amount of future scientific inquiry. Even within this revised and constrained conceptualization of psychological science, enormous work can and must be done if we are to understand the nature of form recognition and other cognitive processes.

3.2. WHY ARE SOME FORM RECOGNITION QUESTIONS DIFFICULT OR IMPOSSIBLE TO ANSWER?

In the preceding section, a trichotomous classification of the questions pertaining to form recognition was proposed. The first class included a group of more or less technical questions that dealt with the methodology of the research or the mathematical and computational models to describe the data. The second class included questions that were essentially aimed at reductive explanation. The third class defined a group of operational questions that could be summarized in two prototypical questions: What attributes of the stimulus affect recognition and what effect do they have? It is to consideration of the second class, those questions considered to be fundamentally intractable, that I now turn. The issue is—Why are these questions not answerable?

To even partly answer this question, one must look at the logical and conceptual roots of psychological science in general. Such an analysis culminates in the general conclusion that the proper course for a future psychological science lies in the direction that behaviorism, albeit of a new and revised form, would take us. From the arguments developed there emerged a position asserting that many of the questions of the second class cannot be answered for the following reasons:

1. because of the intrinsic inaccessibility and the irreducibility of mental processes;
2. because of the neutrality of the psychophysical methods and formal models that can, at best, describe a process but cannot, for reasons of most fundamental principle, provide explanations of it;
3. because of the neutrality of behavior itself; and
4. because of the combinatorial complexity of the involved processes and mechanisms.

This is a general answer that has been discussed in earlier chapters and elsewhere (see Uttal, 1999, 2000); it is not explicated further at this point. However, there are a number of additional special constraints that speak against the possibility of finding answers to some of the patently reductive questions posed in the second class. It is to these particular arguments that I now turn.

3.2.1. Definitional Uncertainty[3]

Many of the battles fought between proponents of opposing theories of form recognition revolve around what can at best be considered inade-

---

[3]I am deeply grateful to my colleague Cyril Latimer who in conversations and in his published articles called my attention to many of the issues raised in this section.

quately defined positions or definitions. Thus, many of the issues that psychological science would like to consider are built on a fragile lexicographic foundation. Consider, for example, the controversy between *local* and *global* precedence. This topic has consumed enormous research effort in recent years, but, in many cases, the definitions of these terms remains vague and uncertain. Rescher and Oppenheim (1955) were among the earliest and the most explicit when they argued that the definition of the two terms was totally inadequate in a scientific sense. They suggested that there was a virtually unlimited number of ways in which a figure could be decomposed into any number of parts and that, without a precise definition of what was meant by "parts" and "wholes," the entire enterprise of establishing the role of either became nonsensical. Latimer (2000b) made a similar argument when he said:

> First, the terms "feature," "holistic," "local," and "global" are relative and any stimulus object will admit of an indefinite number of decompositions and sets of attributes. Accordingly, before there can be any useful discourse on such matters, it must be established, in each and every case, what is to constitute a whole and what are to be regarded as parts and attributes of that whole. In many cases, it is also necessary to state explicitly any background theory and assumptions relating to how objects in question are composed of these parts. (p. 1)

Rarely, indeed, is this wise advice followed when the controversy over whether wholes or parts take precedence in form recognition.

Rescher and Oppenheim further proposed a system for specifically identifying and defining the parts and wholes of a form. Not all agree that their method is satisfactory. For example, Rakover (1998) suggested that the Rescher and Oppenheim scheme is an oversimplification. He argued that it is based on the physical and geometrical properties of the stimulus and these attributes are not necessarily congruent with those that are salient and influential to the human perceptual system.

Several other attempts to define the parts of an object have been made over the years. Both Koenderink and van Doorn (1980) and Hoffman and Richards (1984) used boundaries as a means of defining the constituent parts of a stimulus form. Their goal was to develop an alternative to an obviously unrealistic procedure in which objects were deemed to be made up of more "primitive" shapes. As Bennett and Hoffman (1987) pointed out, however, the idea of shape primitives fails quickly as the universe of forms increases simply because of the need to create more and more "primitives."

Nevertheless, efforts to automatically parse geometric forms continue. Koenderink and van Doorn (1980) developed a partitioning or shape parsing algorithm based on the parabolic contours that can exist on a three-dimensional object. Hoffman and Richards (1984) and Bennett and Hoffman

(1987) proposed a scheme based on *transversality*. The transversality property occurs when two surfaces intersect each other and their tangent planes differ at each point along the intersection. It is this property of objects that signals the fact that surfaces with different shapes are meeting. Transversality, therefore, is an objective, although limited, means of defining the boundaries between different surfaces or, in the present context between the "parts of an object" It does so without any a priori cataloging of a set of parts. Rather, the properties are generated by algorithmically processing the shape of the stimulus form. The procedure by Koenderink and van Doorn (1980) and the newer procedure by Bennet and Hoffman (1987) provide automatic and objective means of defining parts.

However, problems still remain: Are the parts defined by any automatic method the ones that the organic visual system uses to recognize a form? There are two reasons to raise this concern: First, it is not clear that these mathematical partitions are the ones the visual system would produce if it did parse an object. Second, it is not clear that any parts or partitioning strategies are used; it could well be that the whole form is the key element in form recognition. Although, as I argue here, we cannot find a "killer" argument or experiment to make the point, a substantial portion of the psychophysical literature suggests that parsing is not the strategy that has evolved in our form recognition process.

The potential psychophysical irrelevance of any of these parsing or analytic procedures for defining the parts of an object is a particularly important point whose generality should not be underestimated. The application of mathematical principles that have evolved from the needs of and properties of the physical sciences and its objects may not be immediately transferable to the nonlinear, highly cognitively penetrated, multidimensional world of perceptual experience. Illusions and many other unexpected transformations that occur between stimuli and responses are strong evidence that the laws of normal physics and normal geometry may not be adequate to describe the dimensions and interactions of form recognition. This argument is certainly not accepted by all students of the problem (see, e.g., Machado, 1999). Some see mathematics as so general in nature that it can be used to describe any kind of system. Certainly, however, neither the laws governing the relativistic universe of curved space nor a plain old Newtonian one are necessarily the same laws that describe such paradoxical phenomena as apparent motion or metacontrast. Not only is space topologically distorted but even something as fundamental as the sequential order of musical scales becomes confused (Shepherd, 1964b) under certain conditions. Space and time, therefore, can both be perceived differently than defined by the relevant stimuli. This decoupling of physical dimensions from psychological ones is an enormous problem for psychophysical theory in general.

For example, metacontrast is interesting and surprising because it is the apparent result (perceptual suppression) of a subsequent stimulus on the perception of an earlier one. This suggests a backward causation that is anathema to our usual ideas of the unidirectionality of time. Similarly, apparent motion depends on the processing of information at the outset of an experience of something that is yet "unseen"—a phenomenon exemplified by the perceived terminal position of the second dot in the classic Phi phenomenon. Even though, we have not yet "seen" this second dot, we "know" the direction that the first dot must "move" to fill in the gap! This temporal paradox is confounded by an even more implausible phenomenon—the experiencing of a moving dot over a course over which no physical stimulus had been present! What we see is suggested by the stimulus, but obviously not determined by it.

In the light of such paradoxes and the potential for other delinkages between the dimensions of the physical stimulus and those of the perceptual responses, the matter of defining global or local attributes becomes particularly cogent. The problem is especially exacerbated when equivalences are drawn between what are otherwise well defined measures (e.g., spatial frequency) and geometric properties of the stimulus form. Wegner and Townsend (2000) highlight this problem when they said:

> . . . the validity and coherence of the mapping between ranges of spatial frequencies and those aspects of the stimulus that support performance indicative of configural, holistic, featural, and so on, processing is compromised by a lack of definitional precision with respect to the latter constructs. (p. 126)

Wenger and Townsend (2000) then showed that the spatial frequency measures, no matter how precisely defined they may be, have not been adequately bridged to the much foggier concepts of the global or local attributes of a stimulus. Ultimately this failure of definition must lead, by their account, to similar paradoxical conclusions about the nature of the form recognition process. Thus, an additional problem emerges. The precise definition of a mathematical transform with well-defined dimensions creates the illusion that the corresponding psychological dimensions have been equally well defined. This illusion may be the source of many invalid assumptions that are ubiquitous in this field.

The position taken here is closely related to the general difficulty in defining psychological states discussed previously (Uttal, 2001) but it has a distinctly different meaning. Here we are concerned with the definition of the attributes of the stimulus, not the psychological state. However often we may carry out experiments to distinguish global effects from local ones, the actual nature of these respective term remain uncertain. "Features" can be defined in many different ways (e.g., length and width versus spatial frequency components) and the overall configuration depends, in part, on the arrangement of the features. In many situations it is uncertain that the dimensions of a transformed stimulus are those to which the observer is sensitive. For example, as discussed in Chapter 2, how the promising fractal metaphor eventually was shown to have no psychophysical efficacy and how it subsequently all but disappeared from the experimental literature of psychophysics.

The definitional problem, therefore, is enhanced when stimulus attributes are transformed from one domain to another. As discussed earlier, the use of such precisely defined constructs as the Fourier components changes the representation of the stimulus from a natural domain to one totally unrealistic psychologically and neurophysiologically. Clearly, in this and other controversies, insufficient care has been given to a precise definition of the entities under study.

It is important to reiterate that nothing said here about the illusion of precision produced by some mathematical approaches is meant to disparage the use of the unquestionably powerful and precise *Fourier method* to carefully control stimuli. Unfortunately, however, the illusion of a corresponding precision in the psychological domain stimulates a mindset that impels the researcher to seek ill-defined entities such as spatial frequency sensitive channels or "grandmother" neurons. The point is that the powerful and useful *Fourier method* may exert misleading pressures on the theoretician to produce fanciful and erroneous *Fourier explanations* of how we see.

It is also important to point out that as a result of variable and ill-defined primitives, the same finding may have different meanings when examined from the preexisting points of view of different theoretical positions. One of the most obvious results of this assertion is that the description of the results of even the best designed experiment are often subject to a wide variety of hypothetical explanations. Given the looseness that accrues to verbal (as opposed to mathematical or computational) models, this tendency to differentially interpret data is ubiquitous in the history of psychological science. The net result is that the interpretation is often driven more by the theoretical predisposition of the theorist than by the psychobiology of the organism under study.

One example of this sort of disputational confusion is found in a series of papers presented in volume 4 (1986) of the journal *New Ideas in Psychology*. The issue in this controversy was over the part–whole issue, but framed in the context of the "correctness" or "incorrectness" of a Gestalt theoretical interpretation. The debate revolved around the meaning of some well-known geometric illusions: the Necker cube and the Penrose impossible figure. The phenomenal descriptions of the illusions themselves were not the issue; observers consistently report an oscillation of the apparent form in the first case and an equally compelling difficulty in making the impossible figure coherent in the second. Hochberg (1981) used these phenomena to disparage Gestalt psychology. Arnheim (1986a) countered that these data did, in fact, support the idea that the global attribute of the form does affect the perception of its component parts. Hochberg (1986) replied that Arnheim misunderstood what he (Hochberg) was asserting. To which Arnheim (1986b) replied that "there is no point in discussing how to quantify and test the consequences of a given thesis until that thesis is clearly understood" (p. 301). The debate continued in these terms until apparently the editors or the contenders were exhausted.

The words "understand" and "misunderstand," and variations on them were ubiquitous throughout this strange debate. Clearly each of these antagonists was speaking past the other and neither "understood" the other's argument; not only did the words (e.g., "Gestalt," "whole," "part," and perhaps even "theory") mean something different to each of these much admired scholars, but also, the argument was so poorly constructed that both (or neither) may have been correct. Perhaps the most useful clarifying comment in the entire discourse was made by a participant (Vonèche, 1986) who subsequently joined the discussion. His role as intellectual arbitrator was particularly helpful to me, if not to the participants in the debate. Arguing for an eclectic middle ground between Hochberg and Arnheim, Vonèche stated:

> The crux in the matter of Rudolf Arnheim and Julian Hochberg lies in the excessive number of degrees of freedom allowed by terms as vague as "whole" and "parts" The real trouble with wholes and parts is that they can always fit the parameters of any given figure. . . . (p. 303)

Vonèche (1986) and Perkins (1986), another participant who also joined what ultimately turned out to be a multiperson debate, each championed an information-processing approach. That is, both felt it was possible to use the Shannon nomenclature to make definitive statements about the stimuli and to precisely describe the results of an experiment. However, as we saw on page 75, there, too, lies ambiguity and neutrality.

3.2.2. False Dichotomies

Because of the uncertainty in defining terms in scientific debate, there is a powerful, though erroneous, tendency to formulate arguments as if it was a controversy between two extreme dichotomous alternatives. Gould (2000) was particularly insightful when he pointed out the fallaciousness of any approach to scientific disagreement in which controversies are based on "contrasts between inherently distinct and logically opposite alternatives"

(p. 253).[4] In other words, a compromise middle position is most likely to be the most realistic, correct, and inevitable solution to any such debate. This is particularly so in psychological science where the dichotomous extremes are sometimes nothing more than caricatures of reality.

Nowhere in the psychological literature is there better evidence of this continuing tendency to falsely dichotomize than the effort to resolve the controversy between *serial* and *parallel* processing. Yet, it is almost certain that these two extreme positions are but the (hypothetical) end points on a continuum rather than two exclusive alternatives. Some of the most compelling arguments concerning this issue were reported by Shaw (1978; Harris, Shaw, & Altom, 1985) when they showed that, rather than extremes, a much more general model with overlapping and simultaneous processing was a better description than either of the dichotomous extremes. Townsend and Thomas (1994) have also remarked on this same issue and showed how the two extremes—serial and parallel processing—can mimic each other.

The point is that extreme dichotomous positions, often taken as exclusive alternative hypotheses or explanations of data are, in the main, "red herrings" or "straw men" neither of which realistically reflects the complexity of human thought. Rather, they are highly oversimplified models of the complexity and redundant processing that is actually present in the brain.

3.2.3. Computability and Complexity

Definitional and dichotomous difficulties arise for some relatively straightforward reasons. They arise because of the difficulty of capturing the essence of a complex system in a single discrete phrase, especially when there are no physical anchors. The brain and the mental functions that are one measure of brain activity are both characterized by a paucity of simplicity and an abundance of complexity. That is, a single word is hardly able to encompass the range of interactions, feedbacks, feed forwards, and nonlinearities that are reflected in some behaviors. A continuum is almost always oversimplified by caricaturizing it by the activity at any single point along its course. The difficulties encountered when attempts are made to

---

[4]I must admit that I, too, have fallen victim to this propensity in selecting the title of a previous book—*The War Between Mentalism and Behaviorism* (Uttal, 2000). At this stage I wish I had been aware of Gould's advice before entitling this book. The only extenuating thing I can say is that there are, at rock bottom, differences between mentalism and behaviorism that are so fundamental as to suggest that a dichotomous debate may be somewhat more viable in this case than elsewhere. On the other hand, there is also such a range of theoretical positions involved that calling it a "war," as I did, was as incorrect as Gould suggested. I must also note, that as much as I stand chastised by Gould's quite correct argument against false dichotomies and extreme caricatures, I do not agree with him concerning the role of social forces on our science. The only method we have to seek *truth* is the scientific method and any kind of socially relativistic deconstruction of science does no good for the future of our science.

analyze such a system have been well discussed by such thoughtful students of brain and behavior as Shallice (1988); Van Orden, Jansen op de Haar, and Bosman (1997); and Vishton (personal communication).

The point is that it is not only inadequate to characterize a complex system by a singular attribute or property, but that it is also theoretically unsatisfactory to assume a linear sequence of causality. To do so as a pragmatic convenience or in order to simplify for the sake of formal analysis or experimental design would be acceptable only if it was appreciated and made crystal clear that such an artifice was merely a metaphorical tool. It is essential for all concerned to appreciate that such a strategy, however simplifying or convenient, may, in the long run, be theoretically misleading to a disastrous degree. The root cause of the tendency to oversimplify to the point of erroneous triviality is the vastness of the spatial as well as temporal interactions among the myriad components of the brain-mind system. This complexity is something that is often overlooked in designing the unidimensional, highly controlled experiments than can be practically carried out.

Although it may be suggested that this slide toward oversimplification is the result of an insufficiently developed set of research methods, techniques, and equipment, I don't think this is the case. Such an assumption suggests that time will provide us the tools we need. To the contrary, a totally antithetical argument can be made that it is not the inadequacy of our methods, but rather the intractable nature of the problem that is the cause of the lack of reductive or explanatory progress so far.

The ubiquitous penchant toward oversimplification expressed in the work of form recognition scientists ignores the anatomical, physiological, and behavioral complexity of the system we seek to understand. Bremmerman (1971; see the front piece and pages 17 and 237) was among the most vocal early critics of much of what is done in recognition theory, but his arguments have not had the impact they should.

3.2.4. Integrality

Efforts to answer some of the key questions concerning perception or form recognition are impeded by the most fundamental aspects of the nature of the stimuli we use. Although the classic experimental design, as noted, is characterized by manipulation of a single independent variable and the measurement of some equally unidimensional response dimension, it is not always possible to control or even appreciate the complex interaction of interdependent variables; slight changes in a single attribute of the stimulus may have an alarmingly large effect on the overall perceptual experience. Thus, for example, the expression on a face may be totally changed from a happy to a frowning visage by a single, and superficially slight, change in the curvature of the mouth.

The global impact of a single aspect of a stimulus reflects an intimate and inseparable interaction with other aspects that has come to be called *integrality*. A distinction between two kinds of dimensions—separable and integral—has been repeatedly acknowledged over the years, most notably by Shepherd (1964a), Garner (1974), and Monahan and Lockhead (1977). Integral stimulus dimensions are defined as those in which the interactions are so strong, as in the face example, that they jointly determine the overall nature of the stimulus. Separable stimulus dimensions, on the contrary, are those that act independently (e.g., the size and orientation of a ellipse) and, therefore, can be analyzed separately. However, nothing is as simple in this business as it may seem. Even the example of separability illustrated by this tilted ellipse is clouded by potential "oblique" effects that can make what might seem to be separable actually have some integral interactions. Nevertheless, the point made is a strong one: Attempts to segregate or parse dimensions or to estimate the degree of interaction of the dimensions of a stimulus in many cases may be both indeterminate and confounding in an overly simplistic experimental design.

3.2.5. Task Dependency and The Adaptability of Vision

Another impediment to the interpretation of experimental findings obtained from psychophysical experiments is that the brain–mind–behavior system under study is not a stable one. That is, it does not depend on a small number of strategies to solve perceptual problems or use the same one every time. Neither does it necessarily execute the same neural or mental algorithms or processes, even when the tasks at hand may be superficially closely related. To put it bluntly, the results obtained in one experimental situation may not be extrapolatable or even relevant to what may seemingly be another closely related protocol.

To the contrary, the nervous system is equally likely to draw on totally different strategies and processes to solve the wide variety of perceptual challenges, even closely related ones, to which we are repeatedly confronted. The idea of a "bag of tricks" (as opposed to a few standard strategies) was summed up nicely by Ramachandran (1985) and has been further supported by recent work from our laboratory (Uttal, Baruch, & Allen, 1995a, 1995b, 1997) as well as by others (Abdi, Valentin, Edelman, & O'Toole, 1995; Sergent, 1986; Wenger & Townsend, 2000). All of these authors and their experimental results support the conclusion that the visual system is enormously adaptable and adds further to the argument that slight task differences may lead to substantial perceptual strategy differences.

Nowhere is this task dependent strategy better illustrated then in attempts to force fit Fourier analysis to perceptual data obtained in face recognition experiments. As already seen, according to findings from some laboratories, low frequencies are critical, from others, high frequencies determine the results, and a third theoretical position argues for an intermediate range. Koenderink (1984) summed up the point very succinctly when he said:

> It seems clear enough that visual perception treats images on several levels of resolution simultaneously and that this fact must be important for the study of perception. However, no applicable mathematically formulated theory to deal with such problems appears to exist. (p. 363)

However, a much more eclectic and adaptive point of view is expressed by those who are aware of the implications of task dependence. Many in this camp specifically appreciate that task dependence is characterized by two axiomatic premises: (a) The task determines the strategy and (b) there are many strategies that can be used to carry out any perceptual task. In agreement with this position, I argue here that the recognition of a form can be accomplished by any number of quite different strategies by using whatever cues are available. The argument follows that no particular feature, spatial frequency band or otherwise, is uniquely important. A highly caricaturized set of a few lines emphasizing the high-frequency components can be sufficient; so too can a very blurred low-frequency rendition that equally well represents the overall configuration of a form. Indeed, it is highly likely that both types of stimulus and both strategies may be simultaneously at work, perhaps even in cooperative combination with other cues that are not characterized by their frequency domain attributes. It is even likely that the spatial frequency space into which faces are transformed for this analysis is not biologically instantiated or even relevant to what is going on in the brain. The interrelationships among the parts of the original image expressed in the spatial domain may be more likely to determine what is seen. Thus, what is convenient for the experimenter may not be psychobiologically significant. The problem in this case, however, is that we may not know which type of mechanism is operating. This does not mean, however, that we will not be able to determine which attributes of the stimulus are effective in influencing behavior.

3.2.6. The Indeterminacy of Experimental Outcomes

Wenger and Townsend's (2000) comment concerning the irrelevance of Fourier components to the form recognition process quoted on page 84 highlights the uncertainty of the meaning or significance of *any experimental outcome* that attempts to draw conclusions about internal mental processes or mechanisms by inferences drawn from observed behavior.

The implicit disappointment in not being able to nail down definitive answers to so many experimental questions leads many scholars to equivocate in presenting their findings. Researchers with extensive experience in the field of form perception often fall back on a call for more research in a way that may define the unanswerable rather than the unanswered. Kimchi (1992), for example, in one of the most insightful recent reviews, concluded:

> A complete understanding of the perceptual relations between wholes and their parts should await further research and conceptual clarification. . . . This article suggest that it will be a challenge. (p. 36)

Another respected student of object recognition (Hoffmann, 1995) similarly concluded in a extensive review article:

> Once more, we must await future research in order to understand the relationships between the mechanisms of visual behavior control and those used for the conscious recognition of visual structures. (p. 335)

There has not yet been, in spite of many years of research in the field, even the beginning of the kind of convergence on satisfactory answers to the most basic questions concerning form recognition. Indeed, different experimenters looking at the same set of data come to very different conclusions about their meaning given their very different views and assumptions.[5]

If one accepts the generality of the assertion that there is a fundamental indeterminacy of psychophysical data, one is led directly to an acceptance of the tenets of modern behaviorism and a necessary rejection of the currently popular cognitive mentalism. The acknowledgment of the indeterminacy of experimental results is, without question, one of the most fundamental tenets of a nonmentalist behaviorism. Should we ever get to the point of accepting this premise, contemporary scientific psychology would have evolved to a new operational, descriptive, kind of psychological science. In doing so it would have undergone a counterrevolutionary change of colossal importance for the science.

3.2.7. A Final Introductory Comment

So far in this section I have tabulated a number of arguments that speak against the possibility of answering the reductive type questions concerning form recognition that I have classified as belonging to the second class.

---

[5]One of the most frustrating arguments any one in the field of psychology encounters can be phrased as follows: The antagonist asserts: "I can disprove your ideas completely. Let me show you some data I have that 'proves' my point." Rarely is the antagonist who so presents the "killer" data aware of the fact that the counterinterpretation presented is indeterminate or is based on their own biases and assumptions. The logic may be impeccable but the premises invalid! Unfortunately, the debate never gets down to the nature of these underlying assumptions.

It is important to point out, however, that a considerable (and, perhaps, an increasing) body of scientific research is already being carried out within the behaviorist spirit of this indeterminacy assumption. Other than the patently physiological studies that attempt to bridge the crevasse between behavior and neural mechanisms (at either the cellular or ensemble level) there is an increasing tendency for studies of form recognition to eschew reductionism in favor of descriptive models.[6] If this impression is correct, it is clear that a nonreductionist tradition is still alive and that a behavioral and descriptive approach to scientific psychology has not completely disappeared from the current scene.

It is important to note as I conclude this discussion that parametric testing in which one or another independent variable is manipulated in order to determine its effect on a percept is very important. Nowhere else are the complexities of perceptual processing more robustly demonstrated. On the other hand, it is equally certain that the demonstration of a superficially simple (i.e., a functional) relationship between some parameter and a percept is not evidence that the phenomena under study is simply and singularly determined by that parameter. In any experiment, and particularly in any psychological experiment, the controlled variables may alter the results obtained if they, too, concurrently vary. Simple functional, unidimensional relationships do not preclude ultra-complex, mediated processing by the perceptual system. They simply describe the outcome, are neutral with regard to the inner mechanisms, and often produce an illusion of simplicity where there is, in fact, great complexity.

3.3. A SELECTIVE REVIEW OF THE EMPIRICAL DATA[7]

With full appreciation of the enormous conceptual barriers that lay between cognitive and neurophysiological reality and our understanding of how we recognize forms, we must also be cognizant of and celebrate the

---

[6]Of course, this is not universally true. Many cognitive neuroscientists are still attempting to determine which of several possible alternative and patently reductive theories are "correct." But, to me, the literature seems less likely now to deal with simple flow chart or modular information-processing modules than previously. The problem is that it is sometime hard to distinguish between reductive theories and those that, although claiming to be reductive, in fact are only metaphorically or analogically describing the relationships between the stimuli and the responses.

[7]I no longer have the overly optimistic hope of my youth that I can fully review the work of the many authors who have been contributing to form recognition psychophysics. The literature is so vast that, at best, the papers I cite here must be only the tip of an intellectual iceberg. What I have done here is to mention those articles that help me make the relevant conceptual points.

substantial existing database that describes how humans recognize forms. For almost half a century perceptual psychologists, and more recently those intellectual descendents who have designated themselves "cognitive neuroscientists," (see the discussion in Chapter 1) have been studying form recognition in a way that attests to its importance in the field. Much of this work, however, is *incoherent*, not because it is irrational, but rather in the sense that it is internally disconnected. Data pertaining to different experiment paradigms are frequently unrelated even to studies that assay similar processes. Certainly, few of the microtheories that have been developed to represent particular recognition behaviors are cross-connected to others of their kind. Indeed, this is a major problem in the history of empirical research in this field—so much of it has been carried out in isolated fragments without consideration of the interactions that one experiment or theory might have with another. The absence of true replicability is a major handicap of much of this kind of psychological research. There is so much to do and so few willing to go through the tedium of repeating someone's else work. There are few rewards for the replicators; no fame of discovery; no "progress" to be demonstrated to one's patrons. The result of this "microscientific" approach is an incoherent collection of scientific oddities rather than a systematic attack on a very complex field of science.

Such a system feeds on itself. Most results stand both unchallenged and uncorroborated. With such a multiplicity of interesting psychological phenomena, there is always something new to be investigated. A priori hunches are supported by an experiment, and the hunches are reified, becoming the foundations of even more far fetched ideas. Efforts to analyze, to simplify, so that experiments can be carried out lead to trivial or irrelevant findings and, ultimately, to terribly misleading inferences about the actual nature of mental activity.

Nevertheless, we cannot abandon our search for understanding and knowledge. We must work within the constraints of empirical reality. There is much to be learned, many heuristics to be explored, and inferences to be drawn even though the theories may not be iron-clad. Although, we acknowledge that some questions cannot be answered, we must also be willing to make some inferences based on suggestions from the data. In this review my goal is to show that a first approximation to answers about some of the most tantalizing issues in form recognition is possible if we concentrate on the efficacy–transform paradigm that characterize the Type 3 questions defined on page 125.

If there is any single fundamental principle that ties the following discussions together, it is one based on the primary importance of high-level processing of visual forms. The essence of the argument I make here is that top-down influences on form recognition are dominant—that the global, symbolic, and even the semantic attributes of the stimulus are far more relevant than any set of local component features. This assumption is based on the already expressed idea that key attributes of a stimulus are virtually always redundant; that key global information can be equally well transmitted by low or high frequencies, by "features" of many different kinds, or even by symbolic information such as written or spoken words that often bear no geometrical isomorphism to the stimulus form. This contention argues that, in point of empirical fact, it is the interrelationships of various parts (including their meaning) of the form that dominate the actual physical dimensions of the stimulus. For example, where wavelength or luminance was once considered key to perception, recent research now documents that actual experienced color (Land, 1977) or lightness (Gilchrist, 1977), as well as shape of the object is more subject to the relationships among the various parts than to their actual physical properties.

The goal of this section, then, is to convince my readers that even the "simplest" visual experience is so complex and involves such high level and informationally intricate processes that it can be explained neither in terms of the kind of neural or cognitive components that have been proposed by contemporary mentalisms nor in terms of the raw physical properties of the stimulus. As this discussion proceeds, I hope my readers are drawn along to appreciate the enormous complexity of the brain–cognitive–behavior system and the practical and theoretical difficulties that make some of our simplifications border on the absurd.

In making this assertion, I certainly am not alone. Recently, there has been a resurgence of the idea that cognitive penetration—a shorthand for a constructive or interpretive approach to perception—controls perception. Hoffman (2000) expressed this same view as he reviewed the enormous number of illusions that suggest we construct our visual world rather than passively responding to the stimuli projected on our retina. His book is an excellent introduction to the many visual phenomena that suggest there is no sharp distinction between perception and cognition.

3.3.1. Findings Pertaining to the Global–Local Controversy

I begin with a consideration of one of the most contentious and long lasting of the controversies surrounding form recognition: the global–local conundrum. To place it in the context expressed in this chapter, I ask: What global or local attributes of a stimulus form influence perception? And, What is their effect?

The long-term history of the problem—wholes versus parts—is well known.[8] Suffice it to say in the present context that the issue dates back to

---

[8]I presented a brief history of this problem in Uttal (1988). Some of the following material has been expanded and updated from that discussion.

Aristotle, but found its more recent expression in the controversies between the British Empiricists and their followers (based on their fundamental assumption of the association of discrete experiences and sensory components) on the one hand, and the more global views of the Gestalt psychologists who followed the holistic ideas of Mach and von Ehrenfels, on the other. More recently, the ecological school or perceptual science championed by Gibson (1961, 1979), in particular, has argued from a similar holistic point of view.

In spite of its antiquity and persistence, the whole–part or global–local problem has been beset throughout history with the challenge of actually defining what these terms mean. However, there is a related problem that may even transcend the arbitrariness of the lexicographic one. That is, there is still no agreement on the fundamental nature of the problem. What the controversy is about has been interpreted in many different ways. In the past, clarifications of this problem have neither been forthcoming nor enlightening. However, recently a few bright lights have appeared on the scene. Latimer and Stevens (1997) have lucidly pointed out that there is an enormous divergence among researchers concerning the theoretical implications of the data collected with stimuli that varied along some kind of an ill-defined whole–part dimension. According to Latimer and Stevens, the intent of the research varied from one investigator to another. One research theme was directed at the supposed "precedence" of either the local or global attributes of the stimulus. Other experimenters, according to them, attempt to determine whether the processing is actually analytic or holistic. As suggested earlier, however, this may be a chimeric search, a futile quest for a goal unobtainable.

The wide variety of stimuli used and the various manipulations carried out by a substantial number of scholars studying the whole–part problem certainly contributed to the chaotic state of the literature. Although there is no a priori reason to expect that experiments that use faces as stimuli need necessarily provide the same answers as those using more artificial geometric forms, theoreticians would prefer to discover universal laws to explain the diversity of observed phenomena. If no such universal laws actually exist, it is still too often that a "proof" produced with stimuli and procedures from one domain is haphazardly commingled with findings obtained with stimuli from some other domain. The adaptability and flexibility of the visual system to use a variety of different strategies is seriously underestimated by such a conceptual conglomerate.

In the following pages, I review only a sparse sampling of the large number of empirical studies directed at achieving some insight, if not answering, the question of the respective influence of wholes and parts. My emphasis in this section is on the relatively recent work dating from the 1970s to the present. My strategy is to briefly describe exemplar research reports and to comment on the conclusions drawn by their respective authors. It must be kept in mind that many of the problems already identified in this discussion reverberate down through this entire story. For example, the problem of how we should go about defining the parts or, for that matter, the whole is still unresolved.

Object Superiority. One of the major tools in attempts to resolve the whole–part problem is the "object superiority effect." The typical strategy on which this protocol is based shows that a particular part of an object can be seen better when it is part of a whole than when it is presented alone. The idea is based on the assumption that context can provide a perceptual framework within which the "part" can be seen better than when it is isolated. An early example of such a context effect was the work of Reicher (1969) and, shortly thereafter, Wheeler (1970) who were following up a century old experiment reported by Cattell (1886). Reicher showed that letters were better recognized when presented in a meaningful word then when presented alone or in a nonword. The conclusion was that the whole (i.e., the word) added something to the recognition of the part (i.e., the letter) rather than detracting from or inhibiting the letter's recognizability. Although this result does not seem too surprising after the fact, it is important to appreciate that many other studies had shown some kind of an interference between different components of a stimulus and an "inhibition" hypothesis (in which parts interfered with, rather than enhanced, the respective percepts) could not have been rejected a priori.

Following Reicher's pioneering study a number of researchers started applying the idea to geometric forms other than multiletter words. In such an experiment, Schendel and Shaw (1976) used letters and letter fragments as prototype forms and found that critical lines defining which character had been presented were better recognized when the whole character was presented than when just the fragment was presented.

Another example of such a formal study of context effects on an abstract geometric form (as opposed to a letter or word) perception was reported by Weisstein and Harris (1974). They showed that straight line segments were recognized (in terms of their subtended angle) better when a part of an organized form (a Neckar cube-like drawing) than when presented alone both when masking visual noise was present and when it was not. Pomerantz, Sager, and Stoever (1977) carried out a similar experiments in which arrays of symbols (i.e., textured patterns) were presented in a stimulus scene. They also concluded that some contexts substantially increased discrimination of the detected form although others were not effective.

Homa, Haver, and Schwartz (1976), working with faces observed essentially the same effect. They compared the recognizability of parts of a face (i.e., eyes, noses, and mouths) in situations when the parts were scrambled and in situations in which the face was normally organized. The parts were much better recognized when they were part of an organized face than when the parts were scrambled. They concluded by postulating the concept of a perceptual Gestalt.

The emerging conclusion from all these studies was that parts were usually (but not always) detected, discriminated, or recognized better when they were presented in the context of whole objects or entire arrays of symbols rather then when a single part was presented in isolation.

It should be pointed out, however, that there is one glaring source of potential confounding in both the word and object superiority types of experiment. That confound is that an object, in addition to providing a context for the recognition or discrimination of its form, also provides additional information about the nature of the characters of which it is constructed. For example, although an isolated alphabetic character has only itself to convey its individual shape, a group of characters making up a whole word conveys additional semantic and syntactic information about what that individual character might be. Thus, for example, the partial word C_T is loaded with syntactical and sequential usage dependencies that can influence the perception of the missing letter even when the letter is not there. It is likely that all object and word superiority effects are irretrievably confounded and one is hard pressed to distinguish between the effects of geometry and the additional information provided by the syntax of the spatial or alphabetic codes beings used.

Global Precedence. Perhaps the most potent reinvigoration of the study of the problems of wholes and parts in recent years came from the seminal reports by Navon (1977, 1981) on *global precedence*. Navon's original technique involved the use of large letters (the wholes) made up of organized arrays of small letters (the parts).[9] Figure 3.1 depicts the prototypical stimulus used in his studies. Navon's results led him to conclude that the large letter (i.e., the global form) was *precedent*; that is, when presented tachistoscopically, it was more likely to interfere with the recognition of an acoustically presented name for another letter than were the small letters (the parts) whose configuration defined the large letter. On the basis of these results, Navon concluded that the whole (the large letter form) was initially perceived rather than the small component letters. The interpretation, therefore, was that the observer did not reconstruct the form by aggregating the parts, but perceived the global form prior to the perception of the parts.

---

[9] This technique had been previously used by Shor (1971) and by Kinchla (1974) to study interfering effects and target detection respectively.

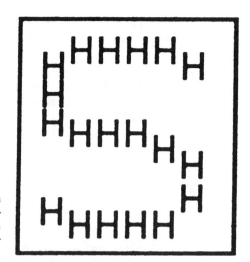

FIG. 3.1. A stimulus object that can be used to study the whole versus part controversy. From Navon (1977) with the permission of Academic Press.

It did not take long for other psychophysicists to challenge this conclusion. By slightly perturbing the design of the experiments, researchers such as Miller (1981) and Kinchla, Solis-Macias, and Hoffman (1983) suggested that the global precedence observed by Navon actually was due to the size scale to which observers initially directed their attention. From their point of view Navon's entire effect was mainly attributable to what the subjects were initially looking at rather than any clash between the local and global attributes of the stimulus letter.

Although joining in the clamor against Navon's conclusion of global precedence, Grice, Canham, and Boroughs (1983) argued that the effect was actually due to "image degradation" of the small component letters. According to their interpretation, the entire global precedence effect effect was mainly attributable to optical resolution factors and high-level cognitive factors were irrelevant. Thus, both top-down and bottom-up theories have been invoked to explain and also refute Navon's findings. Olivia and Schyns' (1997) work supports this conclusion. They showed that the size scale at which the observer directed attention was determined by the information requirements of the experiment and that such a perceptual scaling could be primed by very brief pre-exposures of appropriately scaled stimuli. In other words, they argued that the scale at which attention is initially directed is neither coarse nor fine. Precedence may be either global of local depending on how the experiment is designed.

Clearly, the controversy is still active. Navon (1991) himself has continued to champion a global precedence argument. In that report, Navon suggests that if the effect were due to attentional effects, then attempts to redirect attention should change the results. However, in a series of experiments in which attention was redirected to another place, divided, or to another scale of magnification, he was not able to observe any such attentional influence. Paquet and Merikle (1988), on the other hand, took a somewhat more eclectic poison. They compared the ability of observers to identify the letters in a Navon type display in which a large letter was composed of small letters. They found global precedence for attended stimuli but not for those to which attention was not directed. They observed that global precedence (which they agreed was the usual result) had to be due to factors: (a) "mandatory global processing" and (b) a "postidentification, response selection process . . ." (p. 99). On this basis, Paquet and Merikle (1988) concluded that:

> The present data suggest that that global information must be attended before identification occurs. (p. 99)

Paquet (1999) expressed a strengthened conviction that global factors dominate for stimuli "located outside the attentional focus" and to reinforce her view that this domination is explained by both perceptual and attentional factors.

It appears that none of the proposed explanations even begins to approximate any kind of a resolution of the controversy concerning internal mechanisms. What they did do was determine what influences were effective and under what conditions. Kimchi (1992), in a particularly important review of the problem, tabulated the many factors that can influence the global advantage that is most often seen. Her list includes:

- Overall visual angle: (However, Kimchi also notes that effects of stimulus size are often confounded with any of the other items on her list.)
- Retinal location:
- Spatial Uncertainty:
- Scarcity and number of local elements:
- Goodness of form:
- Exposure duration:
- Attention allocation:
- Differences in the global local structure:

This empirical description, however, does not lead to the reductive explanation for which the researchers have been seeking. Kimchi (1992) made this clear when she commented on how difficult it is to even determine whether the effect is a sensoriperceptual phenomenon or a high-level attentional one.

The important question arising again in this context is whether or not this inability to resolve the question is the reflection of an insurmountable barrier—cognitive inaccessibility—or simply a reflection of the primitive state of our research technology. Clearly, there is little support, given the fragility of the data and the abundance of conflicting opinions, for the idea that progress is being made or that we are converging on an understanding of the role of wholes or parts in form recognition. What does, however, reverberate through this segment of the literature is the priority given to the global organization of a stimulus in determining its perception. Nowhere is this undertone heard stronger than in the study of a particular kind of form—the human face—the topic of the next section.

Face Recognition. Next we consider the special aspect of form recognition when the form is a face. The visual processing of faces has been of interest to psychologists almost forever. Galton (1879), the remarkable polymath, was one of the first to propose a holistic theory of face perception. Since his time, interest in the human face, an especially significant stimulus class, has increased substantially.

An analysis of the literature[10] of face recognition suggests that the most basic questions including the configuration versus feature debate, have no more been answered for faces than for any of the other stimulus types. For example, the question—Are faces special?—has been considered by Farah, Wilson, Drain, and Tanaka (1998) and by Diamond and Carey (1986). These two groups came to diametrically opposed views. Farah and her colleagues argue that faces are special, albeit in inexplicable ways. On the contrary, Diamond and Carey suggest that faces are not different from any other stimulus classes that have been dealt with for extended periods and for which a degree of expertise has been obtained. Both groups, however, suggest that face perception is a function of the molar (= global = Gestalt = holistic = configurational = arrangement, etc.) organization of the whole stimulus shape. This is not unusual; as we see in this section most of the experimenters dealing with whole faces in the picture domain (as opposed to those who use the Fourier frequency domain based approach) as stimuli come to the same conclusion (i.e., faces are dealt with holistically). This is a trend suggested earlier by Bradshaw and Wallace (1971) and Harmon (1973).

Rhodes, Brennan, and Carey (1987) similarly contended, on the basis of their findings in a study using caricatures, that features ". . . may not, in principle, be necessary for representation" (p. 495). They conclude that comparisons are probably the basis of memorial representations and that recognition is carried out by a holistic comparison of the stored memorial image and the current stimulus. Sergent (1986) also argued for a molar strategy noting:

---

[10]Some of the material in this section has been adapted from an earlier article by Uttal published in Wenger and Townsend's (2001) new book.

. . . faces may be encoded and processed in terms of a facial unit, and feature differences may not be treated as such but contribute to the overall configurational dissimilarity between faces. (p. 101)

Many others, on one basis or another, have come to the same "holistic" or Gestalt conclusion including Tanaka and Sengco (1997), Moscovitch, Winocur, and Behrmann (1997), and Donnelly and Davidoff (1999).

Purcell and Stewart (1988), influenced by the earlier work on object superiority, explored a phenomenon they called the *face detection effect*. They discovered that faces were detected better in masking noise when the face was upright and when the parts were normally organized. Inverted faces and faces composed of randomly arranged parts were not detected as well. They concluded from their studies that face perception seemed to be determined more by the global or holistic aspects of the face than by the features or parts themselves. Specifically, they stated:

Our results suggest that a face, as an organized meaningful pattern, is a more potent stimulus than an arbitrary assemblage of the same visual features. (p. 355)

Tanaka and Farah (1993) approached the face recognition problem by concentrating on the identification of facial parts generated and manipulated with computer techniques. They compared the recognition of isolated parts of faces with the recognition of the same parts when they were part of a whole face. Like other object superiority effects, the parts were better recognized when embedded in a whole than when presented alone. When the same experiment was carried out with scrambled or inverted faces, however, the effect was not present. Thus, a well configured face provided a substantial advantage but a disordered one did not. Tanaka and Farah concluded on the basis of these results the hypothesis that face processing is holistic was borne out by these results.

Both Tanaka and Farah (1993) and Purcell and Stewart (1988) provided good reviews of the literature prior to their respective times. Tanaka and Farah performed a particularly useful service by discussing the deficiencies of much of the prior work that supported a part or feature approach to the problem of face recognition. In particular, they noted the following problems with much of the research on this topic:

1. Most prior studies assume that the number of features will not affect a holistic processing system. This, say Tanaka and Farah is not necessarily true.
2. Most prior studies ignore the possibility of parallel processing in which features are never explicitly coded.

3. The tasks used in most experiments are not adequately linked to "normal face recognition."

4. Few experiments compare face recognition to other forms of form recognition so it is not possible to generalize to form recognition in general.

(Abstracted from Tanaka & Farah, 1993, p. 228)

When it specifically comes to face recognition, the Fourier-based or other kind of feature-emphasizing hypothesis leaves us with some extremely ambiguous results. Nevertheless, the predominant opinion expressed by feature theorists of this persuasion is that features, specifically the spatial frequency components, dominate in face perception. But, which frequencies? The data are rambunctiously inconsistent. Since the publication of the now-classic paper of Harmon and Julesz (1973), the idea that low-frequency information can allow virtually complete face perception to occur has been widespread. Ginsburg (1978) adhered to this point of view in his demonstrations of the effect of low-pass filters on face recognition. Harvey (1986) also suggested that it is only the lower frequencies that are maintained in a spatially encoded visual memory and presumably, therefore, only this band of spatial frequencies would be required for face recognition.

However, experiments that claim we see faces because of relatively low-frequency cues are challenged by equally compelling studies supporting exactly the opposite conclusion: that relatively high frequencies cue face recognition. For example, Fiorentini, Maffei, and Sandini (1983) reported that transformed faces in which the relatively higher frequency information was preserved were as recognizable as those in which the lower frequencies were preserved. Caelli and Yuzyk's (1985) work also supported the priority of the high-frequency components because they seem (in their Figure 3) to lead to better face perception than do faces that contain only low spatial frequencies.[11] It is also clear from less formal observations with caricatures or any other kind of line drawing that the high-frequency information represented by such edge information is independently a powerful stimulus to face perception.

The Fourier spatial frequency hypothesis feature argument is further clouded by the reports (e.g., Hayes, Morrone, & Burr, 1986), in opposition to both high- and low-frequency explanations, that it is an intermediate band

---

[11]There is a continuing problem associated with the use of spatial frequency as a measure of faces. Some authors prefer to use cycles per face width although others prefer cycles per degree. Some of our earlier work (Uttal, Baruch, & Allen, 1997) has shown that there are differences in the results of at least some face perception studies as a function of the size of the face. Therefore, cycles per face width is an unsatisfactory independent variable in this type of research.

of spatial frequencies that provides the best stimulus for face recognition. Similarly, although reporting on unrelated work with secondary cueing effects, Parker, Lishman, and Hughes (1996) showed that low- and high-frequency cues were equally effective in improving discrimination scores of two sequentially presented faces. The problem of interpreting the results of experiments using spatial frequency filtered faces as stimuli is, thus, further confounded by the variety of behavioral tasks used.

Costen, Parker, and Craw (1994) reviewed the extensive literature on spatial frequency and face perception and discussed the several different approaches used to determine if there is an essential band of spatial frequencies necessary for face recognition. They too, discovered there is considerable disagreement apparent among the many studies they cite (as well as those I just mentioned) to the local (high spatial frequency) versus global (low spatial frequency) controversy. This is not surprising given the redundant information carried by several different parts of the spatial frequency spectrum of a face. Facial caricatures composed of a few lines and blurred renditions in which no sharp lines are present are both recognizable stimuli.

Following their review of the literature, Costen et al. (1994) concluded that:

> Although these results show considerable variation and exhibit many ambiguities, the general conclusion could be drawn that there is a disproportionate decline in the accuracy of recognition of faces when the medium-low frequencies (approximately 8–16 cycles per face) are removed. (p. 130)

How, then, do we resolve these seemingly inconsistent observations and conclusions? My answer is that they are probably all correct. Given the vagaries of experimental design, I suggest that many different cues, some classified as high, medium, or low frequency as well as others defined along other dimensions, are able to affect the face recognition process.

There is, of course, a more general issue here. Is face perception a unified entity or is it better considered an aggregation of several processes? For example, O'Toole, Wenger, and Townsend (2001) suggested it is a composite of measurement, representation, and task demands. Their general point is that even if we could produce a satisfactory model of representation (also implying a satisfactory model of measurement) we still would not be at the core of the problem: What happens to this representation as the essential perceptual processes take place? No representation—Fourier, principal components, localized features, and so on—can yet adequately "explain" the process we call face recognition. All are, in a certain sense, only metaphors or analogs that help us describe some aspects of the transformations between stimuli and responses, but do not explain how these transformations are carried out.

There are other methodologies that have been used to approach the problem of face recognition. Usually, the same chaos of conclusions emerges in this literature as in the spatial frequency analysis domain. For example, much of the recent interest in research on face perception has been concerned with the deformed, inverted, or masked faces. Interest in this work was stimulated by the fascinating "Margaret Thatcher" illusion (Thompson, 1980) of perceptual normalcy when an inverted face was presented with inverted eyes and mouth. Since then, many other researchers have been concerned with the problem posed by inverting faces and parts of faces and have used the illusion as a way of studying face perception. For example, Rhodes, Brake, and Atkinson (1993) asked, What's lost in inverted faces? They concluded their data support the idea that it is "second order relational features" rather than isolated "first order" ones that are affected by inversion. Faces, to them, were prototypically composed of second-order features that are closely related to each other. They conclude from several experiments that the special sensitivity of faces to inversion supports the idea of what has already been designated by the terms "configurational" or "holistic." They wisely conclude, however, that it is necessary to ". . . make explicit, our notions of configural and holistic coding . . ." (p. 55).

Certainly, the problem of the roles of wholes and parts in face perception has not been resolved. Even though there is a substantial commitment to a holistic interpretation among most current workers in the field, there remains a vigorous elementalist opposition. There is also a middle ground in which cautions or new interpretations are raised about the extant database. Rakover and Teucher (1997), for example, pointed out that many of the effects on the recognition of inverted faces (and the superiority of right-side-up faces in recognition paradigms) attributed to global or configurational effects can also be accounted for in terms of the individual features. They suggest that "We do not propose that facial configurational information does not play an important role in face perception . . ." (p. 760). Their point is that "the configurational information is not necessary for obtaining the inversion effects in a whole face" and that, in some cases, may be "less important than featural information" (p. 760). As usual, the problem is made murky by the difficulty in defining what is meant by configurations and features.

White (2000) also took this same middle-ground stance. He believes that face inversion experiments are best explained in terms of the entire configuration of the face (a holistic type of processing). However, when asked to make judgments about the expression of a stimulus face, subjects seemed to be more affected by the nature of the parts, a demonstration of the integrality of the features at the very least.

In conclusion, the empirical psychophysical literature that is intended to resolve the controversial issue of wholes and parts falls into two contending camps. In general, although not universally, work that uses faces in the picture domain seems to emphasize the predominant effects of the global attributes of the stimulus on perception of virtually all kinds. (I return to consider this in the next chapter where the enormous gap between the majority opinion of a holistic psychophysical system and virtually all formal theories of form recognition are contrasted.) On the other hand, experimental studies that tend to transform the face stimuli into the spatial frequency domain are very inconsistent. Perhaps this is because the visual system is not a Fourier analyzer and does not operate with stimuli that are transformed into the frequency domain. Of course, any good behaviorist would say that this is an unverifiable contention.

Once again, the suspicion arises that the conclusions to which each school of thought eventually comes depends more on their initial assumptions than on the experimental findings. Those that start with faces as stimuli typically emerge as holists; those starting with features find compelling evidence to support the influence of the elemental parts.

To an eclectic critic, it seems likely that both schools may be equally correct and incorrect. But, more fundamentally, it may be that the question itself is unanswerable because of the fundamental inaccessibility of the very cognitive processes that are the targets of this kind of research.

As we begin to delve deeply into the role of the stimulus, we begin to see another worrisome aspect of these kinds of experiments. The particular stimulus of choice in each experiment exerts a profound influence on the general conclusions drawn and theories generated. This problem is considered in detail in Chapter 4, but I forewarn my readers of two complementary caveats now.

1. Different stimuli can produce reliable results that superficially support totally antithetical theories.
2. Any plausible theory can be supported by judiciously chosen stimuli.

The dangers implicit in these caveats are compounded by the arguable inaccessibility of cognitive processes. There is a profound warning here for any mentalist approach to understanding such cognitive processes as form recognition. There is, as well, a call to a new behaviorist approach to the study of perceptual phenomena.

Some Miscellaneous Clues to Holism. The literature dealing with the controversy between the elementalists and the holists is enormous. The experiments are often convoluted and, as I have repeatedly said, the definitions of *wholes* and *parts* are often so loose as to be meaningless. There are, however, a collection of observations and demonstrations that seem to be more direct evidence than many more formal experiments. One set of these phenomena is composed of graphic displays of the importance of the "arrangement" rather than the parts. For example, Koler's (1970) depiction (shown in Fig. 1.1 on page 21 of this book) of a collection of random forms (to the elementalist) clearly makes the point that it is the configuration rather then the parts that makes the difference. Other similar examples of sets of character fonts (Blesser, Shillman, Cox, Kuklinski, Ventura, & Eden, 1973), of various kinds of caricatures, or even the renaissance portraits of people formed from bunches of fruit, flowers, or even fish by Guiseppe Archimboldo (1527–1593)[12] all make the same argument: It doesn't really matter what a figure is composed of, what matters is its arrangement. In other words, the Gestaltists were correct!

3.3.2. Findings Pertaining to the Direct–Mediated Controversy

So far we have seen that, despite a prolonged and active research history, the global–local issue remains unresolved and may be unresolvable. In spite of the considerable research concerning this question and because of the ambiguity of the resulting data, no consensus answer to this question has been reached. In many cases, it seems that the a priori theoretical positions of the respective proponents may be determining both experimental results and the interpretation of those results.

Equally fundamental as the whole–part issue is the controversy between the proponents of what have been designated respectively as the *determinist* (direct stimulus, unmediated, stimulus dominated) and the *mediated* (cognitively interpreted or penetrated) theoretical approaches. In another guise this debate can be framed as an argument between those championing low-level (i.e., peripheral) processes that respond directly to the properties of the stimulus on the one hand and those who see the strong influence of high level (i.e., central) cognitive penetration on the other. The low-level argument is buttressed by neurophysiological work that clearly show correspondences between the stimuli and the neural responses. This is where neuroreductionism has had its greatest successes, in deciphering the low-level transmission codes used by the afferent and efferent pathways. It is, it should be reiterated, *not* likely to be at this level that the conducted signals become the equivalent of the cognitive processes.

The high-level, mediated argument is, in the main, supported by reported psychophysical phenomena and findings. In brief, in many cases the absence of a clear distinction between the transmission aspects and psy-

---

[12]Gestaltists, as well as art historians, would garner a substantial amount of pleasure by looking at the collections of Arcimboldo's work found in Kriegeskorte (1989). These paintings are an excellent demonstration of how wholes (faces) can emerge from judicious arrangements of irrelevant parts.

choneural aspects of the nervous system leads to a confusion between the indisputatively understandable transmission capabilities of the peripheral nervous system and the much more complex (and arguably) impenetrable central neural mechanisms. The effect of a stimulus on the transmission systems and its codes is direct and relatively unmediated; the impact of the physical dimensions of the stimulus becomes less and less significant as the higher level cognitive processes are engaged.

There are philosophical, methodological, and theoretical forces at work that tend to support erroneous "direct stimulus" effects on cognition. Kubovy and Pomerantz (1981) and Runeson (1977), for example, have pointed out that perception science may have been too heavily influenced by the strategies and paradigms of physics. Their point is that physics, both in its classical and modern quantum forms, depends on the analysis of the physical forces to determine the behavior of a system on which these forces operate. In large part (and with the notable example of modern information-processing computers) the parts of a physical system can be isolated in a way that suggests they are independently responsive to each of the impinging forces. This kind of analytic elementalism is a mainstay of modern physical science. From the times of Bacon and Descartes, the method of choice in the physical sciences has been to break up a complex system into its parts in order to study it. It has been assumed that the manipulation of a single parameter of the stimulus, while at the same time holding others constant, could provide the best opportunity to understand the whole system.

However, the human perceptual system probably is not organized in a way that allows it to be dealt with in this manner. The system is, at the least, far more complex and nonlinear in a way that prohibits meaningful analysis into components. Furthermore, anything that is perceived is molded, modified, transformed, distorted, and altered by a highly active and responsive nervous system. There is an interdependency of the various factors, stimuli, and elicited responses that is probably qualitatively different than that occurring in the relatively simple systems encountered in the physical world.

To a degree, computers can be made to share this property of interdependency, but usually we have a very good idea of the nature of the salient transformations made by these *programmable* machines. One of the most fundamental, universal, and transcendent observations about human perception, however, is that what is perceived is not entirely driven by the raw physical properties of the stimulus. In fact, the perceptual result may be wildly divergent from what was predicated on the basis of the raw physical nature of the stimulus.

There are both endogenous and exogenous forces that make the perceptual experience differ from the stimulus. The stimulus itself may be very complex and the resulting percept may not depend on the physics of the stimulus (its physical syntax) as much as it does on the significance or meaning (its informational semantic). Furthermore, the raw map of the physical stimuli may represent only a part of the information in a scene. Relationships among the parts of the stimulus scene may convey much more information than that carried by the physical parameters of the image—particularly if this information pattern is being processed by a highly competent, mediating, information processing, organic observing system like the human being. The end result of this interacting interdependency is that the behavioral indicators of perceptual responses often differ greatly from the dimensions of a stimulus that define the scene.

It should not go without comment, however, that this in itself is not a "killer" argument for mediation. A suitably complex deterministic system can mimic indirectness. A final resolution of the question may be no more at hand than the local–global controversy. However, from a purely behavioral point of view, it is clear that there are vast discrepancies even between some of the most basic of perceptual responses. A behaviorist would argue, however, that all data gathered so far in the history of our science are incapable of definitively resolving this issue.

In this section I review a number of the perceptual responses in which the reported response differs greatly from what would have been predicted by parameters of the physical stimulus alone to support the case for mediation as opposed to direct responsiveness. Obviously, whatever is discussed here is but a small sample of the illusions and unexpected transformations that occur in human perception. Nevertheless, the point being made is clear. Our perceptual experiences *do not* slavishly follow, and in some cases are wildly discrepant with, the physical attributes of the stimulus. The physical attributes included in this discussion include spatial (i.e., form) and temporal patterns (i.e., order) as well as such qualitative properties as the wavelength and such quantitative ones as the intensity of the incident light.

Some of the data discussed in this section were obtained in situations other than the parametric experiment that is the archetype of the modern scientific psychological archival publication. I refer here to the classic demonstrations typified by the many visual illusions demonstrated over the years. A more complete tabulation of those illusions can be found in Uttal (1981). The overall impact of this collection of discrepant perceptual phenomena is a compelling one. We see in ways that are not attributable to the geometry, motion, intensity, or quality of the physics of the light entering our eye. Every experiment or demonstration that exhibits such a phenomenon, therefore, provides a kind of indirect support for a mediated or interpretive theory of visual perception.

Fractured Figures. There may be no better way to start this discussion than to go back to the work of Street (1931) and Leeper (1935). Street developed a test to measure a kind of general perceptual intelligence. It used a type of randomly fractured figures such as shown in Fig. 3.2. Leeper (1935) as well as Reynolds (1985) later showed that the recognition of such fractured forms could be facilitated if the subject was given information about the general nature of the object being presented. Although both agreed that supplemental information was useful in organizing the parts into a coherent form, these two scholars came to opposite conclusions about one significant aspect of the problem: Did simple knowledge of the class of the object help the subject to carry out the perceptual organization? Leeper's original conclusion was that it did. Reynolds, on the other hand, concluded that specific class information did not help: All that was required was the knowledge that a coherent percept could be formed from such a fractured figure. Regardless of who was correct on this particular issue, two im-

FIG. 3.2. A fractured figure emphasizing the role of global configuration rather than local features in determining what we see. From Leeper (1935). Reprinted with permission of Heldref Publications.

portant points emerge from these important classic demonstrations. The first is that the parts of the figure are not critical. A picture can be "fractured" in many different ways and still be capable of being reorganized into a coherent form. Second, cognitive information of one kind or another, as opposed to the specific geometrical cues, is a powerful impetus in accelerating the reorganization.

The Blind Spot. Among the most obvious examples of the impact of cognitive mediation is perception across the "blind spot," the hole in the retinal projection that leaves no corresponding hole in our perceptual field. The anatomy behind this visual phenomenon is well known. The optic nerve enters the retina at a point about 15° in the nasal direction from the fovea—the point of highest spatial resolution. The 6° wide spot is completely devoid of any receptors and is therefore not capable of sensing any light. It is, therefore, optically and physiologically blind. The interesting feature of the blind spot is that we do not under normal conditions perceive this rather wide lacuna in our visual field. Although it can be demonstrated by closing one eye and positioning an object about 15° temporally to the line of regard (the object then "disappears") it is quite surprising how little perceptual impact this relatively large hole has on our visual experience.

As with so many other phenomenal demonstrations, explaining why we do not see the blind spot has become an active enterprise for psychologists, physiologists, and even philosophers. The experimental study of this process is complicated for the most fundamental reasons. One's first impression is that it should be easy to determine if some kind of a filling-in process is occurring by asking subjects what they see in the lacuna. Unfortunately, such an experiment is confounded by some very practical difficulties. First, to carry out this simple experiment, it would be necessary to use a stimulus possessing two mutually inconsistent properties. In the first case, it would be necessary to use a stimulus that could be completed across the blind spot. At the same time it would have to be a stimulus that did not provide any syntactic or semantic cues to what might be present in the blind region on which the observer could base a logical guess. One suggestion would be to use a repetitive or plaid-like stimulus material. However, such a stimulus could appear to be complete by simply connecting the edges on either side of the lacuna even if nothing is seen. To the contrary, something like printed matter could be used, but there is always the danger that the syntax and sequential dependencies of the text would allow the observer to reconstruct the message.

Another major difficulty with trying to see how the blind spot might be perceptually "filled in" is based on the poor acuity, in general, at a retinal eccentricity of 14°. It has been well known for years that the resolving power of the retina at this distance from the fovea is much less than at the fovea (8–10 times worse according to Alpern, 1969). This degraded acuity means it would be extremely difficult for an observer to recognize a stimulus form even if the region were not "blind." The problem is that the acuity threshold for a stimulus in this case is very close to the size of the blind spot itself. This may also help to explain why we are so insensitive to this relatively large hole in our visual field.

Furthermore, the filling in of the blind spot is closely related with another perceptual phenomenon—Ganzfeld fading. Stabilized retinal images and near uniform field fade into perceptual indiscriminability in much the same way that the blind spot is imperceptible. Both Neumeyer and Spillmann (1977) and Ramachandran and Gregory (1991) have shown that artificial blind spots (holes in an otherwise continuous field) fade away. Therefore, determination of what is happening at the blind spot would require some kind of retinal stabilization so that normal saccadic movement of the eyes would not provide cues to the observer. However, such a stabilization is likely to introduce another kind of perceptual blindness—Ganzfeld fading—and thus further confound the experiment.

The end result of these practical problems is that research on the blind spot is extremely difficult to carry out in a rigorous manner with adequate controls being exerted over all of the interacting and confounding variables. The most direct way of approaching the problem (i.e., asking what is seen across the blind spot), is not possible. Indirect tests are therefore required and the logic leading to answers to what seems at first to be a simple question turns out to be more tortured than initially expected.

The general paradigm that has emerged, therefore, is one in which the experimenter attempts to test whether the effect of some property of the stimulus is the same in the blind spot as in an actively responding region of the retina. Not surprisingly, the results of such studies are ambiguous and the issue remains unresolved. One method depends on the detection of aftereffects. Cumming and Friend (1980) were not able to observe any tilt aftereffect when incomplete gratings were used as stimuli and the gratings were designed so that they would have to be interpreted as tilted across the blind spot. On the other hand, Murakami (1995) used an interesting procedure based on the fact that aftereffects are known to be interocularly transferred. The stimulus in this case was one that would produce the inference of motion across the blind spot. The results in this case indicated that the corresponding region in one eye did appear to evoke a motion aftereffect in the other thereby suggesting that a temporal filling-in process across the blind spot was being executed.

Tripathy, Levi, and Ogmen (1996) studied the blind spot by using a two dot alignment procedure across the lacuna and found that the spatial values of the alignment procedure were maintained. This finding suggested to them that the blind spot was not just ignored by having its edges perceptually drawn together. Rather, the edges were functionally as far apart as they would have been across a normal extent of the retina. The uncertainty here is that the spatial values coded by the active regions outside the blind spot may be accounting for the apparent spatial extent of the blind spot.

Other experimenters have approached the problem by eschewing formal parametric experiments and concentrating on demonstrations of the phenomena. Ramachandran (1992), for example, has actively pursued this course of research. His demonstrations led him to conclude there was an active filling-in process that was a subcategory of a more general surface interpolation process.

The paradoxical nature of the blind spot (i.e., we do not see the substantial hole in our visual field), as well as the ambiguous and contradictory results that have been forthcoming in this field have attracted considerable attention, not only in the cognitive neuroscience or psychophysical laboratories but also in the field of philosophy. The argument is between those who see the nervous system as actively filling in the lacuna and those who see the search for filling in mechanisms as a red herring based on a historical misunderstanding. Dennett (1992) and Pessoa, Thompson, and Noë (1998) engaged in a controversy concerning the problem. Dennett's main point is that the "filling-in" process is forced on us by an incorrectly assumed requirement for an isomorphic representation. He considers this to be a vestige of "Cartesian Materialism" in which there must be an exactly equivalent physical (i.e., neural) representation of any thought or concept. Thus, for us not to see the "hole" it must have been "filled in" by some mechanism. Dennett suggested that this is a misconceptualization that ignores a possible alternative, namely, that there is an active cognitive process that interprets the stimuli in a symbolic or nonisomorphic manner. There is no need to postulate filling in, if the brain is organized in a way that a retinal lacuna is simply not seen because it does not exist in the central, symbolic representation.

Dennett's ideas are closely related to older ideas of sensory coding (Uttal, 1973) in which isomorphism is eschewed in its entirety. In this context, codes or neural symbols stand for experiential dimensions but need not be of the same domain. Thus, time may encode intensity and relative amounts of activity in different places encode chromaticity. The important point in the present context is that if a hole exists, it does not have to be filled in or ignored. It is simply "not there" and the constructed experience skips across it as if it had no dimensional existence. Filling in to account for a discontinuity, therefore, as Dennett argues, is a misstatement of the problem, a conceptual error, not a psychobiological phenomena that has to be explained.

Pessoa et al. (1998) disagreed with Dennett and presumably would have with my earlier ideas on the inapplicability of the idea of isomorphic coding. Their argument is that there are many different kinds of filling in and that it is a concept that has much to offer to cognitive neurosciences. They then go on to seek neural correlates of filling in and describe a number of studies that suggest to them it is better to describe filling in as more "the neural completion of a presence rather than 'ignoring an absence' " (p. 737).

Pessoa et al. (1998) dedicated considerable time to comparing neurophysiological data with the psychophysical results of a filled in blind spot. It is important to appreciate two important facts about such a quest. First, it is based on the assumption that there must be an isomorphism of neural activity and subjective experience; that is, that the neurons must display the same dimensions and geometry as the percept. This assumption is at least controversial and at best complete rubbish. Given the symbolic encodings that appear in so many other places in the brain (e.g., greenness being encoded by relative neural response rates), the idea that a demonstration of some perceptual "filling in" is supportive of a neural "filling in" becomes extremely problematical. Furthermore, an argument has been made (Uttal, 1998) that the salient neural mechanisms accounting for the perceptual experiences are simply too complex to be determined. The enormous variety of responses in the brain would provide limitless opportunity to misconstrue an irrelevant response as an essential one. In any case, the electrophysiological data is still ambiguous and we would be hard pressed to definitively determine even where the salient responses are occurring.

Second, the search for isomorphism, in any case, is stimulated by the very kind of misconceptualization that Dennett argued against. The search for spatially isomorphic response patterns in the brain is driven by a predilection for a straightforward, unencoded, nonsymbolic representation system for the brain. There is simply insufficient justification for this naïve view of the organization of the brain. It is likely that such a search will remain unfulfillable.

The blind spot is an example of a phenomenon that has engendered a considerable amount of research over the years because of its paradoxical nature. Its particular relevance to the current discussion lies in the fact that it may be another example of high-level processing, a kind of cognitive reconstruction suggesting that what we see is not determined by the physical stimulus alone. It is, however, clouded by conceptual difficulties. Questions like—How do we see the unseen?—confound and confuse the issue. A much less confusing phenomena is the subjective contour, a topic to which we now turn.

Subjective Contours. Hidden in the fractured figure paradigm is another kind of compelling data supporting the idea that mediation, as opposed to directness, is a fundamental characteristic of organic perception. Simply put, we tend to fill in gaps and lacunae in our visual field by perceptual smoothing, interpolation, and continuation processes that are probably executed at a relatively high level of cerebral information processing. The argument supported by these phenomena, as well as by the others discussed in this section is that what we see is not determined by the stimulus but, rather is itself an interpretation, extending and expanding on the cues offered by the stimulus.

Many of the conceptual problems arising in the interpretation of the blind spot are not present in the study of subjective contours.[13] The geometry of the type of stimulus giving rise to these perceptual experiences is less controversial and the linguistic and philosophical difficulties of coping with "seeing" or "not seeing" something that is not physically there are reduced, if not completely overcome. No longer do we have to worry about spatial nonisomorphisms or topological incongruities, nor do the logical difficulties of explaining missing regions of space impede our discussions. Unlike the blind spot, subjective contours are completion phenomena in which both physical and perceptual "empty spaces" are "filled in."

Subjective contours have been known for more than a century. The first published works in this field to come to my attention were published by Schumann (1900, 1904). However, the illusions were brought to popular attention through the work of a distinguished Italian psychologist—Gaetano Kaniza in 1955. His formidable accomplishment was to design a series of stimuli, including the classic Kaniza Triangle shown in Fig. 3.3, that produced the illusion in a perceptually powerful manner. The actual physical components are referred to as the generating parts. The triangle, so clearly seen, is purely illusory. The Kaniza Triangle has become a mainstay of modern research on filling in and perceptual completion during the latter half of the 20th century. As such, it is a particularly compelling example of stimuli in which the perceptual experience differs greatly from the physical stimulus.

The Kaniza triangle and other similar subjective contour effects have many attributes that make them of interest to perceptual scientists. Not only are the contours completed, but the illusory figures so generated may differ from the parts that generated them in depth or lightness. Most people examining the stimulus shown in Fig. 3.3 report the presence of a bright triangular object lying on a depth plane positioned in front of a background plane on which the generating parts seem to be placed. Such an illusion is most probably the source of many grossly misunderstood UFO reports in which an enormous dark object, delimited by bright light spots (more likely the landing lights of a string of aircraft or a string of flares) is described.

The important aspect of the subjective contours in the present context lies not in the details of what is seen, but rather in the lack of veridicality

---

[13] The term *subjective contours* is but one of the many that has been used to designate these perceptual extrapolations. Other terms include *anomalous contours, illusory contours*, or Kaniza's personal favorite, *quasi-perceptual contours*.

FIG. 3.3. The classic Kaniza triangle
(Courtesy of the late G. Kaniza of
the University of Trieste.)

between the stimulus and the reported percept. They, therefore, represent a compelling argument that the brain–mind system is operating in ways that transcend the simple physics and geometry of the stimulus to determine what we see. This is strong support for the mediating, as opposed to direct determination, side of the controversy. Often the language of the debate is subtly different than the direct versus mediated argument in which it is phrased here. Others have used it as a vehicle to consider such issues as perception versus thinking (Epstein, 1993; Gregory, 1993) or its relation to depth perception (Julesz, 1993), but all of these alternatives are either synonymous with or specializations of the main issue.

Subjective contours have become another one of those "fruit flies" of psychophysical research. They are so charming and interesting and they do offer the opportunity for parametric experiments since the attributes of the physical generating components can be manipulated. For example, Lesher and Mingolla (1993) have explored the role of edges and line-ends in determining the clarity and brightness of the subjective contour illusion. The reported an inverted U-shaped effect on these perceptual dimensions for line density but a monotonic growth function for line width.

Furthermore, Gurnsey, Iordanova, and Grinberg (1999) used adjacent, but offset, gratings to study the detection thresholds for the elicited subjective contours and found that the parameters of the grating spatial frequency, the space between the generating gratings, and the orientation of the gratings all influenced the subjective response. Takemoto and Ejima (1997) showed that even time, another easily manipulated variable, could affect the production of subjective contours. Subjective contours could also produce aftereffects as demonstrated by van der Zwan and Wenderoth (1996). Obviously, the attributes of the stimulus forms that generate subjective contours can be controlled and can affect the strength of the illusion. Equally obvious is that this illusory process exists because of mediated and interpretative processes that go far beyond the information content of the raw stimulus.

There is one disconcerting aspect to recent research on subjective contours. This combination of measurable response and stimulus parameters has been used to support a number of neuroreductive theories of their origin. All of these theories, whether based on the action of single cells (e.g. Peterhans & von der Heydt, 1995) or on the supposed action of major regions of the brain (e.g., Atchley & Atchley, 1998) leave much to be desired given the robust bridge building that should be required to justify these explanatory theories and that is usually not present.

The Contrast Phenomena. Enjoying a much longer period of contemplation than the subjective contours are a closely related group of perceptual illusions called contrast phenomena. The first formal report of the simultaneous lightness contrast, for example, has been attributed to Goethe (1810/ 1971). It was first explored systematically by Hess and Pretori (1894) more than a century ago and interest in this phenomenon continued well into the 20th century (see, for example, Heinemann, 1955). As we now see it is still of interest. The basic phenomenon is well known; a gray area surrounded by a lighter or darker area takes on a lightness that varies with the surround. Darker surrounds make the gray area appear lighter and lighter surrounds make it look darker. This is the prototypical demonstration of another family of illusions that are determined by context rather than the raw physical properties of the stimulus.

Modern theories of the simultaneous lightness contrast have been proposed based on lateral inhibitory interactions in the peripheral portions of the visual pathway. Simultaneous lightness contrast is nearly universally and uncritically assumed to be identical to the Hermann Grid (Hermann, 1870) or the Mach Band (Mach, 1865) effects. However, there are major differences between the two classes of phenomena. The Mach Band and Hermann grid illusions are highly localized near boundaries of light and dark. However, the lightness contrast effect occurs over broad regions of the visual field and display few of the characteristics of these local phenomena. The analogy drawn between the two is probably, therefore, a false one. Although there is a compelling argument that the boundary effects are derived from simple lateral inhibitory interactions in the peripheral nervous system, the contrast effects appear the result of much higher level neural processes—processes so complex they have all the properties of the interpretive, mediated transformations discussed earlier.

Color contrast effects have also been observed for an extended period. Both Helmholtz (1866) and Hering (1887), giants of 19th-century visual science, carried out experiments to describe these phenomena. Similarly, many of the classic visual illusions display size contrast. Given a surround of objects of a particular size, the apparent size of a comparison object is strongly affected; objects surrounded by other objects that are smaller tend to look larger and vice versa. No satisfactory explanation of contrast illusions has ever been forthcoming. Curvature, position, and vertical–horizontal nonveridicalities between the physical stimulus and the reported perceptual experience have all been reported.

The overall impact of this work is, once again, to emphasize the mediated nature of human form perception. Factors other than raw physical attributes of the stimuli lead to interpretive errors or illusions. This represents a kind of discontinuity in the series of transformations between the stimulus and the response that precludes any possibility of understanding the internal mechanisms that account for them.

The Relativistic Context Effects. The contrast phenomena and other related visual illusions are prototypes of a more elaborate type of perceptual phenomena that may be characterized as *relativistic context effects*. Although we cannot tell if they represent a totally different level of cognitive processing,[14] the phenomena we now consider are characterized by an even higher level of mediation than that exhibited by the contrast phenomena. There are several different indicators of a difference between the two groups. First, the relativistic context effects transcend contrast effects in terms of the complexity of the interaction. Conventional lightness and size contrast seemed to be unidimensional and depend on only the relationships between particular aspects of the stimulus. Heinemann (1955), for example, demonstrated smooth functional relationships between the relative luminances of the test and the inducing fields, respectively, in an experiment studying simultaneous lightness contrast. The context effects to which we now turn our attention, however, depend on the processing of what appear to be more subtle aspects of the cues provided in the stimulus scene. In doing so, they often produce catastrophic discontinuities in the percept with slight changes in the stimulus. In this case, the pictorial arrangement or even the symbolic meaning of the scene may affect the perception of its color or lightness. Therefore, several different aspects or dimensions of the stimulus may be simultaneously involved in determining the final perceptual outcome.

Second, some of the relativistic context effects do not seem to depend on the raw physical properties (e.g., the luminances of the stimulus) at all

---

[14]Indeed, as we see on page 164, Purves and his group argue that many of what have been designated as contrast effects are actually subject to the same constraints as the context effects described in this section.

but rather on their meaning, significance, or some inference drawn from their arrangement and the *relative* values of different parts of the stimulus scene. The pictorial values of the scene and very distant relationships may determine the perceived properties in a way that may overwhelm simple adjacency. For example, we see later how the relative luminances of the stimulus scene can define the direction from which an object is being illuminated. It is the effect of the inferred attribute (lighting direction) as opposed to the effect of the raw stimulus attribute (luminance) that distinguishes this exemplar "relativistic context" phenomena from the simpler "contrast" effects. I now consider several such context effects.

A classic lightness context effect which depended on the interpretation of the relative reflectivity of an object was reported by Gelb (1929). He hung a black paper disk in a doorway to a dark room and illuminated the room and the disk through the doorway with a bright white light. Because of the virtually total absorbance of the light entering the doorway (it approximated a perfectly absorbing black box) the room had a very low reflectance. The disk, although dark, did reflect some of the light directed through the doorway. The room, therefore, appeared to be much darker than the black disk. In fact, because of the relative reflectance values, the disk appeared to be very light, even white, according to Gelb's observers. However, if a small, highly reflecting white object was placed anywhere in the door beside the black disk, the apparent lightness of the disk was drastically affected; it immediately reverted to a much darker lightness level.

The interpretation of the Gelb experiment that seems most plausible is the lightness of the black disk was determined by the observer's cognitive evaluation of its reflectivity, relative to the other objects and surrounds in the scene. When the small white object was interjected into the scene, observers had an additional source of data on which to base their relative reflectivity estimates and the scene changed radically perceptually. Indeed one might characterize the change as catastrophic, it was so complete. This is not a contrast phenomena in the classic sense described earlier. The respective luminances of the room and the dark disk did not change. The reflectance relations between the dark disk and the small white object did, however, matter. It provided a basis for a modified computation of the relative reflectances of all components of the scene in a way that determined the perceptual experience.

Gelb's phenomenon has been pursued in a modern context by both Gilchrist (1977, 1979, 1994) and by Adelson (1993). Gilchrist (1977), for example, showed that the perceived lightness of two regions of a stimulus scene depended more on whether the parts were seen as parts of the same object than on their reflectance. Thus, even if a shadow fell on a part of an object, that part and other unshadowed parts would appear to have the same lightness—because, his argument went, they were interpreted to be parts of the same object. If, however, the two regions were deemed not to be a part of the same object, then they would be likely to be perceived as having different lightness.

Adelson (1993) suggested some new illusions that were based essentially on the same principle. He used tile-square shaped patterns designed to produce complex lightness percepts that were inconsistent with the actual physical illumination. Again, the perceived lightness cannot be simply explained by either local inhibitory or relatively low level contrast effects. Rather, they depended on the interpretation of the perceptual organization of the scene by a very active observer. Adelson (1993) summed it up well:[15]

> All of the phenomena discussed above lead to the same conclusion: Brightness judgments cannot be simply explained with low-level mechanisms. Geometrical changes that should be inconsequential for low level mechanisms can cause dramatic changes in the brightness report. It is as if the visual system automatically estimates the reflectances of surfaces in the world and the resulting lightness percepts inevitably sway the judgment of brightness. (p. 2044)

Recent work has sought to work out some of the specific arrangements and relationships that drive these interpretive perceptions. Bonato and Gilchrist (1999) reported that the luminosity threshold varies with the *perceived* size of the stimulus. Li and Gilchrist (1999) extended these results to show that both relative area and relative luminance are incorporated into the mental calculations that determine the ultimately perceived lightness of a stimulus. This work led Gilchrist et al. (1999) to propose a comprehensive theory of lightness perception that accounts for many of the failures of simple constancy. Their interpretation supports the idea that it is the relational and even symbolic aspects of the scene that dominate how we see. Whatever the exact nature of these computations and transformations, clearly these phenomena are accounted for by more than just the raw physics of the stimulus or by simple spatial interaction between adjacent components.

Purves and his group actively pursued this line of research and demonstrated additional evidence that several of the most familiar contrast illusions, usually attributed to low-level neural interactions, are better explained as the outcome of much higher level, mediated, computational processes. Using the approach pioneered by Gilchrist, Purves and his colleagues demonstrated that simultaneous contrast was affected by the pictorial aspects of the stimulus (Williams, McCoy, & Purves (1998); that Mach Bands depended on the lighting (Lotto, William, & Purves, 1999a; 1999b); and that the Cornsweet (1970) effect was also the result of high-level com-

---

[15]Adelson (1993) distinguishes between lightness and brightness. Lightness, to him, refers to apparent reflectance and brightness to apparent luminance.

putations rather than low-level neural interactions (Purves, Shimpi, & Lotto, 1999).

Purves, Shimpi, and Lotto (1999) summed up their conclusions in a way that supports the point of view expressed by Adelson, Gilchrist, and others when they (Purves et al.) said:

> The theory we propose is that perception is a series of associations gener-ated on an empirical basis by the stimulus confronting the observer at any given moment. By virtue of the relative probabilities of the possible sources of the stimulus (that is, what the sources of the same or similar stimuli have turned out to be), all of the factors in the scene that have been germane to the accurate perception of luminance are included in the generation of the per-cept. (p. 8550)

In another article (Lotto, William, & Purves 1999b), the idea is summed up even more succinctly:

> . . . distorted percepts of luminance [such as the Mach Band] are no more or less illusory than any other visual percepts, all of which we take to signify the probabilistic operation of the visual system as it disambiguates scenes ac-cording to a fundamentally empirical strategy. (p. 5249)

Purves and his colleagues make several other important points concern-ing these perceptual phenomena. First, they note that this kind of process-ing is necessary because the stimuli are, in principle, indeterminate. In vir-tually all visual tasks the simple physics of the stimulus scene does not carry sufficient information to uniquely define a single correct or veridical perceptual response. They represent what mathematicians refer to as "ill-posed" problems. Therefore, additional information is necessary to resolve what are inevitably going to be inconsistencies or ambiguities. This infor-mation is generated within the observer in the form of hypotheses and con-straints and must be evaluated in conjunction with the available stimulus cues to produce a useful response. Sometimes this produces discrepant and nonveridical illusions, but in the main, it is adaptive in producing a per-cept that is realistic and veridical.

Second, Purves et al. go a step beyond other theorists in this field to in-volve memory—previous experience. Not only must the computations be extensive on the ambiguous stimulus per se, but some of the additional in-formation must come from previous experience. Thus, even the perception of a parameter as seeming simple as lightness is determined by the stimu-lus, by our cognitive interpretations, and by our previous experience.

The overall impact of all these results is to reinforce ideas of perception as a mediated, active, "intelligent" (if you wish) process rather than just a passive response to the stimulus parameters. It is, however, important to appreciate that none of the authors cited here rejects the idea that the form of the stimulus provides an essential and substantial part of the information necessary to construct the perception. What we are observing is a shift in emphasis from simple effects of raw stimulus attributes and local interactions to much more complex computations carried out by processes that are actively manipulating much more subtle relationships of the attributes of the stimulus than is usually appreciated.

Therefore, one of the most important contributions of this corpus of works is to shift our thinking away from simplistic neuroreductionist theories and low levels of processing to much more complex and higher level neural mechanisms. Unfortunately, this makes us attend to mechanisms of such great cognitive and neural complexity that may forever be unanalyzable.

Complex context calculations of this kind are not limited to lightness; color experiences can also be modulated in what appear to be similar manners. The most striking color context effect ever demonstrated was reported by Land (1977). In these powerful demonstrations, he showed that the perceived chromaticity of a colored patch depended on the relative reflectivity of other colored patches with which it was surrounded. Land used an elegant stimulus consisting of an array of colored patches similar to the exquisite paintings by the artist Mondrian. This important experiment demonstrated that it was not the wavelength of the light being reflected from the colored patches that determined their chromatic experience, but rather the relative reflectances of the different patches. Land convincingly demonstrated that the perceived color of a patch with a constant spectral bandwidth could range over the entire spectrum: Red, green, and blue experiences could be produced by physically identical wavelengths of light!

This was a profoundly important discovery. It should have revolutionized our theories of chromatic perception. Unfortunately, it did not and students are still taught about a deterministic association between wavelength and perceived color. More familiar evidence to the contrary is all around us. Colors, for example, do not change drastically when a scene is viewed through a colored filter such as sunglasses. The most plausible explanation of this phenomenon is of the same genre as the one provided by Land: The relative reflectances lead to some kind of a computation by the brain that dominates the influence of the purely spectral cues.

Some Miscellaneous Clues to Mediation. Finally, a brief mention of other phenomena suggesting that what we see is determined in large part by constructive, mediated, intelligent processes of enormous complexity that are not well modeled in contemporary theory. Stereoscopic depth perception, the awareness of depth induced by the small disparities between the images projected on the two retinas, cannot be the result of either a simple arithmetic fusion or suppression of parts of the images sent to each eye. The resulting image is an interpretive, even logical, processing of the information from each of the eyes to produce a composite image that has aspects that were not present in either eye's image. It is, once again, a highly mediated interpretation of the invariant attributes of the two retinal images that leads to a totally different geometrical interpretation of the scene than is present in either eye's retinal image. This kind of mediated processing is similar to and of the same complexity as the lightness or color context effects discussed in this section.

The many demonstrations of stimulus equivalence or generalization also speak eloquently to the argument for mediation. We respond not to a rigid presentation of particular stimuli, but, quite to the contrary, are able to produce the same perceptual response to many different representations of the same object. A circular disk retains its circularity despite substantial retinal image distortions; a highly abstract caricature can lead to a correct perception as well as a detailed, high resolution photograph. Sutherland (1968), although a pioneering elementalist (see the discussion of his experimental work on p. 191) did perform an important service by listing many findings and demonstrations of various forms of stimulus equivalence. I list them here as exemplars of arguments of how poorly any theory of parts and specific locales serves to explain such phenomena. Unfortunately, Sutherland's suggestion that these phenomena would have to be ultimately explained by a theory that was based on the extraction of parts by neural analyzers certainly has not been fulfilled and probably won't be.

1. Size invariance.
2. Retinal position invariance.
3. Brightness invariance.
4. Equivalence of outline and filled in shapes.
5. Shape confusions.
6. Insensitivity to local distortions such as jitter. (Cited in Reed, 1973, p. 46)

Another strong piece of evidence suggesting that a stimulus does not directly produce a percept is found in studies of transdimensional processing. For example, Lee and Blake (1999) observed that coherent motion itself can lead to the perception of form even in artificial situations in which there are no spatial cues for form present. They used stimuli consisting of small randomly positioned and moving segments (Gabor elements) within large stable regions. No form can be perceived when the small segments are stable. However, when there is coherent motion of the segments, then the shape of the region becomes apparent. The complex nature of the computations that must be carried out to produce this form from motion effect is tabulated by Lee and Blake (1999).

> Specifically, the visual system must (i) compute changes in velocity in each of a number of spatially distributed motion vectors, (ii) register with high fidelity the points in time at which these changes occur, (iii) correlate the times at which these changes occur over neighboring local elements throughout the array, and (iv) identify boundaries associate with abrupt transitions in correlation values among local elements. (p. 1167)

The important point here is that the nervous system is able to extract information from one dimension (time) and, on the basis of quite complex calculations, transmute that information into another (spatial) dimension. This has all the properties of an interpretive process of intractable computational complexity—in spite of the computational model proposed by Lee and Blake.

Nowhere is this transdimensional transformation more clearly illustrated than in the remarkable observations reported by Johansson (1973). He attached point lights to the body of a person walking in an otherwise dark room. The coordinated motion of the small points of light not only cohered into an organized perception of a walking person, but also contained sufficient other cues to allow an observer to estimate the age or sex of the original figure or to later identify a particular individual just from the dynamic pattern of lights they produced!

3.4. SUMMARY AND CONCLUSIONS

There are many other illusions, misperceptions, constructions, and perceptual interpretations that could be listed here. The tendency to perceive occluded bodies as being complete, the difficulty we have in organizing our perception of visually impossible figures, the perception of depth from monocular cues, and reversible or ambiguous figures, all attest to the cognitive penetration, if not domination, of our visual experiences. The conclusion these phenomena must drive us toward is that even these relatively simple perceptual processes are likely to be instantiated in highly complex and high-level neural activities—processes indistinguishable from symbolic and interpretively mediated processes.

If correct, this conclusion has a number of profound implications for studies of visual form recognition. One implication is that neuroreduction is going to be a far more difficult task then heretofore suggested. Simple isomorphic correlation with low-level neural processes, although superficially attractive and seductively simple, is unlikely to be assaying the real complexities of the higher level processes involved in this kind of visual perception. Any putative association between observed neurophysiological responses (I specifically refer here to single neuron studies) and the perceptual experience simply confuses the peripheral transmission of information with its subsequent central coding, interpretation, and decoding. In fact, it is reasonable to argue that subtle codes and processes that are repeatedly being demonstrated by psychophysicists make any neural theories of these phenomena fanciful and probably totally unobtainable. Similarly, the demonstration of the involvement of previous experience argues that many different areas, functions, and mechanisms of the brain may be involved in even the "simplest" form perception process.

The idea that a modular visual process is localized in a particular part of the brain is, in this context, a frail foundation on which to base our understanding of vision. It may be necessary, no matter how unappealing the prospect, to appreciate that such misunderstandings may have misdirected our theories toward low-level isomorphisms and precise localizations in a way that will ultimately be shown to be profoundly incorrect. Such intellectual forces may have arisen out of our desire for experimental and explanatory simplification that may have no correspondence with the complex reality of the human brain.

The potential intractability of some of the problems encountered as we try to explain how the brain could produce perceptual responses has troubled many philosophers and psychologists. Some would argue that "progress" in any direction, even an incorrect one, is preferred to inaction. Others suggest that, however implausible, the glib assertion that we may be making progress is sufficient to obtain the endorsement of the sponsors and patrons of this science. Neither attitude reflects well on our science. Such a duplicitous justification for pursuing what may be clearly unobtainable goals is not desirable in psychobiology any more than any other area of science.

Reductive and computational intractability is widely accepted in other areas of science. Many mathematicians are aware of computational complexities. A multitude of problems designated as NP-complete[16] are now acknowledged to be intractable. Other long sought mathematical goals are also being added to the list of unsolvable problems. For example, statistical mechanics has its own chimerical goal: the exact solution of the Ising

---

[16]Computation complexity theorists have classified problems of various levels of difficulty. P problems are those that can be solved in a deterministic polynomial time by some kind of search algorithm. NP problems are those that can be solved but only in a nondeterminist period of time. NP complete problems are those that probably cannot be solved in any deterministic time period. Many NP-complete problems are considered to be totally intractable. More details on computational complexity can be found in Papadimitriou (1994) and Lewis and Papadimitriou (1998).

model, a means of describing phase transitions when materials change from solid to liquid states or vice versa. It is now appreciated (Istrail, 2000) that the three-dimensional version of this theory is not solvable in any direct manner. For some simple systems it may be possible to use brute force simulations to solve some model systems. However, even then, the material must be relatively homogeneous. Without such a simplifying state of affairs, an exact general 3-D solution is not possible. For realistic (i.e., irregular lattices) 3-D systems, furthermore, the complexity of the problem may make for computational impracticality, even if the solution is not theoretically precluded.

The analogy to the brain is direct. Here, too, is a three-dimensional manifold of interacting elements producing "states," many of which presumably exhibit themselves as perceptual experiences. Unfortunately, even the "crutch" offered by homogeneity to some NP-complete problems is not present: Neurons are irregularly interconnected, interacting in complex ways that do not approximate the quasi-crystalline structure of simple materials. The brain, therefore, seem to be a perfect example of an intractable NP-complete system. If, as we repeatedly observed in this chapter, much of its function is carried out by highly complex cognitive mechanisms widely distributed throughout the brain, it seems highly unlikely that many of the proposed reductive models could ever be solved. The earlier this is appreciated, the less waste and fewer fantastic models of its function, the sooner we turn to a molar behaviorism, as opposed to a fantastic reductionist mentalism, and the sooner we arrive at a true science of form perception.

There is no more appropriate way to end this chapter than to note how disappointing it is to observe psychologists and neuroscientists searching for solutions to problems that are of the same genre as those that mathematicians have already proven to be unsolvable, either because they are in principle intractable or because they are practically unobtainable because of impossibly large computational loads. It is not possible to discern whether it is a lack of mathematical sophistication or simply a conceptual blindness. Regardless, there are many instances throughout our field in which a profound ignorance of developments in other sciences seems to be present.

CHAPTER

4

Theories of Form Recognition

4.1. INTRODUCTION: COMMENTS ON THE NATURE OF THEORIES

The bridge between the previous chapter and this one is anchored by the difficulties of solving NP-complete problems at that end and by the "No Free Lunch" theorem at this end. The No Free Lunch theorem is based on an idea that has been developing in mathematical search theory in recent years that is likely to have important implications for both theories of form recognition and of the brain. Indeed, it has already been identified as one of the key constraints on generalizing neural network theories from one domain to the next.

First, I briefly introduce the No Free Lunch theorem by noting that it was developed as an antithetical response to be an overly optimistic search for what was known as the "Holy Grail" solution to search problems. Initially, researchers speculated that there might be a universal search procedure that would work optimally in all possible situations to determine such attributes as minima or maxima in energy fields or the best possible learning algorithm for a neural net model. However, Wolpert (1995, 1996) threw cold water on the hope for a Holy Grail solution when he showed that the target of the mathematical quest appeared to be as elusive as the biblical one. He established that a universal or Holy Grail search algorithm was simply not obtainable. Rather, he pointed out that no single algorithm can do better than a random search if one considered the average of all possible search tasks. This caveat, he asserted, also holds true for an optimum learning strategy for neural net systems, one of the most popular current approaches to the development of a theory of form recognition.

It is always uncertain whether a mathematical proof such as the No Free Lunch theorem can be translated into an argument relevant to what may seem to be only distantly related biological or psychological problems. To do so requires the psychobiological system be shown to correspond with the mathematical one in terms of its fundamental principles and that the analogies drawn are not simply superficial verbal metaphors. Criteria of complexity and classification sometimes are quite nebulous when attempts are made to build bridges between the two domains. Nevertheless, it does seem that search models of mental activity, as well as the neural activity itself, bear sufficient similarity to the context in which the No Free Lunch proof was originally developed to permit it to be applied to problems of the kind discussed in this book. If this conceptual link can be maintained after close scrutiny, the implications of such a proof are likely to be profound for psychology and the neurosciences. At the very most, it suggests that no universal theory of how the mind works could ever be obtained. At the least, it puts a damper on the more simplistic notions of theory building abroad these days. If Wolpert (1995, 1996) is correct, lurking in the background would always be the possibility that the brain's actions would be indistinguishable from a random process, even to hypothetical research techniques that cannot be imagined today. In other words, the No Free Lunch theorem adds support to the argument emerging from chaos theory, thermodynamics, automata theory, and other scientific perspectives that suggest there can never be any basis for a general model of either the brain or cognition discussed in Uttal (1998). The No Free Lunch argument, thus, raises another barrier to general theory development of the same genre as the one posed by Moore's (1956) second theorem.

We must acknowledge, of course, that this may be a straw man argument, because no such universal theory has yet appeared or even seems to be on the horizon. However, a logical or mathematical argument that demonstrates (or, at least suggests) some impenetrable barrier does provide predictive support for the concept that no future development is likely to provide such a universal theory. It is always easy to say, "we do not yet have the tools to solve this problem, but who can predict the future." However, a general proof of intractability, if substantiated, is a particularly compelling counterargument.

There is another implicit caveat in the No Free Lunch theorem. As well as suggesting there may be an "in principle" barrier to the promulgation of any universal theory of brain–mind, it raises the suggestion that many of the lesser theories of mental activity or behavior, such as those describing the form recognition process or any other cognitive process, may do no better than random excursions in some ultimate scrutiny. This is a subtle point, because it also implies that the neural mechanisms of mind may, in actual fact, be disorderly enough to be uncodifiable in the formal mathematical languages theorists use, which I review in this chapter.

The No Free Lunch theorem, if proven to be both sound (and it looks promising right now) and relevant (yet to be determined), also has implications for any Bayesian theory of cognitive processing. Specifically, Forster (1999) argued that, given this theorem, "there is no a priori justification for the choice of priors" (p. 1) in a Bayesian model. Such a conjecture runs counter to a major assumption of this kind of statistical modeling: the rational development of a sequential convergence on the best answer by means of judiciously chosen successive estimates. Instead, according to Forster, the choice of the priors has to be based, *ex post facto*, on independent assumptions of what worked and what did not. If correct, then the Bayesian approach becomes an unprincipled shotgun approach that should not be expected to converge any better than any other kind of random walk.

The No Free Lunch theorem is only one (and a highly specialized one at that) constraint on "barefoot" theorizing. Some other concerns must be raised before I review the theories themselves. Formal theory building in psychology (in particular) is such a highly regarded activity we tend to overlook that it is fraught with arbitrariness, intractability, paradigm influences, and neutrality that limit its value in fundamental ways. This is not to disparage formal theory as a way of consolidating and condensing empirical findings, but rather to point out that mathematical and computational models are descriptions and not omnipotent insights into the underlying nature of the brain–mind.

For example, an important issue concerns the uniqueness of a given theory. It is certain that not all models and theories presented here are as different as their nomenclature or presentation may suggest. Many of these theories are so nearly equivalent that one can be derived from the other. Such a situation is quite common in science. For example, in the early days of quantum theory, matrix mechanics and wave mechanics, although independently developed, were shown to be essentially identical (i.e., duals of each other).

Closely related is the fact that not all theories of form recognition, even if they utilize the same mathematical principles, may be modeling the same thing. Indeed, a most difficult aspect of any consideration of this set of theories is the determination of what it is, exactly, that their authors are attempting to model or describe. Various theoreticians use the words *form recognition* but the detailed level of the process at which they are working is not always made explicit. This is particularly so in the psychophysical field where nearly every experimenter has a unique protocol and form recognition means many different things to different researchers.

The point is that superficially similar experiments may actually be assaying very different phenomena. It is also true that different experimental designs may be inadvertently studying what are fundamentally the same process. For example, studies of the fusion of sequential stimuli into readable words (e.g., Eriksen & Collins, 1967) are very likely examining the same thing as masking studies (e.g., Uttal, 1971). Even so, the choice of different response measures may produce different estimates of the values of what are essentially identical processes.

Another important (and admittedly highly controversial) point concerning theories deals with the fundamental assumptions involved in any attempt at reductive explanation by means of theoretical models. An important tenet of the behaviorist position is that both cognitive reductionism to hypothetical information-processing components or neurophysiological reductionism to individual neurons or neural nets are unobtainable goals. I have already discussed several of the constraints on reducibility and analyzability that should raise cautions about this reductive enterprise. The argument was that the hope we can obtain definitive and unique information about the internal workings of the brain–mind by inferring what the observed behavior "means" or "signifies" is probably fallacious. In every case, implicit assumptions, other than the explicit ones expressed by an author of a theory, often dictate the plausibility of a reductive model. A theory is based not only on the formal axioms, premises, and assumptions, but also on the unexpressed ones concerning the measurements and presumptive nature of the entities being explored.

Another issue related to the formal equivalences and uncertainty should be raised anew at this point. It has to do with the empirical "facts" obtained by what is an ever growing and currently enormous body of empirical findings. Although it is patently impossible (as so clearly demonstrated by the selective sampling in Chapter 3) to review the entire corpus of empirical data that have been accumulated over the years, it is possible to discern some general features of this effort. For example, one practical fact essential for any student of this field to be aware is that for every datum supporting an analytic or feature oriented model of form recognition, there is an equally strong demonstration showing the correctness of a holistic process. In fact, as we saw in Chapter 3, it actually turns out that on close inspection, that there is no definitive support for either position. The behavioral or psychophysical data are, in the main, neutral and, conversely, all reductively explanatory theories are neutral with regard to the inner workings.

What kind of evidence exists for this assertion of theoretical neutrality? One pragmatic answer to this rhetorical question is that none of the great questions of form recognition (or of visual perception in general) has yet been resolved to anyone's satisfaction. Another answer is the corpus of published research itself. One does not have to delve very far into the great handbooks of perception and cognition to appreciate that their real contribution is their tabulation of the phenomena on our science and not their convergence on an explanatory theory of perception.

Virtually every empirical observation *describes* some aspect of perception, but it is only when additional (and sometime unjustifiable) assumptions are added that these findings are subject to interpretation as an explanatory theory. Therefore, the formal equivalences that may exist between theories, as discussed in the previous paragraphs, are buttressed by a kind of empirical indistinguishability. Theories overlap and can be shown to be equivalent; so too, are our data all-too-often indeterminate with regard to alternative theories—despite their author's strong assertions to the contrary. One's choice of a theory, therefore, depends on a priori and arbitrary assumptions and considerations. So, too, does the choice of one's theory influence the inferred meaning of the empirical observations.

It is unlikely, if not impossible, that any experimental datum will ever provide a "true" reductive explanation of a perceptual phenomenon such as form recognition. Theorists must ultimately retreat to pseudo-explanations based on presumptions and taste, on contemporary ideas from other sciences, on metaphorical heuristics, and on whatever methods are currently available from mathematics or computational science. The most persistent and useful contributions of form recognition research have been descriptions of the phenomena. Who today challenges the Gestalt laws as adequate descriptions of grouping? On the other hand, what contemporary reductionist theory of visual perception is not subject to challenge and, all-too-often, derision. Certainly, visual perception is still taught more or less as a collection of phenomena rather than a coherent set of explanations comparable to the status of some other sciences.

Nickerson on Significance Testing. It is also important in this context to consider the role of statistics in resolving controversies between theories in general and more detailed hypotheses in particular. Nickerson (2000) has heroically reviewed the controversy surrounding the role of null hypotheses significance testing. His comments hold true for distinctions between more elaborate "theories" in psychology as well as in any other science. He noted that significance testing is frequently misused and has historically been subject to contentious controversy from it earliest origins. The problem, according to Nickerson is, as usual, that the barefoot use of tests of significance is based on some hidden assumptions that are not generally appreciated. One, for example, is the false

> Belief that rejection of the null hypothesis establishes the truth of a theory that predicts it to be false. (p. 254)

Another is the false

Belief that statistical significance means theoretical or practical significance. (p. 257)

Nickerson (2000) also pointed out some other criticisms that have been directed at significance testing including:

- The a priori unlikelihood that the null hypothesis is true.
- Null hypotheses significance testing is sensitive to sample size.
- The all or none decisions regarding significance are inappropriate.
- The decision criteria are arbitrary.
- The ease with which the assumptions underlying any statistical test can violated. (Abstracted from Nickerson, 2000, pp. 263–273)

Although Nickerson wisely advised his readers how significance tests can be reasonably used, the caveats that he raised concerning the interpretation of this kind of test for hypothesis testing and theory testing are very germane to appreciating the true nature of theories as discussed in this chapter.

Roberts and Pashler on Goodness of Fit. In a related vein, even more closely pertaining to theories of all kinds, was a recent analysis by Roberts and Pashler (2000). Their concern was with the "goodness of fit" criterion used as a means of choosing among competing theories. They argued that too much credence is given to mathematical models involving several free parameters. Roberts and Pashler criticized this line of thought in much the same way that Nickerson challenged the significance test as an argument for a particular hypothesis. There are, they argued, some hidden assumptions embedded in the use of goodness of fit that result in three serious problems for any theory that depends on such a criterion to "prove" itself as superior to some other formulation.

Roberts and Pashler's (2000) main point was that goodness of fit criteria are not specific concerning what the theory predicts. Specifically they asserted:

Theorists who use good fits as evidence seem to reason as follows: If our theory is correct it will be able to fit the data; our theory fits the data; therefore, it is more likely that our theory is correct. However, if a theory does not constrain possible outcomes, the fit is meaningless. (p. 359)

Roberts and Pashler argued that an important aspect of a theory is its ability to predict what cannot be as well as what can be—in other words, a satisfactory theory must constrain the behavior of the system under study. A simple fit of the data does not justify accepting a theory particularly when there are enough free parameters to permit virtually an infinite number of functions to be modeled.

They also argued that another problem with the goodness of fit criteria is the "a priori likelihood that the theory will fit—the likelihood that it will fit whether or not it is true—is ignored" (p. 359). They real test of a theory, they stated, is its ability to predict unlikely events. It is only when one compares theories that have different predictions that one is in the position of choosing between them in a valid way.

Both Nickerson's and the Roberts and Pashler studies were thoughtful contributions to our understanding of what a theory means and should be considered and attended to by every generation of psychologists. Each of these articles raised compelling arguments against both reductive theories and any attempt to claim uniqueness or validity of one formulation compared to another. They both added support for the contention that mathematical models, at best, are neutral and can only describe (but not expose the inner mechanisms of) cognitive activity any more than can behavioral observations.

On the Idea of Simplicity or How a Razor Can Become a Club. In this discussion of the meaning of theories, it should not go unacknowledged that there is considerable current interest in developing other criteria than goodness of fit or significance for selecting among alternative theories. Constrained by the fact that all theories may be neutral with regard to psychobiological reality, a number of techniques, classic and modern, have been developed that offer a solution to the dilemma when one is confronted with contending theories. The classic criterion, of course, is *Occam's Razor*—simplicity per se. The "razor" or as it is otherwise known, "Lloyd Morgan's canon" is the assertion that the best theory is the one that explains the "most" with the "least." To apply this criterion for choosing among theories or explanation, however, is not as simple as it may at first seem; consensual definitions of the *most* and the *least* are not quite that easy to achieve. Indeed, an entire issue of the *Journal of Mathematical Psychology* edited by Myung, Forster, and Browne (2000) has been recently devoted to developing more specific methods for selecting among alternative mathematical theories. My readers are directed there for several interesting approaches, hopefully fully forewarned by the caveat that "simplicity" may not be a suitable criterion for a system that is highly redundant and has no need for any kind of configurational economy (e.g., the brain). Occam's razor and its derivatives may sound simple, but in fact, they raise as many problems as any other decision rule for choosing the best theory. Despite the superficially rigorous structure and apparently precise language of formal theories of form recognition, they, too, are subject to fundamental conceptual constraints and limitations.

Some "theories," particularly those from the field of experimental psychology, are simply descriptive statements of the results of experiments and are strikingly incomplete. Empirical answers to research questions such as, "What is the effect of inverting a face on the recognition process?" do not constitute theories. Supplemental assumptions and inferences are necessary to "explain" what these observations mean in terms of the underlying recognition processes; it is here that some perceptual theorists go wildly astray.

It must be reiterated that this incompleteness of explanation may be a necessary aspect of cognitive science and represent the results of insurmountable barriers to analyzability and accessibility. It may not be possible for reasons of the most fundamental principle to go from behavioral observations to explanations comparable in the same detail as the computer algorithms programmers generate. I have spoken several times in this book on such problems; here I am concerned with the presentation of an empirical result in the guise of an explanatory theory.

Finally, I must also point out that not all "theories" of form recognition are actually theories of the recognition process. Many posing as such, particularly those from the field of computer science, are image processing algorithms that help to preprocess or prepare images for some subsequent recognition scheme. For example, in many form recognition algorithms it is necessary to normalize or align the stimuli in preparation for the recognition process that follows. In other cases, segmentation of a complex scene into a set of simpler ones or the establishment of boundaries and contours are necessary preprocesses. These preliminary steps are not essential parts of the recognition process. Rather they, are simplifying and normalizing algorithms required to make subsequent computations tractable. For engineers, it is important to appreciate the need for them and understand how they work, but they typically do not help in our search for understanding human recognition behavior.

In the next section I propose a modest reorganization of earlier taxonomies of form recognition. By doing so, it may be possible to unravel the tangle of ideas and concepts that characterize so much of the writing in this field. My goal, restated once again, is to emphasize the salient attributes of certain classic prototypes and selected modern theories rather than to exhaustively survey the entire field. Each example I present, therefore, represents many other similar contributions. Over the years, many seminal ideas have been introduced. Although it is relatively easy to identify the concepts separately (as I strive to do in the historical discussion of classic form recognition models) it is less easy to distinguish among many of the more recent theories because they typically incorporate several (as opposed to a single one) of the earlier ideas. Identifying the key concepts, however, helps us to understand the conceptual basis of modern form recognition theory.

4.2. SOME EARLIER TAXONOMIES

The thesis of this section is that although there are many theories of form recognition, they come in a limited number of types. Some are patently metaphors; some are statistical—proposing only a kind of probabilistic categorization; some are highly specific in their convergence on a particular process; some invoke words, some neurons, and some are based on symbolic metaphors far removed from intuitive common sense. Because of their special interests, the varying levels, and the often ill-defined nature of the form recognition tasks, several scholars have attempted to categorize the different types of theories that one might encounter by suggesting organizing taxonomies. Some of these schemes are simple dichotomies; others are more complex proposing several different classes of theory.

One taxonomic insight that makes special sense to me was Hofstadter's (1985) dichotomous distinction between what he refers to as the "Boolean Dream" (p. 631) and "Statistically Emergent Mentality" (p. 654).[1] Hofstadter argued that any imitation of cognition based on formal rules (such as those making up a computer program) is likely to be totally incorrect as a model of any kind of cognition—including form recognition. Because most of the models described in this chapter are algorithmic, Hofstadter would presumably argue that none of them comes close to a viable theory of the perceiving mind. Instead, he asserts that "the idea of a stochastically guided convergence" to what he called a "globally optimum state" (p. 655) is to be preferred as the foundation for understanding mind. As we see later in this chapter, the concept of a globally optimum state is now gaining great credibility as the foundation of a modern theory of form recognition. Such a model has more in common with statistical mechanics than with the determinist models that dominated so much of earlier thinking.

According to Hofstadter, models based on simple logical rules and algorithmic determinacy such as those proposed by George Boole (1815–1864) or computer programs simply are conceptually erroneous diversions—*no matter how well the simulation may fit the data*. The premises of the algorithmic, Boolean, or computational model are just fundamentally wrong in Hofstadter's opinion. I think he is entirely correct in drawing a line between these two types of theories: the statistically emergent and the Boolean.

This does not mean, however, that the statistically emergent concept is a "Holy Grail" (if I may borrow a phrase from another context) for theories of recognition. Its application, too, is clouded by complexity and numerousness. It must be acknowledged that, even if this conceptual approach is cor-

---

[1]The history of the idea of emergence is a long one. See Tannenbaum (2001) for a discussion of the many times it has been suggested. However, Hofstadter's contrast of *emergence* with the *Boolean Dream* highlights the concept especially well.

rect, the level of complexity at which a process comparable to human thought processes emerges still may be beyond our analytic reach. Emergent mind principles may be no better able to provide us with an acceptable detailed explanation than the Boolean Dream. However, in my judgment, the metaphor of a statistical emergence of a globally optimum state is probably closer to psychobiological reality than is the Boolean one underlying the discrete computational models—including those of the early neural network types. It just may not be possible to go further than uttering the word "emergence" without entering the Boolean morass.

Hofstadter's classification is only one way to dichotomously categorize form recognition theories. Others bisect the theory pie in different ways. For example, Nakatani (1980) distinguished between "qualitative" theories "said to be syntactic or of graph theory" and quantitative ones "said to be analytic or of filter theory" (p. 47). For him, the former category essentially consisted of recognition programs that doted on edges, contours, and parts; the latter category, on the other hand, was characterized by Fourier type filtering algorithms, up until recently a mainstay of recognition theory.

Grimson (1990) also suggested that form recognition models can be divided into two classes: the familiar local class (based on "parameters that are spatially localized, such as edges, corners, or holes") and the global class (based on "parameters that depend on the entire object, such as its surface area or volume") (p. 24).

Pomerantz (1978) offered another version of this same dichotomy when he suggested dividing the field into "(w)holistic" approaches and those in which "shapes are identified by analyzing them into components of some sort" (p. 217). He acknowledged, however, that despite the fact that most models are feature oriented, features do not carry the entire information content of a stimulus. In support of this assumption, he stated:

> The principle difficulty of feature analytic theories of perception, which the Gestalt psychologists repeatedly emphasized, remains: namely, a pattern is more than a listing of the component parts. (p. 227)

The point made by Pomerantz still rings true. Not only do its parts not totally characterize a form, but as we saw in the previous chapter, people usually seem to depend more on the configuration of the parts than on the nature of the parts of an image as they construct a perceptual experience. From these arguments, we may conclude that the dominance of the feature analytic theories in today's theorizing is not so much a result of the psychobiological mechanisms as it is to the mathematical and computational methods available to us.

Other more elaborate (beyond simple dichotomies) taxonomies of form recognition theories have also been developed. Two of the most important are now considered.

4.2.1. Townsend, Landon, and Ashby's Taxonomy[2]

An important multicategory taxonomy of recognition theories was published by Townsend and Landon (1983). All members of the four classes of models that these authors describe can be said to fall into the category of descriptive mathematics and statistics; none is explicitly a neural net model, although some neural net models use the same criteria. Townsend and Landon suggested two major subdivisions: The first includes those that are "based on an internal observation." Exemplars of this class of theories are characterized by the fact that each stimulus event is dealt with separately by the perceptual-processing system. The probability of a correct recognition (i.e., emitting a response with the correct name of the stimulus or the name of the appropriate category), therefore, depends on the evaluation of that stimulus item by a set of internal rules and criteria in the immediate terms of that particular stimulus. In this subdivision of their taxonomy Townsend and his colleagues mainly pay attention to the specific processes such as feature detection that are presumed to exist within the cognitive structure of the observer. The important property of this class is that they occur without recourse to any previous events or even the current state of the observer.

The second major subdivision includes those theories that Townsend and Landon (1983) called "descriptive"—a different use of the word than mine. In this case the role of the individual event is minimized. Instead, the process of recognition is modeled as a kind of guessing or choosing an item from a set of possible responses on the basis of probabilistic (or weighted probabilistic) rules involving context properties that may go far beyond the characteristics of the immediate event. Rather than processing the attributes of a single stimulus, as did the internal-observation theories, models falling into this category merely use the stimulus as one of many influences leading to an appropriate guess or choice of the proper response by the observer.

The first major division, the "internal observation" category, is further broken down into two other subdivisions by Townsend and Landon (1983)—the "general discriminant models" and the "feature confusion" models. General discriminant models are characterized by decision rules and procedures that evaluate the attributes of a particular stimulus and calculate a numeric value or discriminant for all possible responses that could conceivably be associated with that stimulus. This process thus produces a set of

---

[2] The following discussions of Townsend and Landon's (1983) and Watanabe's (1985) taxonomies are abstracted from a more extensive discussion of their work in my earlier book (Uttal, 1988). Because of their relevance to the topic now being considered, it seems worthwhile to at least consider them briefly here. Complete discussions of their work can be found in Uttal (1988).

numeric values associated with the possible responses or categories into which an item may be placed. Which response is chosen is determined in a very straightforward manner: The largest numeric value associated with any possible response becomes the selection criterion leading to the emission of that response. Examples cited by Townsend and Landon of discriminant-type theories include linear-discriminant models, nonlinear-discriminant models, statistical decision theories, template-matching models, correlational models, and feature-discriminant models.

The second category, "feature-confusion models" of the internal observation type theories postulated by Townsend and Landon is characterized by a different criterion. Models falling into this category are purported to actually compute matrices of specific confusions among the set of possible responses. Theories of this genre use the confusion data as a means of determining the rules for generating a reduced set of possible responses from among which the response is finally selected (rather than from the full range of possible responses). The experimental paradigm generating appropriate data for the feature-confusion models must be designed so as to maintain a substantial error rate.

Descriptive theories, the second major heading of Townsend and Landon's taxonomy, are also divided into two subcategories. The first gathers under a single rubric called the "sophisticated guessing-type model," a number of different types of models including the sophisticated guessing models themselves, all-or-none models, overlap models, and confusion-choice models. The second category, which they designate the "choice category," includes but a single exemplar the "similarity-choice" model. For our present purposes it is important to note that the formal mathematical approach of the descriptive models represents a strictly macroscopic theoretical orientation. The mathematical formulae describe, in a formal way, processes that are, at best, only analogous to those presumably carried out in the perceptual nervous system.

The two subcategories into which the descriptive category of Townsend and Landon's taxonomy are broken down—the "sophisticated guessing" models and the "choice" models—are both closely related and, indeed, given a few restrictions, turn out to make much the same predictions.

4.2.2. Watanabe's Taxonomy

Another taxonomy of mathematical theories of form recognition was authored by Watanabe (1985). Watanabe does briefly consider human recognition in his exhaustive discussion of the field, but his main theme is the recognition process as it is executed by the different kinds of mathematical methods used by computers to classify and categorize forms. The relevant portion of his taxonomy looks at recognition as it may alternatively be considered to be a form of:

Entropy minimization
Covariance diagonalization
Statistical decision making
Mathematical discrimination
Structure analysis

The components of Watanabe's taxonomy are virtually all local-feature approaches. The last of the five methods (structure analysis) is explicitly based on such a procedure. It explicitly deals with two-dimensional forms as combinations of local component features. That is, each stimulus object is defined as nothing more than a construction of, for example, vertical and horizontal straight lines, arches, and hooks. The task of the structural-analysis program is to take any stimulus form and specify from which of these component parts it has been constructed. In some algorithms, the order in which these parts have been assembled to produce the original figure can be determined, and this sequence information may also provide useful clues to the recognition of the form.

Two other categories of his taxonomy, the "mathematical discrimination" and "statistical decision-making" methods, on the other hand, invoke feature analyses in a slightly more subtle manner. The objects dealt with by these two methods are typically defined, according to Watanabe, as a multidimensional set of "vectors." What are these vectors? Watanabe indicates they are either "observations" (i.e., the result of different measurements) or the outcome of some kind of distillation procedure in which the number of measurements, dimensions, or descriptors of the original object is reduced. In any case, in an ideal mathematical world, each of these vectors would be orthogonal or independent of the others so that no information would be redundant and, therefore, no processing time would be wasted. Of course, the vectors may have a common causal basis and, therefore, be correlated to some degree (e.g., the height and weight of the members of a population are related), but at the least, each can be measured independently of the other. Described in this way, it becomes clear that these decision-making techniques are also, in terms of their most fundamental assumptions, feature analyzers.

The general category of "covariance diagonalization" includes a cluster of techniques that are operating on almost identical assumptions. Some of these methods are familiar to psychologists (some of whom were among the leaders in developing them), whereas others are quite alien. Two that are familiar include diagonalization of the covariance matrix and factor analysis: Two that are not so familiar to psychologists are the Karhunen–Loeve expansion and self-featuring information compression (SELFIC). All of these methods, however, are characterized by attempts to draw out of a mass of data a smaller number of major or characteristic dimensions, vectors, or features that minimize the number of measurements that have to be made. In other words, all of these methods try to find some common or singular measurement that is closely enough correlated with larger sets of features that it can be used in their place. The extraction of such new features or factors from the many measurements that may make up the raw data of a survey or experiment depends on correlations among the various measurements, and is a means of reducing information to a set of essential, nonredundant measurements.

Finally, let us consider the remaining method alluded to by Watanabe as being prototypical of the pattern-recognition process: entropy minimization. Entropy is defined as the degree of disorder or randomness in a system, and Watanabe (1985) analogized the process of recognition or categorization as being equivalent to removing this disorder. Therefore, categorization was, in his thinking, necessary to discovering the intrinsic order of a system. Entropy reduction, as Watanabe envisaged it, also can be seen to be another feature-oriented approach, for the dimensions to be emphasized in reducing the entropy are the same measurable features or measurements that we have already considered. This state of affairs is, of course, due to today's nearly total deficiency of global descriptors of form. It must be acknowledged, however, that the entropy-reduction technique, more than any others of this taxonomy, does have a potential for a more global interpretation. Indeed, as we see later in this chapter, the models that derive from statistical mechanics are very similar to the entropy minimization procedures described by Watanabe. If there are new developments in identifying holistic attributes, then this model or procedure may be the one best transformable into a global, "arrangement" centered theory.

4.2.3. Uhr's Taxonomy

A third taxonomy of interest was proposed by Uhr (1963). He designated three main classes of form recognition theories.

- Template Matching
- Primitive Analytic Methods
- Sophisticated Analytic Methods
    a. Programs that make use of sets of powerful individual operators.
    b. Programs that analyze the entire interrelated pattern.

Uhr's taxonomy is of special interest because it introduced an idea—the concept of template matching—that was not explicit in either Townsend and Landon's or Watanabe's schemes. Template matching is seen by Uhr as a holistic approach in which the whole image is compared in its entirety with the members of a library of possible alternatives. The category name for that particular alternative or template is then associated with the incoming image.

Unfortunately, the template approach is beset with fundamental problems, some already mentioned, and others highlighted by Uhr. The most serious problem is the absence of generalization (i.e., the templates have to fit very well for a match to succeed and, therefore, the set of templates may have to be very large for the system to work in anything more complicated than a "toy" system). Indeed, as the images become more and more alike, the library must be progressively enlarged. Fine discriminations would, therefore, require huge numbers of templates. This does not seem to be the way the brain works. The brain, presumably, can depend more on its enormous powers of stimulus generalization and general spatial relationships than on a specific set of matching templates.

The fundamental reason behind these difficulties is that the template system is intolerant of variations. However, variance insensitivity seems not only to be a general property of human perception but a necessity in any artificial system or theoretical model to avoid computational or "template library" explosions. Even Uhr expressed his disappointment with this category, as he envisioned it, pointing out that the practical template systems so far developed are actually indistinguishable from some of the "analytic" theories he described later in that pioneering study.

Uhr's second category, "primitive analytic methods," included a large number of methods that he suggested were all dependent on very restricted sets of feature detectors of one kind or another. These devices were tuned a priori to respond to a special feature (e.g., a restricted set of standardized alphabetic characters or straight lines or angles). Not too surprisingly, this category also included neural net type systems, so many of which are dependent on "front end" analysis of a form into its constituent features.

The first subclass ("programs that make use of sets of powerful individual operators") of his "sophisticated analytic methods" category is very similar to the second class—"primitive analytic methods." However, as denoted by the title, more sophisticated methods are used to recognize a form. These more sophisticated methods include the use of increasingly complex components (e.g., curves as well as straight lines) and introduce some kind of spatial adjustments (e.g., accepting displaced stimuli) so that some semblance of invariance could be introduced into the model.

Finally, the second subclass ("programs that analyze the entire interrelated pattern") promised to offer a kind of holistic or Gestalt kind of pattern recognizers. Uhr discussed a number of programs that strive for this ideal kind of goal by using the topology of a form or curve following algorithms that keep track of the trajectory of a continuous outline. None, however, seem to have achieved the holistic goal set by their creators.

4.3. A PROPOSED TAXONOMY OF FORM RECOGNITION THEORIES

The main purpose of this chapter is to propose a newer, but still tentative, classification system of theories of organic form recognition. By its nature, any new taxonomy must itself be highly arbitrary because it, like all of its predecessors, requires a personal estimate of what is important within an intrinsically disorderly group of theories. Because of the increasing conceptual difficulty of distinguishing between current theories, I choose to frame a new taxonomy by seeking their historical roots. In each case I have tried to identify what were the original sources of each of the prototype ideas. Then, the modern status of the field is examined by discussing the three major themes of today's theories—feature theories, global theories, and statistical theories onto which the prototype ideas have converged. Finally, I briefly note some sources to help my readers examine the progress that has been made in the "pattern" recognition field in engineering and computer sciences. The following scheme for organizing theories of form recognition is proposed:

- Classic Sources of The Key Ideas.
  a. The associationist prototype.
  b. The Gestalt prototype.
  c. The unconscious inference prototype.
  d. The neural net prototype.
  e. The single cell prototype.
  f. The adaptive neural net prototypes.
  g. The template prototype.
  h. The probabilistic prototype.
- Modern Elementalisms.
- Modern Holisms.
- Modern Probabilistic Theories.
- Modern Computational Methods.

It quickly becomes evident that the four modern categories overlap to a considerable degree. The elementalist approach to form recognition is so pervasive that its characteristic assumptions can be found virtually throughout the entire system—even among some presented as global approaches. Theories characterized by their authors as global or holistic sometimes carry out feature analyses as an initial part of their protocols or deeply hidden in later levels. Probability criteria, in the form of stochastic or random parameters, can be found throughout the entire group of theories reviewed here, particularly in some of the most promising new ones based on energy minimization or statistical mechanics.

Obviously there is an arbitrariness about which theories are to be considered "classic" and which are "modern." I have made personal choices of the classic ones from among those that seemed to have been seminal in their influence on later theories. Sometimes this historical approach results in a nonsequential chronology. This, however, is unavoidable: Mere chronology is not adequate to distinguish the mundane from the seriously influential.

4.3.1. Classic Theories of Form Recognition— The Prototypes

I begin this discussion by considering the historical origins of some of the classic theories of form recognition. These are important for various reasons; the one common feature they all share is that they were among the first, if not the first, to introduce a prototypical idea that later became a central attribute of many of the modern theories.

4.3.1.1. Associationist Structuralisms—The Traditional Psychological Prototype Theory

One of the curious facts about the terms *form*, *pattern*, and even *recognition* is that they seldom appear in the early history of scientific psychology. Until recently, the study of sensation or perception did not include these topics in the way we think about them today. Nevertheless, harbingers of modern recognition theories can be found in the earliest psychological musings. John Locke spoke about "discrimination" between objects as well as between ideas. Certainly, Wundt (1896) and Titchener's (1899) associationisms anticipated contemporary elementalist theories by emphasizing the components of which a stimulus was composed. James (1890) clearly built on the associationist foundation when he discussed the discrimination of objects in the following way:

> In many concrete objects which differ from one another we can plainly see that the difference does consist simply in the fact that one object is the same as the other *plus* something else, or that they both have an identical part, to which each adds a distinct remainder. (p. 491)

This elementalist and associationist tradition, coupled with the new computer technology has had a continuing and pervasive influence on modern theories of cognition, in general, and form recognition in particular. The structuralist tradition of compiling percepts out of primitive sensory components was perpetuated by this approach. All modern elementalisms can trace their histories back to the concepts of separable parts and features that were dominant until the behaviorist and Gestalt revolutions of the 1920s and 1930s.

4.3.1.2. Gestalt Prototype Global Theories

Counterbalancing the associationist pressures toward component elementalism were the holistic ideas of such scholars as Reid (1846) and Mach (1886). Both of these philosopher–scientists argued that the overall arrangement of the parts was essential in their perception. The culmination of this line of thought appeared in Germany in the first half of the 20th century with the promulgation of Gestalt school emphasizing the primacy of the configuration of the parts over the nature of the parts. The names Koffka (1935), Kohler (1929), and Wertheimer (1912) are forever associated with this theoretical point of view. These authors championed the counter-associationist revolution that held sway until the 1960s when a highly elementalist cognitive psychology provided a new theoretical philosophy that established a new Zeitgeist.

As we see later in this chapter, many of the holistic ideas (which are not easily modeled) still exert a strong attraction to those scientists concentrating on theory building in form recognition. Much of the current charm of the statistical mechanics–energy surface metaphor is that it may provide a mechanism for emphasizing the global form of an object rather than its local features.

4.3.1.3. Helmholtz's Unconscious Inference—An Early Interpretive Prototype

Another important concept that has had wide ranging implications in the historical development of theories of cognition is the idea that percepts and thoughts are constructed interpretations of the stimulus cues and information provided by the stimulus and conveyed through the sensory pathways. This was certainly among the strongest conclusions to be drawn from the discussion in Chapter 3. Our form recognition skills, according to this point of view, are the output of a hypotheses generating system that uses hints and cues from the stimulus and adds constraints and previous knowledge as well as its own processing rules to generate that which is not actually present in the stimulus. Although some production system models of human thought are based on this metaphor, it has had relatively little influence in generating theories of form recognition in particular. Where the idea of construction has had influence is in qualitative theories of human mentation, typically far removed from the topic at hand.

Historically, the idea of interpretive construction has been attributed to Helmholtz (1866). Boring (1950) provided an extensive quotation from Helmholtz's masterpiece *Handbuch der physiologischen Optik* (1866) that clearly defines this important concept for form recognition in particular:

> The psychic activities, by which we arrive at the judgment that a certain object of a certain character exists before us at a certain place, are generally not conscious activities but unconscious ones. In their results they are equivalent to an *inference*, in so far as we achieve, by way of the observed effect upon our senses, the idea of the cause of this effect, even though it is invariably only the nervous excitations, the effects, that we can perceive directly, and never the external objects. (Helmholtz, cited in Boring, 1950, p. 309)

Boring (1950) goes on to note that Helmholtz made three declarations about his concept of unconscious inference that help to particularize what he meant.

1. Unconscious inferences are normally irresistible.
2. Unconscious inferences are formed by experience.
3. Unconscious inferences are, in their results, like conscious inferences from analogy and are thus inductive. (p. 311)

It should be noted in passing that these three statements are fundamentally behaviorist in tone; they describe the process without "explaining" it in terms of some lower level of analysis. Indeed, they do not suggest anything about the underlying inductive (or otherwise) mechanisms that could be accounting for these perceptual constructions. Implicit in Helmholtz' writing is that either serial or parallel, global or local, associationist or Gestalt processes could account for the overall behavior. Having made this point, it should also be noted that the concept of constructive inference proposed by Helmholtz does make more descriptive sense than a rigidly deterministic or algorithmic one given the many discrepancies and non veridicalities between stimuli and reported experiences that fill the empirical literature. At the very least, the concept of inference is not inconsistent with the more formal theories considered in this chapter.

4.3.1.4. Pitts and McCulloch's Prototypical Neuronal Net

It is usually the case that antecedents can be found for any new theoretical position. Certainly there were those who appreciated the psychological relevance of neuronal networks immediately when they were first observed microscopically. Nevertheless, there were identifiable points in the flow of ideas at which everything clicked and what had been obscure became clear. The term *classic clarification* may never have been more appropriately used than when describing the work of Warren S. McCulloch and Walter Pitts. Their contribution sharply defined the border between two periods of perception research—an older qualitative one and the modern period of quantitative models. Two of their articles stand as milestones in the development of the neural net models that were to follow—McCulloch and Pitts (1943) and Pitts and McCulloch (1947).

The McCulloch and Pitts (1943) article was an exercise in formal logic. In that milestone contribution, they proposed a propositional logic based on a system of simple binary neurons. Given that they were both on the staff of the Research Laboratory of Electronics at MIT, it is not surprising to note that this logic was very similar to the ideas percolating at that laboratory during World War II concerning digital logic and to the work on cybernetics led by Wiener and others (see p. 72). Their work had an immediate and major impact. Rashevsky (1948) had a chapter (XLVI) in which the McCulloch and Pitts work was discussed. Others, such as Culbertson (1950), also were moving in the same intellectual direction. Simple neural nets were being analyzed in novel, and even more important, quantitative ways that made exciting promises to those who sought to build bridges between thought and brain. The anatomy and physiology of the nervous system was a hot topic; information theory was exciting many researchers at the time, and, most of all, the digital computer was going through its birth throes.

The McCulloch and Pitts (1943) article invoked a conceptual nervous system of considerably less complexity than the one with which modern neurophysiologists would be satisfied. For example, it acknowledged only all-or-none responses, postulated a system of delays restricted exclusively to synaptic functions, and assumed a rigid structural stability on the part of the nervous system. None of these assumptions are accepted any longer. Nor is their assumption that the total inhibition of a neuron's activity can be controlled by a single inhibitory synapse. Nevertheless, the essential components of at least one kind of hypothetical nervous network are there and the idea of such a network as an "explanation" of cognitive function has become a mainstay of contemporary theory.

McCulloch and Pitts (1943) did make one assertion that is especially remarkable because of its relevance to the debate between mentalism and behaviorism. Anticipating the work of Moore (1956), they stated (concerning their logical system):

> It is shown that many particular choices among possible neurophysiological assumptions are equivalent, in the sense that for every net behaving under one assumption, there exists another net which behaves under the other and gives the same results, although perhaps not in the same time. (p. 115)

Here, once again, is expressed the germ of the antireductionist argument; the concept that both behavior and formal models are neutral with regard to underlying mechanisms. It should be noted that this pioneering report expressed a critical idea that is still not widely accepted.

Their second article (Pitts & McCulloch, 1947) is much more relevant to the topic of this book for it deals specifically with the problem of form recognition. In fact, it was one of the first papers to juxtapose the terms *form* and *recognition* in the modern context. Not only was the vocabulary modern, but so, too, was the general neural net approach used by this extraordinary pair of scholars. Of equal, if not greater, importance was their emphasis on "invariance"; that is, on the recognizability of a form independent of any of the standard transformations (rigid translation, rotation, and magnification) that might be imposed on it.

Once again, the neurophysiology expressed in this article seems antique: They identified the superior colliculus as a site of one of the two form recognition processes and invoked a kind of feedback to motor systems as the source of the invariance computation. Nevertheless, some of their ideas were novel and contributed to many later developments. If one ignores the physiological assumptions and considers only the mathematics, it is clear that their model accounted quite well for the invariance of form recognizability under translation. More up-to-date neurophysiology would only influence the choice of the neural assumptions of their theory and not the process ones described by Pitts and McCulloch's mathematics.

It is also of some interest to note that Pitts and McCulloch (1947) did not use the same kind of propositional logic they described in their 1943 article. In the later work, a kind of conventional integral calculus was used to transform the images in order to carry out the translations. Although they invoked actual eye movements, essentially the same mathematics could be used to shift the image about in the nervous system without any ocular effort by some analog of a two-dimensional shift register. Figure 4.1 is an example of the kind of neural networks that they proposed could implement some of their ideas. It differs hardly in principle at all from much more recent models.

4.3.1.5. Sutherland's Octopus Model—A Prototypical Single Cell Model

The work of Sutherland (1957, 1958, 1959) anticipated what was to become one of the main themes of form recognition work in later years: Single neurons could represent or encode complex perceptual phenomena. Sutherland's theory was neither sufficiently detailed nor quantitative enough to be either validated or repudiated; nevertheless, it contained the essential core of this persisting theoretical idea. The main support for Sutherland's hypothesis came from a small sample of psychophysical results from a very unusual animal—*Octopus vulgaris*—a primitive, but visually well endowed, invertebrate (cephalopod) and some ingenious speculation. Sutherland suggested that a hypothetical neuron (not yet observed in the laboratory at his

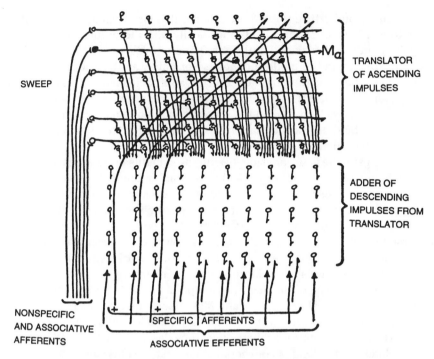

FIG. 4.1. One of the earliest neural network models. This figure and the concepts it embodied stimulated one of the major themes of form recognition theory for the rest of the twentieth century. From Pitts and McCulloch (1947).

time) was activated by a particular geometrical feature of a stimulus. Specifically, individual neurons were assumed to be selectively sensitive to either the horizontal or vertical components of a stimulus and insensitive to diagonals. Thus, figures that were made of horizontal lines would be distinguished from those composed of vertical lines. Predominantly diagonal patterns (exemplified by > or <) would not activate these specialized horizontal and vertical neurons according to Sutherland's theory.

To support his theory (described in Sutherland 1957, 1958), experiments (reported in Sutherland, 1959) were carried out to determine the visual capabilities of these common, primitive, but intelligent animals. The octopi that he used had large, well-developed eyes and apparently an excellent ability to discriminate visual patterns and respond in a way that was adequate for Sutherland's purpose.[3] In fact, the experimental results did not en-

---

[3]It was never made entirely clear why the octopus was chosen as the experimental animal of choice to test the theory, but that, of course, is a provocative question that an experimenter need not answer—intuition often being the best criterion in preliminary decision making as one creates an experimental paradigm.

tirely support Sutherland's (1959) hypotheses and he concluded by noting that,

> the points of disagreement between the results and the theoretical predictions indicate that some additional system of shape classification is at work in the octopus's brain. (p. 141)

As noted earlier, Sutherland's theories and experiments seem somewhat naïve from today's point of view. Nevertheless, they were harbingers of things to come. At about this same time, Hubel and Wiesel (1959) and Lettvin, Maturana, McCulloch, and Pitts (1959) reported their pioneering studies of single cell feature sensitivities. Their results added an enormous degree of validation to neuroreductive theories, like those of Sutherland, that had been formulated in terms of particular neuronal feature sensitivity—however hypothetical the idea may have been at Sutherland's time. These extraordinary neurophysiological findings played an enormous and influential role in later years in supporting popular as well as fantastic theories of neurocognitive relationships. The latter being exemplified by the ideas of Konorski (1967) who proposed that single cellular activity could encode very complex ideas. The "single cell" hypothesis still persists, for example, in the writing of Barlow (1995), but, clearly, theories based on neural networks are now ascendant. Not the least because of the work now to be discussed.

4.3.1.6. Rosenblatt' Perceptrons—A Prototype Multilevel Neural Net

A major intellectual breakthrough in neural net theories occurred with the emergence of the idea that the salient neural networks had to be instantiated as multilayer systems. This idea was strongly impacted by the work of Rosenblatt (1958) who along with Selfridge (1958) (see the next section) were among the first to propose what is essentially the modern version of multilayer neural networks. Rosenblatt's model consisted of two to four layers: (a) a receptor area of the kind we have already discussed; (b) a projection area; (c) an association area; and (d) a layer of response outputs. Figure 4.2 shows one of his early designs. Information was processed in the projection and association areas by manipulating the strength of the connections between the various nodes-cum-neurons. These interconnections could be both afferent and efferent and both excitatory and inhibitory.

The critical feature of Rosenblatt's *Perceptrons*, as he called them, was that the strength of the interconnections between the layers were initially random and then by a process of experience and selective reinforcement would adopt a pattern of differential strengths. The pattern of connection strengths produced by experimentally pairing a particular input pattern

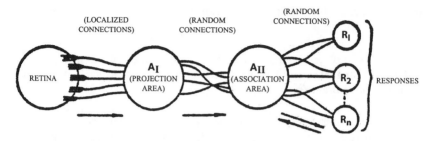

FIG. 4.2. An early model of a perceptron. As envisaged by Rosenblatt, this concept of a multilayered system of unspecialized neurons connected by random links of variable weights was also a major step forward in contemporary theory. From Rosenblatt (1958). Reproduced with permission from the American Psychological Association.

with a particular response would then lead to the automatic evoking of the response when that input pattern was presented anew to the system. The system can be said, by analogy to human behavior, to have "learned to recognize" the input and to associate it with a particular response. Rosenblatt's *Perceptron*, like all subsequent neural net theories, is a highly dynamic arrangement of components and connections; it is inappropriate to assert that any particular arrangement is the unique representation.

Many of the most important ideas of neural net theories were stimulated by this important work. Although this work was criticized and lay dormant for a long time, it is clearly among the milestone developments in this field.

4.3.1.7. Selfridge's Pandemonium—Another Prototypical Adaptive Neural Net

In 1958 Selfridge gave a paper at a meeting held in England that, unlike most other forgotten conference proceedings, was to have a profound effect on thinking about form recognition. Selfridge added several new ideas to the ferment that was developing around the neural net types of pattern recognizers. Like Rosenblatt, he was an early proponent of a system that could learn to recognize objects. Thus, it was not necessary for the system to know in advance what the individual stimuli to be recognized were. Rather, the computer program could be taught to recognize specific forms. Its "learning" was guided by a kind of reinforcement (it was told by the experimenter that a particular set of values—a vector of synaptic-like weights—was to be associated with a particular character) to ever more precisely distinguish between the various stimuli it encountered. In this regard, Selfridge considered his program to be a "search" algorithm that carried out a random hill-climbing procedure guided by the experimenter's reinforcing commands to arrive at a correct identification. The details of Pandemonium were prescient; Selfridge's criterion for searching, as we saw on page 171, is in accord with the No Free Lunch theorem that suggested a random process was as good as anything else in the long run.

Selfridge (1958) developed his theoretical model in the form of a computer simulation of a parallel processing network that could accomplish recognition. This idea had not been unappreciated up to this time but his particular implementation of his Pandemonium model was certainly one of the first, if not the first, formal models to suggest a specific parallel network as the implementation of a recognition system. As such, his work was an important step in the continuing movement toward the simulation of the Pitts and McCulloch (1947) concept of a neural network through Rosenblatt's Perceptron to modern energy state reduction concepts. Selfridge clearly deserves to be considered among the founders of neurocomputing as we know it today.

Selfridge's model was one of the first formal theories that was, for better or worse, specifically based on the component or feature analysis idea. The first stage of his model was made up of a set of detectors that were designed (like Sutherland's hypothetical octopus neurons) to be specifically sensitive to a geometrical component or part of the stimulus image. To understand this idea better, let us consider some of the details of the Selfridge Pandemonium system. Let us assume, to concretize the following discussion, that this sample system is designed to recognize alphabetic characters.

Selfridge's model was composed of four main layers of *demons*, each of which was designed to carry out a specific data processing function on the image—an image that can be seen by even the lowest level of demons. Each of these lowest level demons was tuned to pick up a particular spatial feature of a character such as a straight line, a curve, or an angle. The strength of their output (a "shriek" in Selfridge's terminology thus cueing us to the origin of the term *demon*) was determined by the degree to which that particular feature was represented in the image. The next level of units—the computational demons—was designed to perform some straightforward and relative simple processing. This second level combined the outputs of several of the input demons into an output that also varied in strength (it's shriek level) depending on the particular combination of features to which it was designed to be responsive. The outputs of the computational demons were then fed into the third layer—the cognitive demons—which, in turn, combined certain of the outputs of the computational demons. In the fourth and final layer, a single decision demon was programmed to determine which of the cognitive demons was "shrieking" the loudest. The particular alphabetic character (in this sample case) associated with the loudest shrieking decision demon was then assigned to the processed image.

An especially important aspect of Selfridge's contribution, similar to that of Rosenblatt, was the suggestion that the size of the shriek and the sensitivity of the demon could be adaptively improved. By adjusting the weight or value given to the output of a data or computational demon, the magnitude or shriek of the output of the cognitive demons could be changed. In this early model, these adjustments had to be done by the experimenter; Selfridge finessed the problem of how this could be done automatically, merely suggesting that it should be possible to do so.

Clearly, Pandemonium was a significant step forward and well ahead of most thinking of the time. It incorporated many of the important ideas of later models, if not fully instantiating them. It was, without question, a classic model of a very specific form recognition process that set the stage for the continuing development of ideas in the neurocomputing field.

4.3.1.8. Uhr and Vossler's Prototypical Template Model

As noted earlier, the idea of a template matcher had been around for many years. However, among the earliest researchers to propose a formal model of such a form recognition system were Uhr and Vossler (1961a, 1961b). Although they do not use the word *template* explicitly in their articles, it is clear that the recognition process they modeled was based on a comparison of a single input image with a library of previously stored images. Uhr and Vossler's templates were relatively small—only 20 by 20 cells arranged in a square matrix. As such, they were actually able to deal with very coarse or very small input images. Furthermore, the value of each item in the matrix could be only 0's or 1's—a black or white, yes or no, or binary criterion. The input image was compared successively with each of the templates and the "name" of the one that fit best was associated with the input image. Obviously this primitive system was very limited; they (Uhr & Vossler, 1961b) allude to success with only the 26 alphabetic characters at best. These technical details, however, were not the most serious problems. Some progress could be made in increasing resolution and computational load as faster computers with larger memories became available.

Much more serious for the template methods of this kind is that they continue to be subject to a number of fundamental rather than technical criticisms. They are highly uneconomical in time and processing load; every one of the library of templates must be exhaustively compared with the input image. Template models also are very sensitive to noncanonical positions, orientations, or sizes. If the input image is transformed along any of these dimensions, the template probably will not work very well. If it is transformed in some more subtle way (e.g., by one of the Thompsonian morphometric transformations; see p. 86) the task would quickly become impossible. The only direct way to handle this problem is to drastically increase the number of templates. Doing so, however, not only increased the processing load but also increased the probability of confusions as the increasing number of templates necessarily included increasingly similar ones. In general, all of these problems arise from the basic fact that to work at all, a library of templates has to be complete. There is no logical pyramiding; the number of items in it has to grow at least geometrically as the stimulus universe grows.

One aspect of Uhr and Vossler's contribution was a designed-in adaptation program by means of which the templates "learned" something about the nature of the stimuli during an extensive training period. This permitted the library of templates to increasingly approximate the range of stimuli presented to it. The essence of this aspect of their pioneering contribution, therefore, was to formalize an adaptive version of the template approach. Thus their program was designed not only to evaluate inputs but also to adjust its own parameters as a result of the input images it encountered. This, it should be appreciated, is an alternative to the usual normalization or standardization preprocessing typical of computer vision systems in which the stimulus is altered prior to being presented to the form recognition program.

Template theory is conceptually closely related to *prototype* or *schema* theory. The basic idea of these variants was usually embodied in qualitative, rather than formal, models from the psychological domain that suggested there were standard archetypes or concepts against which a stimulus had to be compared. Like the metaphorical "unconscious inference" the manner in which these standards had to be instantiated in the nervous system (or how they might be in a computer model) was never made specific. Nevertheless, qualitative models of this kind have very long histories. Latimer (2000a), for example, pointed out that Plato's "universal forms," Locke's "abstract ideas," and Berkeley's "general ideas" are early examples of such a theory. Later, according to Latimer, the ideas were introduced to psychology by Bartlett (1932) and Evans (1967), the former suggesting a kind of holistic proto-form and the latter proposing a set of rules for producing that form.

Template and prototype theories can be ordered along a dimension that varies in accord with how precise the match must be for recognition to occur. Templates, in their most pristine form, require a very high degree of geometrical correspondence between the input image and one of the stored templates. Schema or prototype based theories, on the other hand, generally allow a much looser degree of correspondence to match a "general" prototype with the incoming stimulus. However, the conceptual differences between the various approaches are small, at best, and the central idea of exhaustive comparison of a single stimulus with a set of standards unites all of these theories.

4.3.1.9. Luce's Prototypical Probabilistic Theory

Another classic group of theories that served as a prototype for subsequent theorizing about the form recognition process was based on statistical or probabilistic ideas. The principles behind such models have a long history; many of the basic concepts were taken over from economics or other social sciences that antedated 20th-century scientific psychology and its interest in form recognition per se. The modern pioneer in this field is Luce (1959, 1963; Luce & Suppes, 1965) whose application of choice theory to form recognition was spelled out, in particular, in Luce (1963).

Statistical theories of form recognition of the type considered here were generally not intended to be reductive; no attempt was made to define the component processes or mechanisms that underlay the behavior. In point of fact, these theories were and are quintessentially descriptive. From the points of view of both Luce and myself, they were actually more consistent with behaviorism than modern mentalist cognitivism in this sense. Indeed, Luce (1995), himself, discussing the distinction between "phenomenological" and "process" models asserted this same idea when he said:

> Phenomenological models treat a person as a "black box" that exhibits overall properties, but with no internal structure specified within the model. This approach is much like classical physics, in which objects have properties—e.g., mass, charge, temperature—but no explicit molecular or atomic structure is attributed to them. Most psychological theories, including most mathematical modeling of judgment and decision making are of this type; they attempt to characterize aspects and patterns of behavior without asking about the underlying, internal mechanisms that give rise to the behavior. (p. 3)

Luce agrees that this kind of theorizing says nothing about the observed behavior beyond a concise description by means of the appropriate equations or matrices. What it does provide is a formal description of the choice or decision-making behavior involved in recognition or, even more typically, changes in recognition (e.g., during the dynamic processes that occur during discrimination learning).

Theories of this sort may be algebraic or probabilistic, however, it is the probabilistic ones that are of immediate concern. In particular, the classic prototype theory being introduced at this point is what has come to be known as Luce's (1959) probabilistic choice model.

A typical experiment to which such a theory may be applied is illustrated by the following Gedanken experiment. Assume an experiment in which n similar stimuli are presented one at a time and the subject is required to name each as it is presented. The stimuli are assumed to vary only along a single dimension so that they can be placed in order along this dimension. Assuming that the stimuli are numerous enough and similar enough, the data from such an experiment produce a confusion matrix showing the number of times that each stimulus has been confused with each of the others in the stimulus set. The rate of confusing any pair depends on the similarity of the pair—the similarity score being designated by η. η may be considered to be the inverse of the probability of confusing the two stimuli identified by that element of the confusion matrix—the greater is η, the lower is the probability that the stimulus object will be correctly identified. η, therefore, also provides a means of estimating the psychological distance between or similarity of any pair of stimuli. Again, the lower the η, the greater the distance, the less likely two stimuli will be confused.

Once the matrix of similarities is obtained, it is the theoretician's job to model the data. Luce's suggestion was to assume an equation of the form:

$$\eta(i,j) = \eta(i, i+1)\eta(i+1, i+2) \ldots \eta(j-1,j) \tag{4.1}$$

where $\eta(i,j)$ is the similarity of any two objects and the other terms are equivalent similarity measures between other pairs of items in the stimulus set used for the recognition experiment.

To predict the results of the confusion matrix resulting from the experiment, it is necessary to estimate a series of bias parameters $b(k)$ for each of the entries in the confusion matrix. This task is reduced in complexity since $\eta(i,j)$ is, of course, equal to $\eta(j,i)$. Therefore, only k bias parameters are needed, not k^2. Furthermore, as Luce (1963) pointed out:

> In practice, we can only be certain that the conditional probabilities on and near the main diagonal are appreciably larger than zero, and so any estimation scheme had better rely heavily on these entries. (p. 175)

The result of these constraints produced expressions for both the sets of η's and b's that was essentially a probabilistic theory of the data from the confusion experiment. The key contribution of Luce's choice theory, however, is the estimation of the response biases $b(k)$. These response biases are quite closely related to the criterion levels of signal detection theory (SDT) and also to an information theoretical account of recognition behavior. Luce (1963) was able to link these concepts to each other and, in this manner, apply his choice model to the then popular information measure analyses that had also been applied to recognition behavior.

In conclusion, Luce's choice model, like any other theory of cognitive processing, depends very much on the design of the experiment that is intended to be modeled. Experiments using yes–no decisions (i.e., answering the question—are these two stimuli the same or different?) may require different models than those using multiple-choice naming (with its attendant confusion scores) as the response mode of choice. In addition, individuals differ enormously in their performance on many different tests (see, e.g., Halpern, Andrews, & Purves, 1999). Adding uncertainty to such theorizing is that even the best control does not eliminate an almost arbitrary variation in the criteria used by different subjects or even by a single subject at different times. Furthermore, pooling data is also a source of error in the conclusions and interpretations drawn from that data. An illusion of simplicity and order can be induced when data from different experiments or from different subjects are combined that may cloud the actual underlying complexity and variability present among a group of subjects.

The prototype theories I have briefly introduced here contain the essence of almost everything that has subsequently evolved since then in theorizing about or simulating the human form recognition process. Clearly, none of these classic methods was adequate to either fully explain or even come close to mimicking the enormously powerful human capability. Nevertheless, it was in the period from 1945 until 1960 that many of the currently popular ideas first emerged and modern form recognition theories crystallized. The formal models, beginning with Pitts and McCulloch (1947), superceded the speculative qualitative and verbal "just so stories" that had been dominant up to that time in the psychological literature. If nothing else, this transformation from verbal descriptions to quantitative models was an extremely important step forward.

What was the single most powerful enabling force that led to the explosion of new theoretical ideas? The answer is self-evident: It was the post World War II development of the digital computer. Many, if not most, of the new ideas emerged as a result of this extraordinary technological development. Even those theories that were not explicitly computer programs were influenced by the new electronic Zeitgeist, particularly as it developed around the Cambridge, Massachusetts, area. The powerful impact of simply being able to write a simulation program cannot be underestimated.

Strongly supporting the computer driven forces were the new developments in neurophysiology that occurred at about that time. The intracellular microelectrode had been developed by Ling and Gerard (1949) and this technology opened up vast new opportunities to observe the general action of neurons and how they interacted. The combined computer and neuron heuristic was pregnant with possibilities. Many of the pioneers mentioned in this section saw them and produced the striking new prototypical innovations exemplified here.

The groundwork now being established, another wave of new innovation and invention occurred starting around the decade of the 1960s. These modern developments are now discussed to determine just how far the field of form recognition theories has come since the pioneering days.

4.3.2. Modern Theories of Form Recognition—
The Realization

The sample theories now presented are exemplars of the best modern developments in the effort to understand form recognition. As my review of the range of modern theories progressed, it became clear that the putative associationist, Gestalt, neural net, interpretive, single cells, templates, and adaptive categories, were not going to be able to distinguish among the most important developments that occurred in the modern era. Most modern theories and models incorporate ideas from several (if not most) of the prototypical categories presented earlier; therefore, they do not parse as neatly as one would like. Theories that incorporate neural networks are often adaptive; feature theories are often instantiated in parallel processing networks that in some cases mimic the holistic emphasis of the Gestalt approach; neural and entropy minimization theories sometimes coalesce. What I have decided to emphasize, therefore, are a few of the most important current trends in the categories of theories of human form recognition listed on page 186.

Excluded from this discussion is a very large, but what I am convinced is a conceptually deeply flawed, category: single cell theories of form recognition. Although declining in popularity in recent years, this approach was enormously active following the exceedingly important physiological discoveries of Hubel and Wiesel (1962) and Lettvin et al. (1959). From the 1960s to the 1980s, it was virtually impossible to read an article on visual perception that did not cite this kind of research as the foundation for a neuroreductive explanation of a wide variety of visual phenomena.

Nevertheless, before continuing with this critical discussion of the single cell theories of form recognition, it is important to introduce an important caveat. The contributions of these pioneering neurophysiologists should not be minimized or ignored; it is clear that they revolutionized the neurosciences by shifting the emphasis from the simple energetics of a stimulus (its amplitude and time course) to its spatiotemporal pattern.

However, it now seems that these very important neurophysiological discoveries were misapplied when they became the basis for theories of form recognition or, for that matter, any other cognitive function. From the time of the first reports in the late 1950s, there was an almost irrepressible urge to identify the observed activity of single cells as the coded representations of cognitive processes on the part of many psychobiologists. Such a conceptual leap, however, went far beyond the real contribution of these exciting discoveries. To put it simply, they were being applied in a context in which they were not relevant. The enormous abundance of observable neuronal activities occurring whenever the brain is active argues now (as it did then, if these early psychobiological theorists had peered deeper into the underlying assumptions of their bare bones neuronal reductionism) strongly for the fact that the entire single cell theory of cognition is based on a very questionable premise. That premise is that correlated activity in a single neuron *is* the representative code of the perception, thought, or behavior; that is, that a correlated neuronal response is, *ipso facto*, the psychoneural equivalent of mental activity and its consequences.

The logical flaws underlying such an assumption are obvious and I have dealt with them extensively elsewhere (Uttal, 1998) so I do not belabor that point here. Suffice it to say that once one passes beyond the transmission codes of the peripheral nervous system, any such association of a singular neuronal response with a "high level" cognitive process is virtually meaningless. Even there, it is well known that the individual neurons are indeterminate with regard to the stimulus scene: It takes what is presumably a very large population of neurons to represent even the simplest stimulus.

The alternative to this hyper-localized assumption embodied in any theory of single cell representation is the antithetical assumption that an enormous number of widely distributed neurons is likely to be involved in mental activity. Many thoughtful students of the problem, however, currently appreciate that we do not have the slightest idea of the processes by means of which this cumulative neuronal activity is converted in mental activity. Therefore, the arguments for both a statistical, parallel, distributed theory of brain activity and a single neuron theory are now and are likely to remain in the future, indirect metaphors.

The main data supporting the concept that very large numbers of widely distributed neurons must account for cognitive activity are the twin observations that single neurons are typically broadly tuned and that neuronal activity can be observed in widely distributed portions of the brain when cognitive processes are ongoing. Neurons are not narrowly tuned to single stimulus attributes of any kind—a fundamental axiom of the single cell theories. Sharp perceptual discrimination requires the simultaneous activity of many cells both in the periphery and centrally. Single neurons do not come close in their response sensitivity anywhere in the nervous system to encoding the powerful discriminative powers of humans. The apparent chaotic disorganization of such a network of interacting neurons suggests that something like a statistical average of the activity of many neurons must underlay our ability to represent a stimulus form, or for that matter, any kind of a psychological state. The mismatch between the behavior of individual neurons and individual people should have forewarned us about the fatal weakness of any theory of cognition that suggested that single neurons were responsible for the encoding of our percepts, thoughts, or ideas.

Finally, to reiterate an important point—The enormous numerousness and extremely wide distribution of neurons involved in any cognitive process argues that there may be impenetrable barriers to developing a truly neuroreductive account of how the brain produces cognitive activity. This argument is based purely on epistemological issues of the complexity and numerousness of the involved neurons and is not intended to suggest any ontological delinking of neural and the psychological states into different levels of "reality."

Having put single neuron theories aside and raising some caveats about neural network theories, I now turn to a consideration of what criteria and dimensions characterize modern theories of form recognition. One criterion that can be used to classify the majority of form recognition theories that are considered in this section is the degree to which they are dependent on either global organization or local feature concepts. That is, although there may be considerable overlap, most modern theories can be distinguished to the degree they emphasize attributes of the whole form or attributes that are only parts of the stimulus.

Another distinguishing criterion is whether they depend on exhaustive comparisons with a set of templates or prototypes in their approach or seek to compute their way to the final categorization by constructionist or algorithmic procedures.

A third and somewhat more elusive dimension concerns the degree to which a theory is intended to be broadly metaphorical as opposed to the degree to which it is offered as a highly specific explanation of the exact mechanisms underlying form recognition. Many psychological theories, in particular, describe hypothetical systems that operate at a metaphorical or information-processing level invoking concepts and analogies for which we have no direct empirical evidence. On the other hand, some theories deal at a much more specific level with mechanisms and structures that are formulated in highly specific terms and are taken very concretely. It is sometimes hard to distinguish between the metaphorical and the explicitly reductionist for a very profound reason: All of the theories and models are, in the final analysis, descriptive hypotheses.

In fact, it may not be too extreme to suggest that all theories can be nothing more than metaphorical speculations. Earlier theories of cognitive function were explicitly offered as heuristic metaphors or rhetorical aids. For example, the metaphors of a "funnel" or "limited capacity filter" controlling the capacity of attention (Broadbent, 1958) or of attention as a "flashlight beam" (Lindsay & Norman, 1977) were not proposed as realistic mechanisms. Rather, their authors suggested them as ideas that could help us understand some of the functions that characterize attentive behavior.

On the other hand, some of the models discussed here, phrased as they are in the terminology of neurons and networks, or even more subtly in the languages of mathematics or computers, sometimes obscure the fact that these theories are also only rhetorical metaphors for the functions of neural nets that remain (and probably will remain) mysterious. No matter how close the analogy represented by a good fit of an equation or program and an observed behavior, such a theory may, in fact, be no closer to probing the reality of how form recognition occurs than the "flashlight" or "funnel" explain attention.

Finally, there is an ever increasing group of methods that have come to us from computer technology. These methods are not theories in the sense they explicitly seek to explain organic form recognition. Rather, these engineering tools are designed to solve some practical recognition problem by using whatever computational tools are available without regard to any demonstrable biology. In many cases, it should be acknowledged, such program have become the source of inspiration for actual theories of human recognition. Unfortunately, this often has been done in an uncritical manner in which highly improbable assumptions about how computers can be made to "see" are carelessly introduced into discussions of organic vision.

In the following sections, I have selected examples of form recognition theories that illustrate particular approaches. Just as in the discussion of empirical data in the previous chapter, review of the full gamut of such theories is patently impossible.

4.3.2.1. Sample Elementalist (Feature) Theories of Form Recognition

Feature theories are characterized by the foundation assumption that specific local attributes of the form provide the initial and essential input for the decision processes that follow. In many cases, the feature or component theories were naked imitations and minor extrapolations of ideas first developed in computer science circles. For example, any theory that objects are represented psychologically by a set of standard structural components is a direct extension of the computer science work of Binford (1971) and Marr and Nishihara (1978). Given the arbitrariness of the perceptual components sometimes proposed in theories of this type, the fact that they remain empirically unobservable, and the overwhelming argument that they are simply not reported by the unprimed human observer, there is little scientific support for this metaphor for object recognition.

Other popular feature theories dealt with even more abstract ideas. I have already discussed the Fourier Analysis approach to form recognition. Even though this theory evolved into a highly specific neurophysiological model, it seems also to be declining recently in popularity. Nevertheless, it is important to reiterate that this kind of feature theory, in which the "features" are spatial frequency components,[4] does provide a powerful mathematical tool to describe and manipulate visual patterns.

---

[4]Sinusoidal spatial frequencies were the original components in the classic Fourier analysis, but there has been a progression of newer "basis functions" used in similar kinds of analysis. For example, Watson (1983) suggested a new set based on functions produced by multiplying sinu-

Julesz's (1981, 1984) "Texton" theory of texture discrimination discussed on page 67 is another example of a feature oriented approach. The component features of his model of shape discrimination are elements that must be discriminated on the basis of their individual local statistics, but these properties are as much features as are corners or angles. Indeed, when violations of simple rules occurred to challenge his analysis in terms of statistical properties, Julesz turned to alternative explanations involving specific sensitivities to particular geometrical patterns such as corners and arrows.

Others have simply assumed a priori that parts are essential for recognition and have developed a variety of means of parsing out the parts from a complex scene. Hoffman and Richards (1984), for example, developed algorithms for decomposing parts based on the principle of "transversality"—a means of distinguishing the boundaries between intersecting objects based on the nature of the respective intersections. This technique and others like it developed by computer scientists to segment images are precursor image processing utilities required to normalize images and not really theories of the recognition problem.

The most popular of the modern psychological feature theories of form recognition was proposed by Treisman in the 1980s (see Treisman & Gelade, 1980). Her model became a dominant theme in the 1990s and was most completely presented in the distinguished Bartlett memorial lecture (Treisman, 1988). Influenced strongly by some of the physiological studies suggesting that different areas or parts of the nervous system processed differed attributes or features of a stimulus form, Treisman carried out a number of experiments that suggested these feature or attributes (including, e.g., color, orientation, direction, and size) were processed separately by different cognitive as well as neural mechanisms. She hypothesized that an individual neural map was formed for each of these features.

The next important postulate of the Treisman model is central and is, perhaps, the most significant aspect of her theory. She assumes that, although initially analyzed and represented separately, these different attributes must be brought together again—or "conjoined" by focused attention. According to her, the hypothetical effect of this attentive effort is to create a master map that provides the input to (or serves as) consciousness as well as providing the necessary controls for behavior. It is at this level of the conjoined map that we perceive or behave, according to the Treisman model.

---

soidal and Gaussian functions. This alternative set had the advantage of looking much more like the receptive fields of retinal neurons. Recently, as discussed on pages 82–83, Stewart and Pinkham (1991, 1994) have proposed an even more abstract idea based on Hermite eigenfunctions that permit virtually any set of basis functions to be used and none to be more natural a priori than any other. This idea is particularly attractive because it does not make any particular commitment to a particular set of basis functions.

In the last decade of the 20th century, a number of other psychological researchers have pursued some of the ideas originally proposed by Treisman. For example, Ashby, Prinzmetal, Ivry, and Maddox (1996) proposed a formal theory of how the features could be recombined. Their theoretical approach, like that of Treisman and her colleagues, was based on perceptual phenomena that heavily depended on the concept of "false" or "illusory conjunctions." False conjunctions, for example, occur when a color and a shape are incorrectly combined and perceived to characterize a conjoined stimulus in an incorrect place when, in fact, they were actually located at separate locations in the visual field.

This brings us to one of the most important generalizations of the entire field of psychophysical research—the idea that what you put in largely determines what you get out. Earlier in this book I concluded that the preponderance of the psychophysical data supported the idea that holistic processing rather than part or feature processing best characterized human vision. This generalization was framed within the context of experiments that used whole patterns or objects such as faces as stimuli. Within the context of stimuli that are presented as wholes, holism is still the most compelling conclusion.

What then are we to make of the data obtained in experiments by Treisman and Ashby and their respective colleagues presented as support for their feature based theories? It may be argued that their experimental designs used stimuli that were more likely to assay the effects of a putative feature processing mechanisms than tap into holistic processes. Or, to phrase it somewhat differently, their experiments were constructed in such a way that the easiest explanation was one based on features or attributes. The typical experimental material used throughout the entire corpus of empirical studies used to support Treisman's "feature integration" theory are letters or other simple geometrical shapes and colors, typified by a red circle or a green letter. (See, e.g., Hazeltine, Prinzmetal, & Elliot, 1997; Johnston & Pashler, 1990; Treisman & Gelade 1980). The choice of stimuli like these and the parallel decision to limit the response domain to how long it takes to locate a particular colored shape (i.e., search time) produces strong pressures pushing an investigator toward feature-based explanations. In other words, if independent variables are defined in terms of features, as they are throughout this entire experimental program, then one is most easily led to develop feature type explanations and theories. If, on the other hand, one's choice of stimuli includes more holistic forms, then one is more naturally directed to global type theories.

To sum up this line of argument, what appears to be the "best fitting" theory depends strongly on the selection of the stimuli and other aspects of the design of the experiment as well as on the experimenter's initial assumptions. Once one has chosen the independent and dependent variables, the *best* (or, perhaps, the *easiest*) theory is largely predetermined. The theoretical implication of this line of thought is that the outcome, both empirical and theoretical, of any study of cognitive processes is all-too-often predetermined by initial empirical and theoretical decisions. That the chosen context is so important in determining the theoretical outcome is due in large part to two other generalizations:

1. Any behavioral result is fundamentally indeterminate or neutral with regard to the underlying mechanisms, and
2. the strategies that are used by the brain to solve problems are, in point of actual fact, varied, numerous, and inaccessible.

Our powerful perceptual system, accordingly, is able to deal with many different challenges with which it may be presented by applying any one (or combination of) a large number of different perceptual tools. Therefore, none of the theories of form recognition that have been proposed is "wrong" (if one judiciously limits their impact to the descriptive level); each has something to say about how a particular class of perceptual problems may be solved. However, what is wrong is concluding that one or the other alternative is right to the exclusion of other possibilities.

The dual concepts of analysis and recombination (or "binding" as it has come to be called) that pervade the feature integration-type theories are hypotheses that seem to be supported by what are conceptual interpretations of some very solid neurophysiological evidence from the peripheral nervous system as well as some much less solid conjectures concerning how central cognitive systems might operate. The primary hypothesis that objects are decomposed into their component features and then recombined, as we have seen is ubiquitous throughout the entire field, presently as well as throughout its history. Boring (1950) noted that the idea that a stimulus could be broken up into attributes or components go back to Hermann Lotze and Oswald Külpe well into the 19th century. Clearly, both tradition and a kind of superficial analytic simplicity have played important roles in the development of feature theories.

Clearly, the Treisman-type model is a variant of the information-processing models that incorporate hypothetical and invisible components (i.e., levels of representation) that must be inferred from behavioral data. The main problem faced by this theoretical approach is the classic one of the inaccessibility of the cognitive processes under study. Virtually all theories of cognitive processes are constrained by this same indirectness. Although there is no question that the phenomena observed by Treisman, her colleagues, and successors are probably accurate and faithful descriptions of human perceptual behavior, the conceptual leap to this particular feature theory is a long and, from my point of view, untenable one. It is driven by the choice of stimuli, superficially consistent with the measured behavior, and dependent on a convenient, though possibly erroneous, conceptual schema. In the final analysis, all reductive theories of perceptual process are constrained by the fundamental inaccessibility of the very processes that are the targets of the study.

4.3.2.2. Sample Global Theories of Form Recognition

The search for an exemplar global theory of form recognition is not without its difficulties. I have already mentioned that computational and neurophysiological technologies are inherently elementalist and, to a substantial degree, they provide the conceptual foundations of most current theories. Thus, the instantiations of even the most global of theories still reflect component oriented premises. Furthermore, it is extremely difficult to construct a mathematical model that adequately simulates a global theory. It seems likely, given what we do know about the microanatomy of the brain, that cognitive processes like form recognition will be ultimately based on a very large number of components operating collectively in ways that we do not know how to simulate. Indeed, if the number of neural units required to achieve a level of complexity sufficient to produce cognitive processes is very large, a valid reductive model of form recognition or a truly comparable level of artificial intelligence may be much more elusive than even some of the optimists among us now think.

Are There Any Holistic Theories? We can, therefore, ask: Are there any theories that are patently holistic? An affirmative answer to this question can be seen in one of the most primitive kinds of form recognizers—the template matchers. In a simple sense, acknowledging all of their attendant inefficiencies and clumsiness, template matchers do attempt to "recognize" a form by comparing its entire shape with the entire shape of each item in the library (e.g., see the work of Shepherd, 1999). The comparison between an input form and the library of comparison items is, in principle, at least, carried out, not on the basis of any local feature or group of features, but rather on the basis of the whole form.[5] However, the necessity for exhaustive search (either in parallel or in serial order) and the requirement for an enormous library of forms suggest that this particular brand of holism is not likely to be representative of psychobiological reality.

Another candidate to exemplify the global approach is the Lie transformation group hypothesis proposed by Hoffman (1966). Hoffman's model

---

[5]In point of fact, however, the programs that instantiate the template matching process are, like all other digital computer models, executed on computers that deal with local parts in sequential order. The only distinction between *local* and *global* programs is how and when the recognition decision is made.

deals with the topological transformations that can be applied to visual forms as well as to many other domains of scientific inquiry. Many of the transformation groups he proposes mimic the global dynamics of visual perception. In a general sense, his descriptions are oriented toward depicting and transforming the entire shape of a form. Nevertheless, many of the most obvious kinds of form similarity are not accounted for by any of the Lie groups. (Caelli, 1977).

Other closely related, though much less formal global theories, have been proposed from time to time. Pribram, Nuwer, and Baron (1974) suggested the metaphor of holography as a highly distributed model of memory and attention. Such an extreme form of distribution almost automatically implies a kind of holistic representation of the stimulus form and an insensitivity to its local properties.

Blum (1967) had earlier proposed an essentially holistic response to the shape of an object based on the propagation of the shape by processes akin to the growth of a bacterial strain on a medium. Each point on a form initiated growth and each subsequent new point acted as a further focus of growth, according to this idea. The net effect was that resulting growth contours were dependent on the shape of the original stimulus form. The shape and interaction of these growing contours, therefore, were presumed to differentially encode the original form. The global aspect of this model was that the shape of the ultimate growth contour was not dependent on any particular feature but collectively on the entire form. Although Blum's exposition was, like many of the other precomputer versions, more of a metaphor than a detailed theory, it was based on a kind of sensitivity to the overall shape of the form rather than its local features. The concept of a growing pattern is also of interest in that it presages some of the ideas inherent in the energy minimization models that were to follow.

All of these theories, however inadequate they may have been on other counts, were expressions of a primarily holistic or global point of view concerning form perception. Features were eschewed and the entire form was presumed to operate collectively to characterize the stimulus or to determine an appropriate response. The answer to our question, then is: Yes, a few.

Is Parallelicity Tantamount to Globality? This brings us to the category of the parallel processing, distributed neural network models of perception. Before considering theories of this kind, it is necessary to consider a more fundamental issue: Is parallelicity tantamount to globality? The answer to this question is both certain and negative. The many neural network models of form recognition that exist today come in a wide variety. From the earliest developments, however, parallel processing versions of feature oriented neural network models can be found (e.g., see the discussion of Selfridge's Pandemonium on p. 194). Despite the fact that computational elements of the model may appear to operate across the whole input space, an initial analysis of the object into its features is carried out by most of the neural net models that have been proposed so far. This commitment to analysis of the local features of the input stimulus is clearly illustrated in the pioneering work of McClelland and Rumelhart (1981) as well as many other theories that have been proposed since then. The three layer McClelland and Rumelhart neural net, like so many others of this genre, started off by analyzing letter forms into their simple geometrical components including horizontal, vertical, and oblique lines. Interestingly, this theoretical model was intended to "explain" word superiority effects, a context effect that seems wildly unconnected to the spatial geometry that was the usual grist for the form recognition theoretical mill. Because local features are an integral part of so many neural network (i.e., distributed) theories, it is clear that distribution and globality cannot be identified with each other and that the answer to the question just asked must be *no*!

Page (2000) also considered the distinction between the *localist* and *distributed* means of representing forms within parallel distributed processing networks. He concluded that it is entirely possible for such a distributed network to be implemented based on either global and local premises. His main concern, however, was with the ultimate representation rather than the method of processing. The key criterion of a distributed system for Page was that the entire network be responsible for the encoding of the attributes of a memory or an object. The key criterion of a localized representation is that a single component of the network can represent an object. The important point in the present context, however, is that Page also concluded that distributed neural network theories can be based on either local or global premises.

Although closely related, it should be obvious that the antagonistic concepts of local and distributed processing and the dichotomy of holist versus feature processing, are not the same. Page's distinction was between two ways of representing information internally inside the system after processing has been completed. The whole–part issue deals with the ways in which the information is processed before arriving at that representation. Nevertheless, both considerations support the idea that there is nothing that restricts a distributed neural net system from being either local or global in its foundation assumptions.

To emphasize this point, there are many other modern examples of distributed neural net system theories that are based on feature detectors as a initial processing mode. For example, Carpenter, Grossberg, and Mehanian (1989) developed a method for boundary segmentation that could be used as the front end of a decision-making recognition system. Based on earlier work from Grossberg's laboratory (Grossberg & Mingolla, 1985), this system used a hierarchy of feature detecting components. The early ones were sensitive to contrast differences and they subsequently fed simulated neurons encoding higher levels of spatial sensitivity analogous to those observed in the organic nervous system. This concept of a feature detecting neural net has long been a mainstay of the many publications coming from Grossberg's laboratory (see, e.g., Carpenter & Grossberg, 1987; Grossberg, 1976).

Fukushima's Cognitron. On the other side of the theoretical coin, there are parallel distributed neural net models that come close to being essentially global systems. One was suggested by Fukushima and his colleagues (Fukushima, 1981; Fukushima & Miyake, 1978; Fukushima, Miyake, & Ito, 1983). In particular, one of the earlier models (Fukushima & Miyake (1978) was based on an iterative feedback method that did not involve any a priori or explicit introduction of local features analyses into the algorithm. Instead, these authors suggested that the key idea in their recognition machine is the self-organization of the "neural" network of their simulation. In addition to the usual feed-forward from one layer to another in a five layer neural net system, they proposed that the final layer should have an additional property—its synapses had to be modifiable and, thus, could direct a self-organization of the system that depended on repeated presentations of the same input patterns. The result is that each of a number of *different stimulus forms ultimately produced a unique distributed configuration of all of the simulated neurons in the network.* This final distributed *state* was itself the distinguishing code for recognition, not the emission of a response signal from a single decision node as is much more usually proposed as the final step in neural net models of form recognition.

The idea that the overall state of the system is the final encoded outcome has much to say for it as a guiding concept. It is often the case that we confuse the selected response with the final representation of the object. Indeed, throughout the neural net modeling movement, there has been a tendency for the investigator to present a single selected output of the system as the solution to the recognition problem. The unique and highly compelling argument of Fukushima and Miyake's approach is that there is no explicit selection of a "correct" identification modeled by a maximum of activity in one of many response nodes as exemplified by the Pandemonium idea. Rather, the final stabilized configuration or state of all of the nodes in the network becomes tantamount to the identification process itself. The selection of the response is, from this point of view, merely an ancillary process that takes place after the final "recognition" state has been achieved.

The point is that there is no "decoding" that would require the action of a homunculus-like decoder. It is the raw (and overall) pattern of neural activities produced by the multiple original presentations (the training) that instantiates the identification process. The set of all such system states represents the universe of forms that the system has encountered. To word it in another context—*the self-organized patterns themselves are the "psycho-neural equivalents" of the experience.*

The problem is that, even though the patterns of activity may be sufficient to internally solve the recognition problem for the subject, it is impossible for an external observer to directly ascertain their state. Thus, an experimenter must ask the subject to verbally assign some name or category or to emit an observable response to indicate what has been recognized. This indicator, however, is a supplemental activity, an artifact of the need to observe the operation of what is otherwise a closed system.

In a neural net model, as in a psychological experiment, it is the external observer's need to find out what is going on that demand the extra steps required to summarize the overall state of the system. This can be done by carrying out the final decision and response steps in order to provide a single criterion response or by displaying the state of every node in the network. For the modest number of neurons in simulated networks of the kind being discussed here, the latter method can often be accomplished without selecting a specific response mode. Fukushima and Miyake (1978) do exactly that: Some of their figures show the ultimate pattern of activity that is arrived at for each sample stimulus from what may be considered to be a holistic or global point of view.

It is interesting to note that for a more complex network of many neurons, the problem becomes very similar to the representation task discussed in Chapter 2. This analogy supports the idea that it is the state of the system that is important in both the initial and final stages of the recognition process. Evaluation of the representations at each end of the process are only necessary for the convenience of the investigating scientist. The state is sufficient for the system itself. One might pun in words from a totally different context—*L'Etat c'est moi!*

Even though the system that Fukushima and Miyake (1978) developed was too small to realistically simulate the form recognition properties of the human visual system, it did incorporate some concepts that were quite rare throughout the entire field of artificial intelligence and theoretical modeling. As noted, one of these was the idea that the global state of the system was the key correlate of the recognition process. Another was the fact that it was self-organizing. All that had to be done by the experimenter was to repeatedly present the training stimuli and the system automatically organizes itself to produce the final distribution of neural activity. Thus, the final perceptual experience was a joint function of the stimulus and the functional rules built into the neural net. Such a conceptualization of the problem has the ring of a fundamental truth in the study of organic vision—albeit, like all other reductive explanations, it may be impossible to verify.

Another important idea inherent in the Fukushima and Miyake model is that once organized by the repetitive training cycles, the system is capable of what they called "associative recall." That is, the system was able to establish an appropriate pattern of responses even if the input was only a fragment of the form to which the system had originally been trained. Furthermore, the system was robust enough to produce the appropriate overall pattern of response even when the input pattern was embedded in significant amounts of random visual noise. Finally, if totally novel patterns were presented to the system (consisting of either totally random visual noise or totally novel regular forms) the system responded by either producing a new distribution pattern or by producing nothing at all. Thus, this model had the additional advantage of minimizing the tendency to confuse old stimuli with new ones.

Uttal's Autocorrelation Theory of Form Detection. A theory of form detection (as opposed to recognition) that enjoys many of the nonfeature aspects of the early Fukushima and Miyake model can be found in Uttal (1975). This theory of the extraction of regular forms from noisy backgrounds, based on the autocorrelation function, also used a completely parallel and distributed approach without any feature sensitive operators. The autocorrelation function (AC) was expressed as:

$$AC = \iint f(x,y)f(x + \Delta x, y + \Delta y)dydx \qquad (4.2)$$

where $f(x,y)$ is a two-dimensional form and $f(x + \Delta x, y + \Delta y)$ is the same form shifted to a new position $\Delta x, \Delta y$. The autocorrelation function, therefore, is a process of comparing a stimulus form against itself for many different values of $\Delta x, \Delta y$. It was this algorithm's intrinsic and overall sensitivity to linear and periodic patterns that allowed the program to discriminate between an orderly form and random noise and to correctly rank order the psychophysical detectability of many different forms.

Like the Fukushima and Miyake model, after the algorithm had been executed, the network arrived at a particular state of organization that represented the autocorrelation of the input pattern. The state was unique for each input form. As far as the system was concerned, this state was tantamount to the solution of the problem posed when a form was to be detected. Again, it was only when the experimenter sought some means of categorizing the state that a second step of processing had to be executed. The choice of a state evaluator in this case was a "Figure of Merit" that quantified the spatial relationships among all of the nodes in the final layer of processing. The very arbitrary figure of merit carried out this function by carrying out some ad hoc numerical and statistical operations to summarize the collective activity of all points in the autocorrelation space. The Figure of Merit (FM) was represented by:

$$FM = \frac{\sum_{n=1}^{N}\sum_{i=1}^{N}(A_n A_i)/d_{ni}}{N} \tag{4.3}$$

where N is the number of peaks in the autocorrelogram, A_n and A_i are the amplitudes of a pair of peaks and d_{ni} is the Pythagorean distance between them. The products of all possible pairs $(n \times i)$ are computed, each is divided by the distance between them, and then they are all added together and divided by the number of peaks. This results in a single number *FM* which predicts the detectability of a particular shaped target in interfering visual noise. It must be reiterated, however, that this subsequent evaluation of the state of the system is not really necessary except to satisfy the needs of the external observer to quantify the outcome.

Autocorrelation has repeatedly been alluded to as a powerful means of dealing with a number of perceptual phenomena. For example, Werkhoven, Snippe, and Koenderink (1990) used it to model motion perception and Ben-Av and Sagi (1995) have demonstrated its value in modeling perceptual grouping.

In sum, the essential idea behind both the Fukushima and Miyake and the several applications of the autocorrelation theory is that it is not necessary (except for the observational purposes just mentioned) to go beyond the final system state to the selection of a response or output unit or to a develop some arbitrary metric of that state. In point of basic principle, any such supplementary step is extraneous to the detection or recognition processes per se. The establishment of the final network state *is* detection or recognition.

What is proper to emphasize, in place of this effort to quantify or categorize a distributed state, is the range of plausible mechanisms that could allow a system to go from an input pattern to the final representative state. A wide variety of learning and other processing algorithms has been suggested over the years. In particular, considerable attention has been paid to the problem of the decision rules that govern changing the strength of the interconnections between nodes in neural network models. In the earliest system (e.g., Selfridge, 1958) the experimenter manually changed these values. Subsequent methods utilized simple feed-forward criteria such as the number of times a connection was activated (Hebb's rule, 1949). The closely related "delta rule" (Widrow & Hoff, 1960) was one of the first to compare the desired state of the system with the current state and then to adjust the lower levels of the neural net to minimize the discrepancy. Intervention by the experimenter was typically also required to establish the desired state when this criterion was used.

Newer models sought to automate this process by invoking various kinds of feedback methods such as the back propagation technique. Back propagation (Rumelhart, Hinton, & Williams (1986) was a step toward the holy grail of neural net theory—a self-organizing principle that removed external intervention by the experimenter and substituted rules that permitted the network to learn and recognize on its own. Back propagation adds backward flowing signals to the forward flow of information. It attempts to minimize an error or discrepancy between the desired final state and the current state by evaluating the partial derivatives of the error pattern in a two-stage process—one forward pass and then a subsequent backward pass. Although automatic in this sense, the rules for changing the strengths of the connections between the neural net nodes are deterministic. It is therefore, possible, depending on the ultimate configuration that is desired, that the system could converge to a false minimum. This problem became the stimulus for the next stage of development of neural network theories.

The Energy Minimization and Stochastic Approaches. Two important new ideas were introduced into neural net modeling in recent years. First, a search for solutions to this false minimum problem was stimulated by the work of Hopfield (1982) when he proposed a novel conceptual approach to this kind of simulation. He suggested that the overall pattern of activity in a neural net could be considered to be analogous to an "energy surface" or a "cost function." The basic idea proposed by Hopfield derived from classic physical ideas in which systems were deemed to be quasi-continuous and be able to self-adjust to an optimal final system state by minimizing the internal "stresses."

The second influential idea in the last two decades of neural net theorizing was the introduction of stochastic or random processes into the model to solve the false minimum problem. By so doing, probabilistic models allowed the system to occasionally "leap out" of a false energy minimum and continue to seek the true minimum.

The combination of Hopfield's inspired analogy of a neural net as an energy surface and the ability of random factors to overcome some of the potential errors introduced by ill-posed problems resulted in some stunning innovations. Simulated annealing, for example, a method originally proposed by Kirkpatrick, Gelatt, and Vecchi (1983), is a straightforward application to neural net theories of the classic idea that an agitated surface cools to a final, stable state in a way that is dependent on the cooling rate. In a simulated annealing program, the probability of altering the strength of an internodal connection is a joint function of the input to that node and the simulated temperature. As the "temperature" is lowered, the system tends to converge on an equilibrium state that represents a minimum of the energy misdistribution throughout the entire system—an intrinsically global concept. This relationship can be represented by the expression:

$$P = \frac{1}{1 + e^{\frac{I}{T}}} \tag{4.4}$$

where P is the probability that a connection to a node changes, I is the input to the node, and T is the simulated temperature. As T declines, the probability of changing the strength of a connection is reduced and the system gets more stable. Since P is a stochastic term, the final outcome of the annealing process is not entirely predetermined. Even though the local minimum equilibrium state at which the final "cold" system arrives may not be the lowest in the system, the random factor built into this formulation permit the system state to occasionally move out of the false minimum and increases the probability that it will ultimately arrive at the true minimum.

As just noted, a key idea of the simulated annealing approach is the introduction of stochastic (i.e., random) factors into the system analysis. However, probabilistic algorithms require much more processing than does a deterministic system. This tends to make such models operate relatively slowly. On the other hand, stochastic solutions may often achieve a correct final state better than can a deterministic system. The latter is very likely to simply oscillate between equally stable states rather than having the flexibility to converge on a *good* if not the *best* solution. Other approaches that take advantage of similar ideas from statistical mechanics include Monte Carlo simulations (see Binder & Heerman, 1988 for a discussion of this method), however, these random search methods are typically even slower than the simulated annealing technique.

Another method incorporating stochastic and probabilistic ideas that has enjoyed a great deal of enthusiastic support in the neural network community in recent years is the Boltzmann machine. This idea was originally proposed by Hinton and Sejnowski (1986) and is also based on an analogy with a thermodynamic system moving towards a final equilibrium state. The key idea in the Boltzmann model is the same as that underlying the statistical analysis of gases. Although associated initially with a high degree of variability in the energy of each particle in the system, there is a tendency for the system to settle down into a stable state in which the energy is much more evenly distributed. The basic idea, like that of a heated gas, is that high-energy particles give up energy to the low-energy particles and this transfer provides a force driving the system toward the final stable state.

Like the simulated annealing method, with which it is closely related, the Boltzmann machine concept incorporates probability principles (specifically the Boltzmann probability distribution) that allow it to solve problems that would confound a deterministic neural-net system. The probabilistically controlled sequence of states through which the system progresses is not predetermined, but can vary randomly. Such a system is much less likely to become "stuck" in some erroneous intermediate state. The Boltzmann probability distribution is defined as an exponential function in the following way:

$$P(S) = Ke^{\frac{-E_s}{BT}} \tag{4.5}$$

where $P(S)$ is the probability of finding a component of a multicomponent system in a state S, K is a constant, $-E_S$ is the negative of the energy of the energy of the State S, T is the temperature, and B is the Boltzmann constant; the latter being equal to $1.3806503 \times 10^{-23}$ Joules per degree Kelvin.

The Boltzmann probability distribution used in contemporary neural net models is derived from previous efforts to characterize the distribution of velocities of the molecules in a gas. It has also proven to be useful in describing the equilibrium seeking behavior of chemical systems. The strategies of statistical mechanics that are modeled by this theory are still considered to be the best way to explain, for example, the global properties of a container of gas—particularly the relation between its temperature and pressure. A major benefit arising from Boltzmann's statistical distribution, therefore, is that it allows physicists to describe the macroscopic behavior of a system of microscopic elements without paying attention to the idiosyncratic behavior of the individual components that make up the system. The promise is that these same stochastic principles can be used to describe the macroscopic behavior of a system like the organic brain without resorting to an exhaustive determination of the behavior of each neuron. This was the basis of the idea that was to become the conceptual core of Hinton and Sejnowski's Boltzmann machine.

The neural net implementation of a Boltzmann machine that distinguishes it from previous neural net models is its stochastic nature; that is, random parameters are incorporated into the model. However, as formulated by Hinton and Sejnowski, Boltzmann machines also differ from previous neural network models in including an additional, but invisible, hidden layer within the model. The activity of this hidden layer and the strength of its constituent connections are controlled in part by these random parameters and in part by the incoming stimulus pattern.

Like any other neural net model, the distributed network in which these concepts are instantiated must be trained to carry out the recognition or other intended process. The key criteria for changing the weights of the interconnections, as noted, are probabilistic rather than deterministic. The decision rule for a Boltzmann machine may also be similar to the one proposed for simulated annealing in equation 4.4. Since the change in strength of a connection is probabilistically determined and this equation allows for both increase and decreases in its energy, a certain proportion of the time, the energy increases above the level needed to allow the system to leap out of a local or false minimum.

This kind of energy minimization or relaxation process still has some obvious potential pitfalls—both practical and theoretical. Like simulated annealing it is relatively slow. Similarly, the system may not converge to a final equilibrium state: It may oscillate under certain conditions. Furthermore, like the previous methods, it is not always certain that the energy state, once achieved, is the correct one, the true global as opposed to a fallacious local minimum. In addition, there is always the problem that the essentially serial digital computer algorithm, may become so complex that it may take an explosively large amount of time to be evaluated. On the other hand, the probabilistic models do enjoy means of occasionally "hopping" out of these false minima. For those interested in the details of this important approach to form recognition, two excellent references are Hinton and Sejnowski (1986) and Hertz, Krogh, and Palmer (1991).

If, for the sake of argument, one can separate the discrete methods inherent in computational modeling of simulated annealing or Boltzmann machines from the physical principles on which they are based, it can be seen that they represent a very interesting way of conceptualizing the brain in what is fundamentally a holistic or global approach. For the moment, let us concentrate on the fundamental assumptions on which such systems are based. The basic idea instantiated in these models is quite different from the one on which the older neural net models were based. The traditional neural net model is quintessentially a discrete one. A more or less regular array of computational nodes is connected by an almost crystal-like pattern of interconnections. Highly deterministic decision rules both guide and constrain its performance.

The Boltzmann and the simulated annealing models differ from the older models in two important ways. First, of course, is the introduction of stochastic processes. However, what is perhaps even more important is the presumed scale of the process. Both permit us to conceive of a system in which the simulated neurons are very much more numerous, much smaller, and randomly interconnected by a highly irregular plexus of collaterals than the usual neural network. Indeed, the various units may be, in principle, so finely connected to each other either directly or indirectly and over large as well as small distances. Thus, all the components of such a system are influenced by all portions of a stimulus form. In other words, however similar the practical programming requirements of the old and new systems may be, there is lurking in the conceptual background of the new approaches the concept of continuity across a surface, of action not in terms of discrete units or local interactions, but of a much more heavily interconnected and, from some points of view, quasi-continuous system. Of course, the brain is also discontinuous and microscopically discrete. This anatomical fact cannot be denied, but there is a different point of view inherent in thinking about a system in this alternative manner—more analogous to the many microscopic molecules of a glass or a box of gasses than to the relatively coarse resolution of a computer or the usual neural net model.

Therefore, if the synthetic neurons of this hypothetical network are small enough, numerous enough, and adequately interconnected, the model can be thought of as closely approximating a global form processor. Individual nodes would be influenced by distant locations and converge by stochastic processes to an overall state that would reflect a kind of minimum energy representation that is the presumed equivalent of the perception of a form. This is a different way of conceptualizing the problem from the discrete node, local action, feature oriented, deterministic model so popular today. Given the seamless, unified, nature of consciousness and perception as reported in behavioral responses and by the nature of our own self-awareness, this may be a significant conceptual step forward.

Indeed, it is not even necessary that each neuron in the network is constant in its encoding. The final outcome (i.e., perceptual experience) of the process could be determined by a statistical measure of all of the activity of all of the units that are involved. The momentary activity of any single unit or even local region would not matter. Rather, the overall statistical state of the ensemble would be definitive in determining its "perceptions" or "overt responses." This point of view also suggests that the statistics of the final state would be determined not by the stimulus alone, nor by a deterministic rule, nor solely by its previous experience, but rather by the statistical or cumulative activity of a very large number of individually unimportant components responding to many influences.

It would be difficult to carry out a real simulation of such a quasi-continuous network. The main reason that such an experimental test is not likely is one of simple combinatorics. Computers, both current and contemplated, would be hard pressed to handle the necessary load that would be generated both by component numerousness and by a high degree of random interconnectedness. The number of combinations required to simulate an organic brain may be far beyond any conceivable simulation.

This practical difficulty should not, however, be of concern to contemporary neuroscientists. If we look back on the roots of the physical challenges that drove the development of the original Boltzmann distribution, it is obvious that many of the same difficulties were faced then as now. The heart of the solution proposed by physicists was to look at indicators of global action rather than attempt anything as foolhardy as an exhaustive listing of the behavior of components. The same strategy should apply now. Attempts to simulate discrete neural networks may actually be holding us back from an insightful and valid understanding of how the brain operates. In addition, such a strategy may be misdirecting our attention to overly simplistic networks that are patently incapable of implementing the kind of information-processing principles to which we should now be paying attention. In other words, the conventional computational neural net model may be becoming as inadequate as a theory of brain action as the hydraulic models were in their time. The simulated annealing and Boltzmann machine concepts offer alternatives well worth considering.

4.3.2.3. Modern Statistical Theories of Form Recognition

The statistical approach to theories of form recognition pioneered by Luce (1959, 1963) and others have continued to stimulate theories that involve random processes in opposition to deterministic ones. In 1986, Ashby and Townsend proposed a theory of recognition they called General Recognition Theory (GRT). GRT, building on Signal Detection Theory (SDT), was based on the statistical distributions of noisy forms in a hypothetical perceptual space. In particular, two-dimensional data was assumed to be plotted into different regions of the space. Based on the nature of the form and the uncertainty or noise in which it was embedded, decisions had to be made about which of the alternative categories (i.e., regions) a form could be best located. Because there was always some overlap of the potential spatial regions (in the same way there was in the one-dimensional space of the classic Signal Detection Theory) there could be no absolutely correct identification or recognition of a form. The answer to the recognition question—What form is it?—could only be made based on certain assumptions of the distribution of the noise. Therefore, there was always a measurable probability (p) that the form would be incorrectly recognized, just as there was a probability (1-p) that it would be correctly recognized.

The GRT, as presented by Ashby and Townsend (1986) was essentially a static model; the distributions were assumed to be stable over time. Recently, the GRT has been updated and expanded by Ashby (2000) to include the temporal dynamics of a more realistic kind of perceptual processing; that is, the noise was not only assumed to be spatially distributed but it changed from one moment to the next. According to Ashby, one advantage of such an approach is that this model can now aid in the prediction of reaction times for the recognition task as well as in describing the recognition task itself. Thus, a fundamental advantage of such a dynamic model is that it more completely reflects the situation in which our sensory systems are actually functioning; one in which stimuli vary over time and, more germane to the present discussion, one in which their effects and the relevant decision criteria are also changing.

The new dynamic extension of GRT proposed by Ashby (2000) assumes that the "data," the incoming sensory representations of the form, are fluctuating randomly. The problem then becomes one of estimating the correct output from this time varying signal. In the static case in which the inputs were stable in time, the decision was straightforwardly dependent on the region in which the vector representing the several dimensions of the stimulus placed that stimulus and the distribution of the noise that made this localization uncertain. One simply decided on which side of a decision line or discriminant value the stimulus fell and that was that.

In the synthetic world described by Ashby's stochastic model, however, the situation is much more complicated; both the stimulus parameters and the decision boundaries are changing randomly and the former influences the latter. Where a single stable discriminant value (D) or decision boundary could be used to chose response A if $D > X$ or response B if $D < X$ (where X is the criterion value), the dynamic uncertainty of the new model made the use of such a simple criterion unsuitable. In this case, the simple "exclusive or" decision rule of the static case no longer works.

A new kind of criterion was, therefore, necessary to guide the decision-making (i.e., the recognition) process. The criterion now becomes a stochastic process itself. To avoid classification errors (i.e., localization errors in the perceptual space) Ashby suggested that it was necessary to introduce a third category of response. Where X, a single value had previously distinguished between only two possible responses (*choose either A or B*), the new situation requires that a third possible response be added—*continue sampling*. This additional category was required because of the uncertainty that had been introduced by the dynamic and random behavior of both the stimulus and the decision rule values. No longer was it simply a matter of knowing fixed values for the mean and standard deviation of the noise in the two-dimensional space. Rather, sampling must be continued until a sufficiently high level of D is achieved (i.e., $D \geq X$) to indicate that the correct response should be A or a sufficiently low level (i.e., $D \leq Y$) is achieved to indicate that the correct response should be B. For values Z between X and Y (I. e., $Y < Z < X$) the data had to be considered to be indeterminate and the sampling continued.

Ashby's stochastic model turns out to be closely related to other mathematical tools such as random walk or diffusion processes in which the various values of the perceptual representation of the stimulus are allowed to wander about until they also satisfy some decision criterion. The random factor acts, as it did in the Boltzmann machine model, to insert at least a measurable probability that the problem can be solved correctly in a situation that would be otherwise indeterminate. In this case it requires that the model continues to process information until enough data has been collected to exceed the high or low levels of the criterion respectively. The key idea in this present context lies in the advantage of adding the random factor to produce an uncertain, indecisive middle of the range of the decision boundary values. This is, of course, directly analogous to the suggestion that a stochastic component should be added to the simulated annealing or the Boltzmann machine models.

Ashby's expansion of the basic idea of the GRT to the stochastic and dynamic version is an excellent example of the kind of thinking that goes into a model dominated by statistical concepts. It makes the interpretation of the recognition process more realistic by pointing up the fact that our perceptual responses and decision rules are constantly changing as new information floods in. However, it must be appreciated that this approach is very far from championing or even suggesting any kind of neural or cognitive reduction. As Luce (see p. 198) pointed out, this is a purely descriptive approach to understanding what is going on inside the head and it is completely devoid of any mechanistic explanations of how these processes are actually being instantiated in specific mechanisms. It is, in this sense, another method that is quite consistent with a modern behaviorism.

4.3.2.4. Modern Engineering Methods for Form Recognition

So far in this discussion, I have concentrated on theories that are specifically intended to be models of human form recognition. It must be understood that in terms of sheer volume, this category is but a small part of the enormous corpus of engineering effort intended to achieve quite a different goal—the development of computer vision techniques for recognizing forms in practical engineering situations. Of this latter huge body of work, there are several things that must be said.

First, nothing that has been accomplished in this field compares very well with the skills of the human observer. No matter what engineering technique is examined, none is yet able to even begin to approximate the enormous perceptual power of the human observer when it comes to detection, discrimination, and recognition. Tiny variations from a canonical position, size, or orientation or a slight difference in the domain of targets for which a computer method has been designed usually lead to disastrous error rates. Major changes in the universe of items to be recognized can lead to errors of such absurdity that one would long for the simple failures of false recognition. A considerable amount of the effort that goes into developing computer form recognition systems is, therefore, actually aimed at normalizing the image rather than recognizing it.

Second, the technology of the engineering field in large part has run ahead of the data and theory of cognitive neuroscience. It is rare, once one progresses past the initial metaphor of a neural net to find any significant influence of biology or psychology on the development of computer vision systems. Robotic systems depend on the limits and constraints of available engineering tools and concepts and, only in the rarest current cases, does inspiration come from psychobiology. Although some perceptual phenomena have been influential in designating the tasks that a computer vision system should strive to accomplish, our ignorance of the organic processes has forced the computer technology to go its own way. The flow of information, ideas, and heuristics has, in the main, been in the opposite direction—from computer sciences to psychology.

Third, it can not be denied that some useful progress has been made in engineering practical form recognition devices. However, as just noted, virtually all such useful systems are limited to very narrowly defined universes. Alphabetic character recognizers have been very successful and sometimes they have even been able to deal with several different fonts simultaneously. But, if such a system is called on to deal with a completely different class of images (e.g., identifying faces) it, of course, fails completely. Adequate generalization is still not a characteristic of any computer vision system (Dreyfus, 1972, 1992). The systems that operate the best are those that constrain the target universe of items to be recognized to highly standardized fonts such as the system used on bank checks or supermarket bar codes.

Fourth, because of the enormous corpus of work in this field, it is patently impossible to review it sufficiently well to satisfy readers of a book such as this. In its stead, I only mention some of the recent books that I have found to be useful as I reviewed this extensive field of engineering.

1. Chen, Pau, and Wang's handbook (1993) collects together a variety of articles dealing with many different aspects and techniques of the form (i.e., pattern)[6] recognition field. The articles discuss basic methods as well as applications and delves deeply into the architectures of a variety of engineering systems.

2. Although Ullman (1996) is concerned with the psychology of vision more than most of the other engineering books in this mini review, his main emphasis is on the computer techniques involved in form (object) recognition. More philosophical and thoughtful than most of the others, he provides a useful service in discussing the practicalities of image alignment and image fusion. Of particular value are his discussions of classification and segmenta-

---

[6] I parenthetically identify the words that the authors of each of these books in this field uses as synonyms for "form" to suggest the variety of vocabularies currently in use.

tion. The book is also noteworthy for discussing a number of the conceptual problems relevant to the concerns raised in this book.

3. Wechsler (1990) presents a sophisticated discussion of the many problems involved in computer vision at a broader lever than just form recognition. This book is particularly well organized in terms of the problems faced, rather than the techniques invented to solve those problems. Representation, recognition, and invariance are dealt with as intellectual challenges. It also presents one of the best discussions of complexity and the limits it imposes on computer vision in general.

4. Grimson (1990) offers a specialized view of the form recognition problem. He conceptualizes it as a search problem and describes several strategies for carrying out searches. The discussion is heavily couched in the language and details of geometric features and the constraints that are produced by both two- and three-dimensional geometries. After considering what are the criteria for evaluating form recognition programs (efficiency, correctness, robustness, scope—see his p. 401) Grimson concludes that the system best fitting these criteria may be one based on a library of prestored comparison forms. This "template" approach led him to emphasize the task of correctly indexing this library in order to optimize the search algorithms.

5. Anzai (1989) deals with many of the standard procedures used throughout the field of form recognition. In addition, he presents a clear discussion of the ideas underlying the special strategies involved in the use of parallel processing computers and neural networks. This book emphasizes the problems associated with the representation of the form to be processed.

6. The best reference on image processing, in general, is Pratt (1991). This book is not particularly concerned with form recognition, but it is one of the most complete and serious studies of the many different techniques that have been developed to process two-dimensional images. Many of the methods presented here are necessary precursors to the development of recognition systems. Image sampling, intensification, restoration, Fourier transformations, and the practical details of edge processing and segmentation are all considered in detail. All of which are essential knowledge for anyone interested in developing practical computer vision system.

7. Finally, the journal *Pattern Recognition* (Call Number Q327.P36) is published quarterly and is ubiquitous in libraries around the world. Every issue is filled with new algorithms and new ideas that can quickly overload the most dedicated aficionado of this field.

4.4. DISCUSSION AND CONCLUSION

My review of theories of form recognition has covered a wide range of different topics. Nevertheless, it must of practical necessity be incomplete. The literature in this field is enormous and the samples presented here are but a very few of the many contributions that have been made to this research enterprise. From a certain point of view what is true for a review like this one is also true of the goal of the field itself. Just as there is too much in the libraries and journals to be processed within the confines of one book's covers, there is also much too much information in even a relatively simple stimulus for even the best of our modern computers to fully process in a reasonable time. To complicate the problem even further, it is clear that human form recognition theories are going to have to eventually depend on the availability of "knowledge" to supplement the simple geometric analyses—the aspect of the problem that dominates all of the models we have discussed. A few theoreticians have realized the enormity of the task set for themselves by attempting to simulate the intelligence of the human recognizer. Again it is Bremermann (1971) who summed up what may be the main difficulty when he asserted:

> The difficulties in pattern recognition, quite generally, are combinatorial. Almost horrendously large numbers of possible configurations, possible states, etc., are encountered. The basic problems to be solved are *quantitative*; how to reduce the amount of data processing involved, how to find shortcuts through the chaotic maze of possible states. These difficulties are not solved by most of the qualitative "theories" that appear in the literature. Nor will they be solved by merely creating general, *formal languages* for pattern recognition. (pp. 31–32)

On the other hand, it is also important to note that the task of recognizing forms can be accomplished. We humans are walking existence proofs that powerful vision systems capable of recognizing forms are not only possible but have a probability of "1" of realization. In spite of this "existence proof," there is a broad consensus that we currently have no insight into how this process is accomplished within our brains. It would be nice if we could optimistically assume this was only a temporary state of affairs and that, given enough time and scientific breakthroughs, it could be overcome. However, a complicating factor, to which I have alluded many times in this book, is that not only do we not now know, but it is reasonable to argue that we *cannot know* the answers to many of the questions that are being asked.

It is important to appreciate that even if one takes an optimistic view of how far we have come in satisfying the compelling practical need for artificially intelligent *form*, *pattern*, *object*, or *shape* recognition systems, these engineering successes are not tantamount to understanding how people perceive. Clearly the engineers have gone off in directions that are no longer imitative of human perception. Their techniques are dependent on and constrained by the properties of computers and image capturing equipment. In those situations in which they do approximate human vision, it is clear that they are usually based on quite different rules and algorithms than are likely to be used in the human brain. The behavior may be analogous, but the underlying principles are probably quite different. A computer pattern recognition system typically makes numerical measurements of properties, features, or distances and these measurements are formed into a vector. These numerical values are then compared with other vectors accumulated from previous measurements for a match and the closest match is de facto recognition. A good example of this strategy can be found in some modern face recognition systems that measure distances between many possible pairs of landmarks to form the vector and then compare that set of measurements with a library of prestored "face vectors."

It seems highly unlikely that humans carry out face recognition by a process of accumulating specific measurements and then comparing them with a library of possible alternatives. One of the strongest pieces of evidence that this is not the way humans operate is the multiplicity of ways in which the recognition can be made; specific measurements just don't seem to be needed.

Therefore, many of the theories that are considered in this chapter, however interesting, may be based on assumptions and techniques that are motivated by convenience and practical computability rather than by the psychobiological realities of the brain's actual organization.

A brief review of some of the universal features of these theories may help to make this point. In the last half century a new neuroscientific metaphor has gradually replaced those of previous centuries. Based on novel developments in neurophysiology and computer science, the idea of a neural net has become the prototypical contemporary model. With some exceptions (to be mentioned shortly) the standard model is of a deterministic system of largely regular and discrete components interconnected by relatively local links. The line of intellectual development of neural net models can be traced from McCulloch and Pitts (1943) through Selfridge (1958) to today's PDP (Parallel Distributed Processing) models. Even newer theories incorporate subtly, but distinctly, different ideas, namely the introduction of stochastic processes, very far reaching interconnections, and perhaps even more fundamentally, an appreciation of the vast number of neurons that would be required to do something useful like recognize a form. This has led to the introduction of ideas from statistical mechanics that were originally developed to describe the cooling of a glass or the distribution of velocities of gas molecules in a tank without exhaustive enumeration of the behavior of individual particles. It also led to the ideas that were, it can be argued, not analogizing discrete neural nets per se but, rather, conceptually continuous surfaces whose behavior is guided by the need to achieve distributed energy equilibrium states. This is a fundamentally new and very attractive conceptualization of a model of organic form recognition that has intrinsic global coding capabilities.

If we examine the fundamental assumptions of this new approach, it does appear that such a scheme is based on principles that are biologically more realistic than the computationally tractable, discrete neural net models. The one real instantiation of such a system, of course, is the organic brain, the exact details of which are probably forever beyond simulation, imitation, and analysis because of the realized potential for a combinatorial explosion and the "apparent randomness" that bedevils all cellular neurophysiological studies of the nervous system. Nevertheless, the key ideas of randomness, extreme numerousness, universal interconnectivity, and ultimately an approximation to continuity may have more to offer than today's coarse models of computationally tractable, locally interacting, modest size, discrete neural networks in the continuing search for the underlying principles of neural processing.

The logical conclusion toward which this discussion has been proceeding approaches Hofstadter's (1985) idea of "statistically emergent mentality" as an alternative to the "Boolean dream" (p. 654) of the conventional neural network. The problem with the "emergence" metaphor is exactly the one just highlighted; it was, is, and probably will always be impossible to carry out a simulation that would allow us to examine the details of this emergence. Thus, form recognition theorists are caught between the horns of a dilemma. Should they continue to exercise simplistic theoretical models that many agree are not likely to be psychobiologically realistic? Or, to the contrary, should they accept the fact that the best of these theories is only a distant metaphor and they would be better advised to return to the descriptive, molar, emergent (i.e., behavioral) approach that preceded this 20th century burst of theoretical activity?

In conclusion, it is important to keep in mind that the emergence of global properties from the statistical tendencies of the components of a complex system is not a supernatural development. It is more likely to be the natural outcome of concatenation of a sufficient number of units. There is nothing in this concept to deny the fact the global behavior of a complex system is implicit in the nature of the components. The fact that it may be, for practical combinatorial reasons impossible to understand or simulate this emergence does not detract from the fact it may be a more accurate conceptualization of the fundamental basis of the logic that governs our minds and our behavior.

5

Summary and Conclusions

5.1. INTRODUCTION

The previous chapters reviewed several aspects of the many problems faced by psychologists when they attempt to understand form recognition. Proposed methods for internally representing stimulus images have been considered; a sample of the psychophysical literature that is relevant to the problem has been reviewed; and the main alternative theories of the process have been explored. Throughout this discussion, I have emphasized how the technical, empirical, theoretical, and even conceptual topics that were raised speak to the problems faced when we try to understand how the powerful recognition capabilities of the human visual system are carried out.

It is now time to summarize the material to see if a coherent story, if not an explanatory theory, can be extracted from what has so far been discussed. Coherency, in this case does not, I must remind my readers, mean completeness. Throughout this book, I have repeatedly pointed out that some of the easiest questions to ask may be impossible to answer for both practical and fundamental reasons. Therefore, nothing in this concluding chapter should be considered to be final: The conclusions drawn are, at best, tentative and incomplete conjectures. What I do hope to do is present one psychologist's view of where we are and what seems to be the most compelling current interpretation of the data that have been uncovered and the theories that have been invoked in the study of form recognition.

Several main points are made in this concluding chapter.

- A descriptive behaviorism, rather than a reductive mentalism, is the best possible approach to studying form recognition.
- Such a modern revitalized behaviorism does not exclude perception as a legitimate topic of research as long as one adheres to certain constraints in the interpretation of empirical findings.
- We must accept the fact that some questions cannot be answered. Therefore, disputes between many of the alternative theories and hypotheses that have been presented as putative explanations of the form recognition may not be resolvable.
- Nevertheless, there is a point of view (hardly a formal theory) that does seem to emerge from the review of findings and explanations that is carried out in this book. A major goal of this chapter is to present that point of view.

Prior to drawing any conclusions, some comments are required concerning the behaviorist position that has been stressed throughout this book. There appear to be three fundamental questions that must be asked concerning the plausibility of this entire scientific enterprise. These questions are:

1. Can perceptual phenomena be reductively explained in the lower level terms of neurophysiology?
2. Can the apparently unified mental experiences be analyzed into cognitive modules?
3. Are the underlying processes and mechanisms of any perceptual experiences, including form recognition, accessible to empirical research?

Throughout this work, I have repeatedly alluded to a particular set of answers to these three questions. The background and arguments for the answers are spelled out in detail in three earlier books (Uttal, 1998, 2000, and 2001) and I need not repeat them here. Suffice it to say that the answers to these three questions should be:

1. Because of the complexity of the nervous system (among other arguments, which all derive from this basic point) any attempt to understand mental activity in terms of the essential level at which it arises (the pattern of interconnections between vast number of neurons) is futile.
2. Because the assumptions that are necessary for dividing up cognitive processes into mental modules are so untenable, any hopes of analyzing any mental activity into subcomponents is futile.
3. Because of the many intervening processing stages between reports and the underlying logical activity, intrapersonal perceptual activity is inaccessible.

If these three fundamental answers are correct, then what are we left with? The answer to this question is a revitalized and purified kind of psychophysical behaviorism stripped of some of its antique postulates and modified by the addition of several new fundamental rules and properties. This revitalized behaviorism is characterized by the following properties.[1] It must be:

• *Psychophysical:* Classical psychophysics has provided us with an excellent model of a scientific psychology. In it, stimuli and responses are anchored to physical dimensions and parameters and response modes are kept as simple as possible. Psychophysics has been enormously effective because it has developed a system of standardized procedures (e.g., the method of limits, forced choice procedures, signal detection theory, etc.) that helped to avoid or, at least, to understand some of the biases that could creep into interpretations of empirical findings. In this manner it is possible to characterize the transformations between stimuli and responses and to determine which attributes of a stimulus are salient; that is, which have effects and which do not. We can also measure the transformations that characterize the relationships between stimulus and response relationships. Beyond that, I argue, psychology is on treacherous grounds.

• *Mathematically and behaviorally descriptive:* Inasmuch as reductive explanations are prohibited by epistemological concerns, we must appreciate that all theories and models can, at best, only describe the behavior of a complex system of as great complexity as the brain. The best way to accomplish this description is by the use of mathematics with its tight rules and logic. However, all mathematical theories (including computational and neural net versions) are in fundamental principle equally incapable of determining the underlying mechanisms that account for the observed behavior—as is behavior itself. Leaps of inference from behavioral data to reductive explanation, no matter how ingenious, cannot be validated. Goodness of fit of a mathematical model with empirical observations, likewise, does not justify reductive conclusions. In short, both mathematics and behavior are *neutral* concerning the specific nature of underlying mechanisms.

• *Neuronally Nonreductive:* Because the brain is a vast matrix of many neurons multiply and idiosyncratically interconnected; because the organization of this neuronal matrix is the ultimate psychoneural equivalent of mental activity; and because complexity theorists have taught us about the intractability of NP-complete problems (of which the brain is likely to represent a valid example) the hope of reductively explaining any aspect of the mind (e.g., form recognition) by a neural model cannot be fulfilled. This does

---

[1]This list of the desirable properties of a revitalized behaviors is presented in a highly reduced form. Fuller discussions of each point are presented in Chapter 4 of my earlier work (Uttal, 2000).

not mean that neural nets cannot be made to simulate some aspects of cognitive processes, but instead, that such a simulation cannot validate the separable neurophysiological assumptions of a mathematical model.

• *Experimental*: No science can be pursued in the absence of a regular, continual, and rule-constrained grappling with nature or, more specifically, the kind of nature with which that science is concerned. Ideas, speculations, hypotheses, and theories must be tested and the major means of doing so for scientific psychology is controlled experimentation. This does not mean that all observations are unequivocal nor that all questions can be answered by laboratory or naturalistic methods of investigation. Nevertheless, like democracy, this is the best we have.

• *Molar*: Because of the epistemological limits on reduction to either neurons or cognitive modules, the main approach of any scientific psychology should be a molar one. Of course, in the peripheral world of sensory and motor functions, some low-level analyses are possible. However, when it comes to higher level cognitive processes, a holistic, unified approach is the proper one.

• *Empiricist$_1$ and Nativist*: Throughout the history of behaviorism, one of the heaviest and least sustainable intellectual burdens it carried was the overwhelming emphasis on the learning (Empiricism$_1$) as opposed to the innate—Nativist—determinants of behavior. Clearly, modern developments in genetics make it clear that the nature–nurture issue is far more complicated than any simplistic empiricist$_1$ theories would suggest. The appropriate resolution of this age old controversy has to be an eclectic one in which both factors are acknowledged to be important in the determination of behavior.

• *Empiricist$_2$ and Rationalist*: The debate between champions of direct, stimulus determined behavior (Empiricist$_2$) and those who believe it is mediated by active processes in the organism has also bedeviled traditional behaviorist approaches. This debate was also exacerbated by humanistic ideals of "free will." There is sufficient evidence of nonveridical processing in the visual system resulting in distortions and misinterpretations of the incident stimulus pattern to support the hypothesis of an active, mediated cognitive system. However, although I may be personally convinced that both direct and mediated factors must be at work, I am convinced that this question cannot be resolved. My doubts are based on the assumption that there is no way to determine the underlying mechanisms from the psychophysical reports. In other words, it is possible, perhaps even likely, that an ultra complex "direct" system could produce responses that are indistinguishable from the most complex, mediated behavior. Indeed, this issue is the prototypical example of the fragility of any attempt to "explain" underlying mechanisms from external observations. What is clear is that, whether direct or mediated, the organism plays a powerful dynamic and transformational role in determining what is perceived.

- *Antipragmatic*: Throughout the history of American psychology in particular, from the pragmatism of Pierce and James to the therapeutically and humanistically oriented modern applied psychologies, practical values have dominated much too much of our science. This has happened to the detriment of psychology as science rather than as a putative contributor to the "well being" of society and of the individual. It is virtually impossible to argue against such noble practical goals, but all too often psychologists have substituted criteria of "social value" for scientific objectivity and the quest for truth and basic understanding. I propose to leave to the practitioners among us, the therapeutic functions. In return, I ask them to leave to scientific psychology the quest to achieving long-term goals of understanding and knowledge for their own sakes. The applied mentalists who, for one reason or another, choose to defend both accessibility and cognitive reductionism are welcome to proceed, but in the final analysis, any success psychotherapy is able to demonstrate is more likely to be attributable to inspired intuition or the special empathy enjoyed by certain gifted individuals than to the results of rigorous scientific investigation.[2] Theories of the nature of psychobiological nature should remain unpolluted by social needs or trends but, to the contrary, be based on an objective and independent evaluation of natural observations by unbiased observers.

Given this point of view, what kind of questions can be asked for which there is a reasonable chance of finding answers. On page 122 I described three kinds of questions that can be asked: the technical ones, the reductive ones, and the descriptive ones. These questions can be generally characterized by the following three prototypical question classes:

1. How do we technically handle the measurement and representation of stimuli and responses.
2. What are the internal physiological or cognitive processing mechanisms that account for the observable behavior?
3. What variables of the physical stimulus affect form recognition?

And

What is the functional (i.e., transformational) relationship between the parameters of the stimulus and the parameters of the response?

As expressed there, only 1 and 3 are, from the behaviorist point of view, answerable. The point being made here is, in general, that many of the questions asked by cognitive and neuroscientifically oriented psychologists

---

[2]See Dawes (1994) for a richer and fuller treatment of this assertion.

of Class 2 are, for reasons of fundamental principle, unanswerable. If this is correct, psychologists must accept this constraints on our science and limit our efforts to answering those questions that are tractable. This boils down to essentially limiting the science to questions of Class 3, supported by those of Class 1. I believe that such an acceptance also supports the principle that the guiding philosophy of scientific psychology should be some form of behaviorism.

In the remainder of this chapter, I have two goals. First, I want to list without further citation or argument what I believe are the universal metaprinciples and emerging general principles of an achievable form recognition science. Finally, I discuss what seems to be a plausible interpretation of the empirical data and theoretical models that have been discussed throughout this book.

5.2. EMERGING PRINCIPLES OF FORM RECOGNITION

This section is composed of two parts. The first is a statement of two overarching metaprinciples that have guided my thinking about the study of psychology for many years. The second part is a collection of less universal principles and conclusions that have emerged in the course of the research carried out on the specific topic of this book—form recognition.

5.2.1. Some Metaprinciples Concerning the Ontology and Epistemology of Scientific Psychology[3]

Any compendium of emerging principles must be prefaced by certain general metaprinciples concerning the nature of a scientific psychology. Each of these is a statement of a fundamental assumption on which all subsequent logic and argument is based. I have made these explicit in each of my recent books and repeat them here for emphasis and to avoid an all-too-likely misinterpretation of the overall argument made in this book.[4]

1. *Psychoneural Equivalence*: It is necessary, I have discovered, to repeatedly remind my readers that the denial of the accessibility of mind and of the reducibility of cognitive processes to neural mechanisms—for practical reasons—is not a rejection of the fundamental *ontological* premise of scientific

---

[3]A fuller statement of these and related principles can be found on pages 182–184 of Uttal (2000).

[4]Specifically, it is necessary to present these metaprinciples to avoid the misinterpretation that, in some obscure way, my view embodies or supports some cryptodualism. It does not, and my basic ontology remains materialist, physicalist, and monist.

psychology. That premise, which I have elevated to the status of a meta-principle, asserts that mental activity of all kinds is totally attributable to and accounted for by the interactions and activity of the vast array of neurons that make up our nervous system, in general, and our brains, in particular. To assume otherwise is to push psychology out of the family of natural sciences. This is a statement of a monistic ontology or of an identity theory that does not accept multiple kinds of reality.

2. *The Inaccessibility and Irreducibility of Mental Processes*: Given the ontological statement of psychoneural equivalence, one must go beyond that foundation ontological premise to accept certain epistemological constraints within which psychological science must operate. Given that mental processes are inaccessible and irreducible, we must accept the fact that reductionist explanations can never be achieved. The important point here is that this is a practical matter, a limit on our ability to obtain knowledge about something that is undeniably real. That is, this second metaprinciple does not deny the reality or existence of either mind or brain. What these constraints do assert is that it is impossible to build valid bridges of understanding between the two domains (structure and function) of measurement. The major reason for this limit on our science is the nonlinear complexity and numerousness of the components of the nervous system. The brain, in other words, has all of the properties that suggest it is classifiable as an intractable NP-Complete problem in the language of mathematics.

5.2.2. Emerging Principles of Form Recognition

Now that my ontological and epistemological premises have been stated, I can summarize this book by listing, without further argument or empirical data, the principles of form recognition that are evidenced in the discussion of the previous chapters.

1. Perception was largely ignored as a research topic during the classic period of behaviorism because it was assumed that mental processes could not be assayed.

2. A modern view suggests that if the research domain is constrained to questions of the efficacy of stimulus parameters and the transformations between stimuli and responses, progress can be made in the study of perception of all kinds.

3. Despite repeated calls to the contrary, contemporary cognitive mentalist perception theory still adopts reductive goals that are fundamentally impossible to achieve.

4. The motivating forces and metaphors driving contemporary reductive theory in form recognition are computers, neurophysiology, and the absence of a good mathematics for representing configurational properties.

5. The reductive explanatory assumptions of a theory can and must be separated from the descriptive mathematical ones.

6. All mathematical descriptions are neutral with regard to underlying mechanisms.

7. All representation methods so far proposed are domain limited. That is, they are suitable only for a limited universe of forms. They do not generalize very well to visual stimuli types other than those for which they were specifically designed.

8. Although mathematical and computational convenience is a desirable step in the development of methods to represent or encode forms within a theory, nothing is known about the way that forms are actually represented in the higher reaches of the nervous system.

9. For that matter, there is still a general paucity of information about the rules, logic, and methods by which any cognitive process is carried out by the nervous system.

10. The choice of a representation system of stimulus forms for a computer model is intended to reduce the computational load. There is no a priori reason for choosing one over another.

11. Although many different types of representation have been proposed, many turn out to be mathematical duals of each other and, thus, do not represent distinctly different methods. Sometimes the particular application generates a specialized vocabulary and, by so doing, obscures the actual identity of superficially different methods.

12. Methods of generating forms that depend on random processes often do so at the cost of unexpectedly and uncontrollably producing stimulus forms that have some particular saliency that can defeat the purpose of an experiment.

13. The empirical data obtained from an enormous base of research on form and shape perception is heavily polluted by a priori ideas and theories. The preliminary selection of the type of stimulus to be used in any experiment can produce results to support almost any point of view or plausible theory.

14. Much of what psychologists do in their study of form recognition is displacement activity rather than attacks on the key problems.

15. Many definitional difficulties, usually ignored in the design of experiments, make it difficult to answer questions concerning the form recognition process. For example, even such well-used parameters characterized by the words *global* or *local* are inadequately defined by their proponents. Such terms as *features* are so idiosyncratically defined that it is impossible to compare studies of what are often very closely related phenomena.

16. Mathematical procedures that are guaranteed to produce fictional components from wholes (e.g., Fourier analysis) are sometimes uncriti-

cally extrapolated to represent reductive models of the underlying neurophysiology.

17. Disagreements between extreme or dichotomous theoretical positions are usually resolved by compromises and an emerging appreciation that extreme positions may only represent the ends of a continuous dimension.

18. It is highly unlikely that human form recognition is guided by a single method or strategy. The extreme adaptability of the visual process suggests that it may be composed of a constellation of many different methods that are selectively called into play depending on the task at hand.

19. All data obtained in psychophysical experiments are neutral with regard to the underlying mechanisms.

20. Cognitive penetration—an umbrella term for a host of different high level mental processes that influence perceptual responses—also obscures and obfuscates any attempt to infer underlying processes from behavioral observations.

21. The semantic and symbolic aspects of a stimulus pattern may be as effective or more effective in determining the perceptual response than the geometrical or other physical aspects of a stimulus.

22. The human visual system is extremely powerful in dealing with variations. That is, it generalizes in effective ways from one stimulus to another.

23. The human visual system is exquisitely sensitive to the holistic properties of a stimulus, demonstrated by its ability to process such challenging stimuli as faces or symmetrical forms.

24. There is no distinction between a sensory and a perceptual experience. Both are enormously complicated and the simplest "sensation" must invoke processes as complicated as those involved in the most complex perception.

25. Four basic psychophysical questions repeatedly arise in the study of form recognition: Are parts or wholes precedent? Is recognition based on comparison or construction? What role does learning play? What is the role of context? Questions of this type, dealing with the nature of the underlying processes may be unanswerable. Top-down approaches cannot work because of the inaccessibility of the processes. Bottom-up approaches may not work because of the complexity and numerousness of the neural components involved in even the simplest cognitive action.

26. The selection of a particular response may be an irrelevant part of the recognition process. The responses may be necessary to measure the newly transformed state of the system resulting from the interaction of the stimulus and the organization of the system as an indicator of what happened, but it may not be a property of the recognition process per se. In other words, recognition without overt behavior is certainly possible.

27. The learning of response categories may also be a distinguishable part of the recognition process. Although it is clear that prior experience can modulate the recognition process, "learning" may only establish that state of the system and also not be a part of the recognition process per se.

28. Spatial and temporal relationships, and even semantic context, appear to play much more prominent roles in form recognition and visual perception than was previously believed.

29. Many mathematical theorems argue that the challenge introduced by problems such as form recognition are insurmountable. NP-complete proofs and the refutation of quest for a Holy Grail for search algorithms suggest intractability of the form recognition problem and the impossibility of any kind of a reductive theory.

30. All theories of form recognition, regardless of how well they fit the obtained data of an experiment, are neutral with regard to underlying mechanisms.

31. Most current theories of form recognition are based on some kind of feature analysis. However, this approach seems to be an artifice arising from the fact that we do not have a good method of formally handling the global attributes of a form.

32. Form recognition by an exhaustive comparison of an input stimulus with a set of templates seems to be a profoundly flawed method from several points of view. However, many, if not most, modern methods are implicitly based on such an organizing concept.

33. In the last half century, there has been a progressive evolution of form recognition theories based on the concept of a neural network. The idea of a parallel processing network, in which Hebbian synapses have played a central role, has evolved into a stochastic, energy minimization approach.

34. Because of the enormous number of neurons involved in any cognitive process, critics like Bremmerman (1971) and Dreyfus (1972, 1992) have argued that artificial intelligence, of a level comparable to that of human intelligence and including form recognition, is unobtainable.

35. Few theories of form recognition are adequately sensitive to variations in position, size, or rotation in the way the human is. Therefore, many such theories have preprocessors to standardize or normalize an image prior to its being presented to the recognition module. These preprocessors are often misunderstood to be integral parts of the recognition process itself in psychobiological theories.

36. It is important to appreciate that no theory is likely to be universally correct. One conclusion to be drawn from the psychophysical data is that people use many different strategies and that, therefore, there may be many answers to the single question: How do we see forms?

37. Although it may have had it its original roots in the heuristic of a biological neural net, modern neurocomputing in engineering has moved far beyond this original impetus. Nowadays, the constraints on engineered systems are those of the hardware and software technologies and not of the psychobiology of the nervous system.

38. In any event, the idea of a computer-like form recognition process in the organic nervous system may be fundamentally incorrect. Form recognition, like all other cognitive processes, may be an emergent process of a complex matrix of neurons that follow completely different rules than the Boolean ones used by computers. Most current theories depend on the accumulation of metric measurements and deterministic evaluations of them. Humans are more likely to see by the interpretation of unscaled relationships.

39. The newest developments—stochastic properties and energy minimization—seem to be closely approximate organic brain processes. As such, they provide a more realistic interpretation of how our brains work.

These, then, are what I consider to be among the most important principles and metaprinciples emerging from this review of the science of form recognition. The next section describes a conceptual theory based on this review.

5.3. SOME CONCLUDING THOUGHTS ON THE NATURE OF FORM RECOGNITION

This concluding section opens with an apology and a caveat. The apology is that I am about to do that which I have argued that a behaviorist should not do: speculate about internal workings of a cognitive system. The caveat is that nothing that is said here should be taken as a formal proposal of a theory of form recognition.

What is clear is that we are dealing with a system of enormous complexity, involving vast numbers of neurons, and operating by rules of representation and interaction that we know virtually nothing about. There are, however, certain hints suggesting some things about how the brain might be organized. These suggestions, I repeat, are not to be interpreted as the components of a formal theory, merely as another plausible way to look at the way the brain may be organized. I repeat, there are no "killer arguments" that can either confirm or reject any of them.

Some of these conjectures are behavioral and others are neurophysiological or anatomical.

1. Dimensional isomorphism is counterindicated in many aspects of perceptual processing. For example, the experience of "greenness" must be rep-

resented by some temporal or spatial aspect of the responses of neurons, not by their color. Therefore, it is likely that many other kinds of cognitive processing may also be encoded in a symbolic rather than a congruent manner.

2. The human observer is exceedingly sensitive to the global aspects of a stimulus in many visual tasks. Notwithstanding that some experiments also show a sensitivity to the parts or components of a stimulus, the general tone of psychophysical research suggests that the Gestalt psychologists were more right than not about the overall configuration of stimulus form being the essential factor in visual perception.

3. Because of the enormous amount of evidence showing nonveridicality between stimuli and responses, it is, therefore, suggested that high-level cognition has a profound impact on our percepts. This strongly argues that our perceptual experience as well as other more obvious cognitive processes are mediated by logical and interpretive processes that go far beyond the basic physical parameters or geometry of the stimulus scene. Such a disconnect further complicates simple deterministic models of visual perception.

4. Because the assumptions necessary to justify the parsing of cognitive process into subcomponents are so unrealistic, it is likely that not only can we not do so, but that the whole "block diagram" approach of contemporary cognitive mentalism is untenable.

5. The ease with which well-designed experiments can be made to provide empirical support for almost any plausible theory suggests there is no single brain strategy or mechanism to explain a cognitive process. Rather, the "mind" has available to it a wide variety of cognitive and neural tools that can be applied in different situations. Therefore, it is likely that even if we could tease out some neural basis of some cognitive function, it would not be unique. There may be as many ways to solve a perceptual problem and, therefore, as many "mechanisms" as there are ways to "skin a cat."

6. Because of the logistical problems with any kind of a template theory in which an incoming stimulus is exhaustively compared with a library of prototypes, it is extremely unlikely that such a mechanism operates in the nervous system. As most form recognition models are based on such a process, they are collectively inaccurate conjectures concerning the nature of the process.

7. Given the low probability of a template matching process, some kind of a *constructionist* or *state seeking* process seems to be the main alternative. We can speculate that a stimulus operates on the heavily interconnected matrix of the nervous system to alter its current state. The new state is itself the "solution" to the problem. A response may be associated with that state by prior learning and its transformation of the initial state of the network. However, the learning and the response selection processes, although necessary pre-

cursors or required to indicate what has happened to an external observer, are actually not critical to our understanding of the form recognition process. An excellent theoretical expression of this "state seeking" conjecture can be found in the work of Fukushima and Miyake (1978).

8. Although it is impossible to definitively determine what metaphor or analogy is closest to what is going on in the nervous system, the ideas of simulated annealing and the Boltzmann machine have a certain charm about them. They are both based on the global reactivity of an energy surface whose behavior is modulated by stochastic (i.e., random) processes. In both of these models, the idea of energy minimization over a surface or throughout a volume is central. Although the thermal forces they invoke as a metaphor obviously cannot exist in the brain, the idea that "energy" or "activity" seeks a stable state of either energy or information is extremely attractive.

9. All of the cognitive and perceptual processes so far discussed can be assumed to operate on some kind of a statistical basis. That is, it is the "central tendency" of the activity of a vast array of neurons that determines the response of the system, not the idiosyncratic activity of individual neurons. That myth (the single neuron hypothesis) was the result of vast amounts of data forthcoming from microelectrodes concerning the activity of single neurons and the confusion of tractable peripheral transmission codes with the intractable neural mechanisms of higher level cognition.

In conclusion, however interesting or even fun these conjectures might be, the goal of a neuroreductive explanation of cognitive processes (of which form recognition is an outstanding exemplar) is most likely hopeless. There is an increasingly large corpus of mathematical proofs suggesting that many of the questions we would like to answer about the relation of our brains and our mental activity are formally intractable. NP-Completeness, the refutation of the Holy Grail hypothesis, thermodynamics, automata theory, and Chaos theory all point in the direction of a substantial "in principle" barrier to bridge building between these two domains. A strictly scientific psychology of the future, therefore, must be some form of a revitalized behaviorism. If this point of view is correct, then it is hard to justify the predominantly reductive orientation of so much of contemporary cognitive theory. Calls for "progress" of any kind and at any intellectual cost hardly do justice to a scientific analysis to some of the most profound questions of human existence.

References

Abdi, H., Valentin, D., Edelman, B., & O'Toole, A. J. (1995). More about the difference between men and women: Evidence from linear neural networks and the principle component approach. *Perception, 24*, 539–562.

Adelson, E. H. (1993). Perceptual organization and the judgment of brightness. *Science, 262*, 2042–2044.

Alpern, M. (1969). Movements of the eyes. In H. Davson (Ed.), *The eye. Vol. 3: Muscular mechanisms* (2nd ed., pp. 1–214). New York: Academic Press.

Ames, A. (1955). *An interpretive manual for the demonstrations in the psychology research center.* Princeton, NJ: Princeton University Press.

Anzai, Y. (1989). *Pattern recognition and machine learning.* Boston: Harcourt Brace Jovanovich.

Arnheim, R. (1974). *Art and visual perception: A psychology of the creative eye, the new version.* Berkeley: The University of California Press.

Arnheim, R. (1986a). The trouble with wholes and parts. *New Ideas in Psychology, 4*, 281–284.

Arnheim, R. (1986b). A reply to Hochberg and Perkins. *New Ideas in Psychology, 4*, 301–302.

Ashby, F. G. (2000). A stochastic version of General Recognition Theory. *Journal of Mathematical Psychology, 44*, 310–329.

Ashby, F. G., Prinzmetal, W., Ivry, R., & Maddox, W. T. (1996). A formal theory of feature binding in object perception. *Psychological Review, 103*, 165–192.

Ashby, F. G., & Townsend, J. T. (1986). Varieties of perceptual independence. *Psychological Review, 93*, 154–179.

Atchley, R. A., & Atchley, P. (1998). Hemispheric specialization in the detection of subjective objects. *Neuropsychologia, 36*, 1373–1386.

Attneave, F., & Arnoult, M. D. (1956). The quantitative study of shape and pattern recognition. *Psychological Bulletin, 53*, 452–471.

Attneave, F. (1972). Representation of visual space. In A. W. Melton & E. Martin (Eds.), *Coding processes in human memory.* Washington, DC: Winston.

Bargh, J. A. (1997). The automaticity of everyday life. In R. S. Wyler (Ed.), *Advances in social cognition.* (pp. 1–47). Mahwah, NJ: Lawrence Erlbaum Associates.

Bargh, J. A., & Chartrand, T. E. (1999). The unbearable automaticity of being. *American Psychologist, 54*, 462–479.

Barlow, H. B. (1978). The efficiency of detecting changes of density in random dot patterns. *Vision Research, 18*, 637–650.

Barlow, H. B. (1995). The neuron doctrine in perception. In M. S. Gazzaniga (Ed.), *The cognitive neurosciences*. Cambridge, MA: MIT Press.

Barr, A., & Feigenbaum, E. A. (Eds.). (1981). *The handbook of artificial intelligence: Vol. 1*. Stanford, CA: Heuristech Press.

Bartlett, F. C. (1932). *Remembering: A study in experimental and social psychology*. Cambridge, England: Cambridge University Press.

Ben-Av, M. B., & Sagi, D. (1995). Perceptual grouping by similarity and proximity: Experimental results can be predicted by intensity autocorrelations. *Vision Research, 35*, 853–866.

Bennett, B. M., & Hoffman, D. D. (1987). Shape decompositions for visual recognition: The role of transversality. In W. Richards (Ed.), *Image understanding* (pp. 215–256). Stanford, CT: Aldex.

Bigun, J., Duc, B., Smeraldi, F., Fischer, S., & Makarov, A. (1998). Multi-modal person authentication. In H. Wechsler, P. J. Phillips, V. Bruce, F. F. Soulie, & T. S. Huang (Eds.), *Face recognition: From theory to applications*. Berlin: Springer.

Binder, K., & Heerman, D. W. (1988). *Monte Carlo simulation in statistical mechanics*. Berlin: Springer-Verlag.

Binford, T. O. (1971). Visual perception by a computer. Paper presented at the *Proceedings of the IEEE Conference on Systems and Controls*, Miami, FL.

Blesser, B., Shillman, R., Cox, C., Kuklinski, T., Ventura, J., & Eden, M. (1973). Character recognition based on phenomenological attributes. *Visible Language, 7*, 209–223.

Blum, H. (1967). A transformation for extracting new descriptors of shape. In W. Walthem-Dunn (Ed.), *Models for the perception of speech and visual form* (pp. 362–380). Cambridge, MA: MIT Press.

Bonato, F., & Gilchrist, A. L. (1999). Perceived area and the luminosity threshold. *Perception and Psychophysics, 61*, 786–797.

Bookstein, F. L. (1978). *The measurement of biological shape and shape change*. Berlin: Springer-Verlag.

Bookstein, F. L. (1987). Describing a craniofacial anomaly: Fine elements and the biometrics of landmark locations. *American Journal of Physical Anthropology, 74*, 495–509.

Bookstein, F. L. (1989). Principle warps: Thin-plate splines and the decomposition of deformations. *IEEE Transactions on Pattern Analysis and Machine Intelligence, 11*, 567–585.

Bookstein, F. L. (1991). *Morphometric tools for landmark data: Geometry and biology*. Cambridge, England: Cambridge University Press.

Boring, E. G. (1942). *Sensation and perception in the history of experimental psychology*. New York: Appleton-Century.

Boring, E. G. (1950). *A history of experimental psychology*. New York: Appleton-Century-Crofts.

Braunstein, M. L., Hoffman, D., Shapiro, L. R., Andersen, G. J., & Bennett, B. M. (1986). Minimum points and views for the recovery of three-dimensional structure. In *Studies in the Cognitive Sciences* (No. 41). Irvine, CA: School of Social Sciences, University of California, Irvine.

Bradshaw, J. L., & Wallace, G. (1971). Models for processing and identification of faces. *Perception and Psychophysics, 9*, 443–448.

Bremermann, H. J. (1971). What mathematics can and cannot do for pattern recognition. In O.-J. Grusser & R. Klinke (Eds.), *Pattern recognition in biological and technical systems*. Heidelberg, Germany: Springer-Verlag.

Bremermann, H. J. (1977). Complexity and transcomputability. In R. Duncan & M. Weston-Smith (Eds.), *The encyclopedia of ignorance*. New York: Pocket Books.

Brindley, G. S. (1960). *Physiology of the retina and the visual pathway*. London: Edward Arnold.

Broadbent, D. E. (1958). *Perception and communication*. London, England: Pergamon Press.

Brown, D. R., & Owen, D. H. (1967). The metrics of visual form: Methodological dyspepsia. *Psychological Bulletin, 65*, 243–259.

Butler, D. L. (1991). Simple geometrical fractals. *Behavior Research Methods, Instruments and Computers, 23*, 160–165.

Caelli, T. M. (1977). Criticisms of the LTG/NP theory of perceptual psychology. *Cahiers de Psychologie, 20*, 197–204.

Caelli, T. M., Julesz, B., & Gilbert, E. (1978). On perceptual analyzers underlying visual texture discrimination: Part II. *Biological Cybernetics, 29*, 201–214.

Caelli, T., & Yuzyk, J. (1985). What is perceived when two images are combined? *Perception, 14*, 41–48.

Campbell, F. W., & Robson, J. G. (1968). An application of Fourier analysis to the visibility of gratings. *Journal of Physiology (London), 197*, 551–566.

Carpenter, G. A., & Grossberg, S. (1987). A massively parallel architecture for a self-organizing neural pattern recognition machine. *Computer Vision, Graphics, and Image Processing, 37*, 54–115.

Carpenter, G. A., Grossberg, S., & Mehanian, C. (1989). Invariant recognition of cluttered scenes by a self-organizing ART architecture: Cort-X boundary segmentation. *Neural Networks, 2*, 169–181.

Casti, J. L. (1996). Confronting science's logical limits. *Scientific American*(October), 102–105.

Cattell, J. M. (1886). The time taken by cerebral operation. *Mind, 11*, 220–242.

Chen, C. H., Pau, L. F., & Wang, P. S. P. (1993). *Handbook of computer recognition and computer vision.* Singapore: World Scientific.

Cherry, C. (1957). *On human communication.* New York: Wiley.

Coren, S., Ward, L. M., & Enns, J. T. (1999). *Sensation and perception.* Orlando, FL: Harcourt, Brace Jovanovich.

Cornsweet, T. N. (1970). *Visual perception.* New York: Academic Press.

Costen, N. P., Parker, D. M., & Craw, I. (1994). Spatial content and spatial quantization effects in recognition. *Perception, 23*, 129–146.

Cottrell, G. W., Dailey, M. N., Padgett, C., & Adolphs, R. (2001). Is all face processing holistic? The view from UCSD. In M. Wenger & J. Townsend (Eds.), *Computational, geometric, and process perspectives on facial cognition: Contexts and challenges.* Mahwah, NJ: Lawrence Erlbaum Associates.

Craw, I., Costen, N., Kato, T., & Akamatsu, S. (1999). How should we represent faces for automatic recognition? *IEEE Transactions on Pattern Analysis and Machine Intelligence, 21*, 725–736.

Culbertson, J. T. (1950). *Consciousness and behavior: A neural analysis of behavior and consciousness.* Dubuque, IA: Wm. C. Brown.

Cumming, G., & Friend, H. (1980). Perception at the blind spot and the tilt aftereffect. *Perception, 9*, 233–238.

Cutting, J. E., & Garvin, J. J. (1987). Fractal curves and complexity. *Perception and Psychophysics, 42*, 365–370.

Dawes, R. M. (1994). *House of cards: Psychology and psychotherapy built on myth.* New York: The Free Press.

De Valois, R. L., & De Valois, K. K. (1988). *Spatial vision.* New York: Oxford University Press.

Dennett, D. C. (1992). "Filling-in" versus finding out: A ubiquitous confusion in cognitive science. In H. L. Pick, P. Van den Broek, & D. C. Knill (Eds.), *Cognition: Conceptual and methodological issues.* Washington, DC: American Psychological Association.

Diamond, R., & Carey, S. (1986). Why faces are not special: An effect of expertise. *Journal of Experimental Psychology: General, 115*, 107–117.

Dodwell, P. C. (1970). *Visual pattern recognition.* New York: Holt, Rhinehart, and Winston.

Donnelly, N., & Davidoff, J. (1999). The mental representation of faces and houses: Issues concerning parts and wholes. *Visual Cognition, 6*, 319–343.

Dreyfus, H. L. (1972). *What computers can't do.* New York: Harper and Row.

Dreyfus, H. L. (1992). *What computers still can't do.* Cambridge, MA: MIT Press.

Duff, M. J. B. (1969). Pattern computation in pattern recognition. In S. Watanabe (Ed.), *Methodologies of pattern recognition* (pp. 133–140). New York: Academic Press.

Dürer, A. (1525). *Underweysung der Messung mit dem Zirckel un Richtscheyt, in Linien Ebnen und ganzen Corporen.* Nuremberg.

Ehrenfels, C. F. v. (1890). Uber Gestaltqualitaten *Vierteljahrsschrift fur wissenschaftliche Philosophie, 14,* 249–292.

Epstein, W. (1993). On seeing that thinking is separate and on thinking that seeing is the same. *Giornale Italiano di Psicologia, 20,* 731–748.

Eriksen, C. W., & Collins, J. F. (1967). Some temporal characteristics of visual pattern recognition. *Journal of Experimental Psychology, 74,* 476–484.

Evans, S. H. (1967). A brief statement of schema theory. *Psychonomic Science, 8,* 87–88.

Fahlman, S. E. (1979). *A system for representing and using real world knowledge.* Unpublished thesis, Carnegie-Mellon University, Pittsburgh PA.

Farah, M. J., Wilson, K. D., Drain, M., & Tanaka, J. N. (1998). What is special about face perception? *Psychological Review, 105,* 482–498.

Fiorentini, A., Maffei, L., & Sandini, G. (1983). The role of high spatial frequencies in face perception. *Perception, 12,* 195–201.

Fitts, P. M., & Leonard, J. A. (1957). *Stimulus correlates of visual pattern recognition: A probability approach.* Columbus: Ohio State University.

Fitts, P. M., Weinstein, M., Rappaport, M., Anderson, A., & Leonard, J. A. (1956). Stimulus correlates of visual pattern recognition: A probability approach. *Journal of Experimental Psychology, 51,* 1–11.

Fodor, J. (2000). *The mind doesn't work that way.* Cambridge, MA: MIT Press.

Forster, M. R. (1999, August). *Notice: No-free-lunches for anyone, Bayesians included.* Paper presented at the 11th International Conference of Logical, Methodology, and Philosophy of Science, Cracow, Poland.

Fourier, J. B. J. (1822/1878). *Theorie Analytique de la Chaleur.* Paris: F. Didot.

Fourier, J. B. J. (1878). *The analytical theory of heat (Trans. from the 1822 Edition).* Cambridge, England: Cambridge University Press.

Fukushima, K. (1981). *Cognitron: A self-organizing multilayered neural network model.* (Report No. 30). Japan Broadcasting Co. Tokyo.

Fukushima, K., & Miyake, S. (1978). A self-organizing neural network with a function of associative memory: Feedback-type Cognitron. *Biological Cybernetics, 21,* 201–208.

Fukushima, K., Miyake, S., & Ito, T. (1983). Neocognitron: A neural network for a mechanism of visual pattern recognition. *IEEE Transaction on System, Man, and Cybernetics, 13,* 826–834.

Gall, F. J., & Spurzheim, J. C. (1808). Recherches sur le system nerveaux en general, et sur celui cerveau en particulier. *Academie de Sciences, Paris, Memoires.*

Galton, F. (1879). Composite portraits, made by combining those of many different persons into a single resultant figure. *Journal of the Anthropological Institute, 8,* 132–144.

Garner, W. R. (1962). *Uncertainty and structure as psychological concepts.* New York: Wiley.

Garner, W. R. (1974). *The processing of information and structure.* Hillsdale, NJ: Lawrence Erlbaum Associates.

Garner, W. R., & Hake, H. W. (1951). The amount of information in absolute judgments. *Psychological Review, 58,* 446–459.

Gelb, A. (1929). Farbenkonstanz der sehfinge. *Handbuch der Normalen und Pathologischen Physiologie, 12,* 594–678.

Gerlernter, H., Hansen, J. R., & Gerberich, C. L. (1960). A FORTRAN compiled list processing language. *Journal of the ACM, 7,* 87–101.

Gemen, S., & Gemen, D. (1984). Stochastic relaxation, Gibbs distributions, and the Bayesian restoration of images. *IEEE Transactions on Pattern Analysis and Machine Intelligence, 6,* 721–742.

Gibson, J. J. (1961). Ecological optics. *Vision Research, 1,* 253–262.

Gibson, J. J. (1979). *The ecological approach to visual perception.* Boston: Houghton Mifflin.

Gilchrist, A. L. (1977). Perceived lightness depends on perceived spatial arrangement. *Science, 195*, 185–187.

Gilchrist, A. L. (1979). The perception of surface blacks and whites. *Scientific American, 240*, 112–124.

Gilchrist, A. L. (Ed.). (1994). *Lightness, brightness, and transparency.* Hillsdale, NJ: Lawrence Erlbaum Associates.

Gilchrist, A., Kossyfidia, C., Bonato, F., Agostini, T., Cataliotti, J., Li, X., Spehar, B., Annan, V., & Economou, E. (1999). An anchoring theory of lightness perception. *Psychological Review, 106*, 795–834.

Gilden, D. L., Schmuckler, M. A., & Clayton, K. (1993). The perception of natural contour. *Psychological Review, 100*, 460–478.

Ginsburg, A. P. (1978). *Visual information processing based on spatial filters constrained to biological data* (Tech. Rep. No. AMRL-TR-78-129). Wright Patterson AFB, Ohio: Aerospace Medical Research Laboratory.

Girvan, R. (1999). *The Mandelbrot Monk.* Available at http://www.users.zetnet.co.uk/rgirvan/udo.thm

Globus, G. G. (1992). Toward a noncomputational cognitive neuroscience. *Journal of Cognitive Neuroscience, 4*, 299–310.

Goethe, J. W. v. (1810/1971). *Goethe's color theory* (Matthaei, R., Trans.). New York: Van Nostrand.

Goldstein, E. B. (1998). *Sensation and perception.* Monterey, CA: Brooks Cole.

Gollwitzer, P. M. (1999). Implementation intentions. *American Psychologist, 54*, 493–503.

Gould, S. J. (2000). Deconstructing the "science wars" by reconstructing an old mold. *Science, 287*, 253–261.

Graham, C. H. (Ed.). (1965). *Vision and visual perception.* New York: Wiley.

Graham, N. V. S. (1989). *Visual Pattern Analyzers.* New York: Oxford University Press.

Green, R. T., & Courtis, M. C. (1966). Information theory and figure perception: The metaphor that failed. *Acta Psychologica, 25*, 12–36.

Gregory, R. L. (1993). Seeing and thinking. *Giornale Italiano di Psicologia, 20*, 749–770.

Grenander, U. (1993). *General pattern theory.* Oxford, England: Oxford University Press.

Grice, G. R., Canham, L., & Boroughs, J. M. (1983). Forest before trees? It depends where you look. *Perception and Psychophysics, 33*, 121–128.

Grimson, W. E. L. (1990). *Object recognition by computer: The role of geometric components.* Cambridge, MA: MIT Press.

Grossberg, S. (1970). Neural pattern discrimination. *Journal of Theoretical Biology, 27*, 291–337.

Grossberg, S. (1976). On the development of feature detectors in the visual cortex with applications to learning and reaction-diffusion systems. *Biological Cybernetics, 21*, 145–159.

Grossberg, S., & Mingolla, E. (1985). Neuronal dynamics of perceptual grouping: Textures, boundaries, and emergent segmentations. *Perception and Psychophysics, 38*, 141–171.

Gurnsey, R., Iordanova, M., & Grinberg, D. (1999). Detection and discrimination of subjective contours defined by offset gratings. *Perception and Psychophysics, 61*, 1256–1268.

Gutta, S., & Wechsler, H. (1998). Modular forensic architectures. In H. Wechsler, P. J. Phillips, V. Bruce, F. F. Soulie, & T. S. Huang (Eds.), *Face recognition: From theory to applications.* Berlin: Springer.

Hake, H. W., & Garner, W. R. (1951). The effect of presenting various numbers of discrete steps on scale reading accuracy. *Journal of Experimental Psychology, 42*, 358–366.

Halpern, S. D., Andrews, T. J., & Purves, D. (1999). Interindividual varaiation in human visual performance. *Journal of Cognitive Neuroscience, 11*, 521–534.

Hanson, N. R. (1958). *Patterns of discovery: An inquiry into the conceptual foundations of science.* Cambridge, England: Cambridge University Press.

Harary, F. (1972). *Graph theory.* Reading MA: Addison-Wesley.

Harmon, L. D. (1973). The identification of faces. *Scientific American, 27*, 71–82.

Harmon, L. D., & Julesz, B. (1973). Masking in visual recognition: Effects of two-dimensional filtered interference. *Science, 180,* 1194–1197.

Harris, J. R., Shaw, M. L., & Altom, M. J. (1985). Serial position curves for reaction time and accuracy in visual search: Tests of a model of overlapping processing. *Perception and Psychophysics, 38,* 178–187.

Hartley, R. V. L. (1928). Transmission of information. *Bell System Technical Journal, 7,* 535–563.

Harvey, L. O., Jr. (1986). Visual memory: What is remembered? In F. Klix & H. Hagendorf (Eds.), *Human memory and cognitive capabilities, mechanisms, and performances* (pp. 173–187). Amsterdam: Elsevier Science.

Hausdorf, F. (1919). Dimension und ausseres Mass. *Mathematische Annalen, 79,* 157–179.

Hayes, T., Morrone, C., & Burr, D. C. (1986). Recognition of positive and negative bandpass filtered images. *Perception, 15,* 595–602.

Hazeltine, R. E., Prinzmetal, W., & Elliott, K. (1997). If it's not there, where is it? Locating illusory conjunctions. *Journal of Experimental Psychology: Human Perception and Performance, 23,* 263–277.

Hebb, D. O. (1949). *The organization of behavior.* New York: Wiley.

Hecht, S., Shlaer, S., & Pirenne, M. H. (1942). Energy, quanta, and vision. *Journal of General Physiology, 25,* 819–840.

Heinemann, E. G. (1955). Simultaneous brightness induction as a function of inducing and testfield luminance. *Journal of Experimental Psychology, 50,* 89–96.

Helmholtz, H. v. (1866). *Handbuch der Physiologischen Optik.* Leipzig: Voss.

Hering, E. (1887). Uber die theorie des simultanene contrastes von Helmholtz. *Pflueger's Arkives fur die Gesamte Physiologie des Menschen und der Tiere, 41,* 1–29.

Hermann, L. (1870). Eine erscheinung des simultanen contrates. *Plueger's Archives Fur die Gesamte Physiologie des Menschen un der Tiere, 3,* 13–15.

Hertz, J., Krogh, A., & Palmer, R. G. (1991). *Introduction to the theory of neural computation.* Redwood City: CA: Addison-Wesley.

Hess, C., & Pretori, H. (1894). Messende untersachungen uber die gesetzmassigeit des simultanen Helligkeits-contrastes. *Albert von Graef's Archiv fur Klinische und Experimentelle Ophthalmologie, 40,* 1–24.

Hick, W. E. (1952). On the rate of gain of information. *Quarterly Journal of Experimental Psychology, 4,* 11–26.

Hinton, G. E., & Sejnowski, T. J. (1986). Learning and relearning in Boltzmann machines. In D. E. Rumelhart, J. L. McClelland, & T. P. R. Group (Eds.), *Parallel distributed processing: Explorations in the microstructure of cognition. Vol. 1. Foundations.* Cambridge MA: MIT Press.

Hochberg, J. (1981). Levels of perceptual organization. In M. Kubovy & J. R. Pomerantz (Eds.), *Perceptual organization* (pp. 255–278). Hillsdale, NJ: Lawrence Erlbaum Associates.

Hochberg, J. (1986). Parts and wholes: A response to Arnheim. *New Ideas in Psychology, 4,* 285–293.

Hochberg, J., & Hardy, D. (1960). Brightness and proximity factors in grouping. *Perceptual and Motor Skills, 10,* 22.

Hochberg, J., & McAlister, E. (1953). A quantitative approach to figural goodness. *Journal of Experimental Psychology, 46,* 361–364.

Hoffman, D. D. (2000). *Visual intelligence: How we create what we see.* New York: Norton.

Hoffman, D., & Richards, W. (1984). Parts of recognition. *Cognition, 18,* 65–96.

Hoffman, W. C. (1966). The Lie algebra of visual perception. *Journal of Mathematical Psychology, 3,* 65–98.

Hoffman, W. C. (1985). Geometric psychology generates the visual Gestalt. *Canadian Journal of Psychology, 39,* 491–528.

Hoffman, W. C. (1994). Conformal structures in perceptual psychology. *Spatial Vision, 8,* 19–31.

Hoffmann, J. (1995). *Visual object recognition: Handbook of perception and action. Vol. 1: Perception* (pp. 297–344). London: Academic Press.

Hofstadter, D. R. (1985). *Metamagical themas: Questing for the essence of mind and pattern.* New York: Basic Books.

Homa, D., Haver, B., & Schwartz, T. (1976). Perceptibility of schematic face stimuli: Evidence for a perceptual Gestalt. *Memory and Cognition, 4,* 176–185.

Hopfield, J. J. (1982). Neural networks and physical systems with emergent collective computational abilities. *Proceeding of the National Academy of Sciences, USA, 79,* 2554–2558.

Hubel, D. H., & Wiesel, T. N. (1959). Receptive fields of single neurons in the cat's striate cortex. *Journal of Physiology, 148,* 574–591.

Hubel, D. H., & Wiesel, T. N. (1962). Receptive fields, binocular interaction, and functional architecture in the cat's visual cortex. *Journal of Physiology, 160,* 106–154.

Hyman, R. (1953). Stimulus information as a determinant of reaction time. *Journal of Experimental Psychology, 45,* 423–432.

Istrail, S. (2000, May). *Statistical mechanics, three-dimensionality, and NP-completeness. I Universality of intractability for the partition function of the Ising Model across non-planar lattices.* Paper presented at the 31st ACM Annual Symposium on the Theory of Computing (STOC 2000), Portland, OR.

Ittelson, W. H. (1952). *The Ames demonstrations in perception: A guide to their construction and use.* Princeton, NJ: Princeton University Press.

Jacobson, L., & Wechsler, H. (1988). Joint spatial/spatial frequency representation. *Signal Processing, 14,* 37–68.

James, W. (1890). *The principles of psychology.* New York: Henry Holt.

Johansson, G. (1973). Visual perception of biological motion and a model for its analysis. *Perception and Psychophysics, 14,* 201–211.

Johnston, J. C., & Pashler, H. (1990). Close binding of identity and location in visual feature perception. *Journal of Experimental Psychology: Human Perception and Performance, 16,* 843–856.

Julesz, B. (1962). Visual pattern discrimination. *Institute of Radio Engineers Transactions on Information Theory, IT-8,* 84–92.

Julesz, B. (1981). Textons, the elements of texture perception and their interactions. *Nature, 290,* 91–97.

Julesz, B. (1975). Experiments in the visual perception of texture. *Scientific American, 234,* 34–43.

Julesz, B. (1978). Perceptual limits of texture discrimination and implications to figure-ground separation. In E. L. J. Leeuwenberg & H. F. J. M. Buffart (Eds.), *Formal theories of visual perception.* New York: Wiley.

Julesz, B. (1984). A brief outline of the Texton theory of human vision. *Trends in Neurosciences, 7,* 41–45.

Julesz, B. (1993). Illusory contours in early vision and beyond. *Giornale Italiano di Psicologia, 20,* 869–878.

Julesz, B., Gilbert, E. N., Shepp, L. A., & Frisch, H. L. (1973). Inability of humans to discriminate visual textures that agree in second order statistics-revised. *Perception, 2,* 391–405.

Kabrisky, M. (1966). *A proposed model for information processing in the human brain.* Urbana: University of Illinois Press.

Kandel, E. R., & Tauc, L. (1965). Heterosynaptic facilitation in neurons of the abdominal ganglion of Aplysia depilans. *Journal of Physiology, 81,* 1–27.

Kaniza, G. (1955). Margini quasi-percettivi in campi con stimolazione omogenea. *Rivisita di Psicologia, 49,* 7–30.

Kendall, D. G. (1989). A survey of the statistical theory of shape. *Statistical Science, 4,* 87–120.

Kimchi, R. (1992). Primacy of wholistic processing and global/local paradigm. A critical review. *Psychological Bulletin, 112,* 24–38.

Kinchla, R. A. (1974). Detecting target elements in a multi-element array: A confusability model. *Perception and Psychophysics, 15,* 410–419.

Kinchla, R. A., Solis-Macias, V., & Hoffman, J. (1983). Attention to different levels of structure in a visual image. *Perception and Psychophysics, 33,* 1–10.

Kirkpatrick, S., Gelatt, Jr., C. D., & Vecchi, M. P. (1983). Optimization by simulated annealing. *Science, 220,* 671–680.

Kirsch, I., & Lynn, S. J. (1999). Automaticity in child psychology. *American Psychologist, 54,* 504–515.

Klein, D. B. (1970). *A history of scientific psychology: Its origins and philosophical backgrounds.* New York: Basic Books.

Klemmer, E. T., & Frick, F. C. (1953). Assimilation of information from dot and matrix patterns. *Journal of Experimental Psychology, 45,* 15–19.

Klemmer, E. T., & Loftus, J. P. (1958). *Numerals, nonsense forms, and information* (AFCRC-TR-57-2): USAF Operational Applications Laboratory.

Koenderink, J. J. (1984). The structure of images. *Biological Cybernetics, 50,* 363–370.

Koenderink, J., & van Doorn, A. (1980). Photometric invariants related to solid shape. *Optica Acta, 7,* 981–996.

Koffka, K. (1935). *Principles of Gestalt psychology.* New York: Harcourt Brace.

Kohler, W. (1929). *Gestalt psychology.* New York: Liveright.

Kohonen, T., Oja, E., & Lehtio, P. (1981). Storage and processing of information in distributed associative memory systems. In H. Hinton & J. Anderson (Eds.), *Parallel models of associative memory* (pp. 105–144). Hillsdale, NJ: Lawrence Erlbaum Associates.

Kolers, P. (1970). The role of shape and geometry in picture recognition. In B. S. Lipkin & A. Rosenfeld (Eds.), *Picture processing and psychopictorics* (pp. 181–202). New York: Academic Press.

Konorski, J. (1967). *Integrative activity of the brain.* Chicago: University of Chicago Press.

Kovalevsky, V. A. (1980). *Image pattern recognition.* New York: Springer.

Kriegeskorte, W. (1989). *Guiseppe Archimboldo.* Cologne, Germany: Benedikt Taschen.

Kriz, J. (1996). Fractal coding and Gestalt principles (In German). *Gestalt Theory, 18,* 148–156.

Kubovy, M., & Holcombe, A. O. (1998). On the lawfulness of grouping by proximity. *Cognitive Psychology, 35,* 71–98.

Kubovy, M., & Pomerantz, J. R. (1981). *Perceptual organization.* Hillsdale, NJ: Lawrence Erlbaum Associates.

Kumar, T., Zhou, P., & Glaser, D. A. (1993). Comparison of human performance for estimating fractal dimension of fractional Brownian statistics. *Journal of the Optical Society of America, 10,* 1136–1146.

Land, E. H. (1977). The retinex theory of color vision. *Scientific American, 237,* 108–128.

Lappin, J. S., Doner, J., & Kottas, B. L. (1980). Minimal conditions for the visual detection of structure and motion in three dimensions. *Science, 209,* 717–719.

Latimer, C. (2000a). Abstract ideas, schemata, and hyperstructures: Plus ca change. . . . *Psycoloquy, 10,* 1–2.

Latimer, C. (2000b). *Computer modeling of cognitive processes.* Available at http://www.cs.indiana.edu/Noetica/OpenFormIssue1/Latimer.html.

Latimer, C. R., & Stevens, C. J. (1997). *Some remarks on wholes, parts, and their perception.* Available at http://www.cognet.soton.ac.uk/psyc-bin/newpsy

Lee, S. -H., & Blake, R. (1999). Visual form created solely from temporal structure. *Science, 284,* 1165–1168.

Leeper, R. (1935). A study of a neglected portion of the field of learning—The development of sensory organization. *Pedagogical Seminary and Journal of Genetic Psychology, 46,* 41–75.

Leeuwenberg, E. L. J. (1971). A perceptual coding language for visual and auditory patterns,. *American Journal of Psychology, 84,* 307–349.

Leeuwenberg, E. L. J. (1978). Quantification of certain visual pattern properties: Salience, transparency, similarity. In E. L. J. Leeuwenberg & H. F. J. M. Buffart (Eds.), *Formal Theories of Visual Perception* (pp. 277–298). Chichester, England: Wiley.

Lesher, G. W., & Mingolla, E. (1993). The role of edges and line ends in illusory contour formation. *Vision Research, 33,* 2253–2270.

Lettvin, J. Y., Maturana, H. R., McCulloch, W. S., & Pitts, W. H. (1959). What the frog's eye tells the frog's brain. *Proceedings of the Institute of Radio Engineers, 47*, 1940–1951.

Lewis, H. R., & Papadimitriou, C. H. (1998). *Elements of the theory of computation.* Upper Saddle River, NJ: Prentice-Hall.

Li, X., & Gilchrist, A. L. (1999). Relative area and relative luminance combine to anchor surface lightness values. *Perception and Psychophysics, 61*, 771–785.

Licklider, J. C. R., & Miller, G. E. (1951). The perception of speech. In S. S. Steven (Ed.), *Handbook of experimental psychology.* New York: Wiley.

Lindsay, P. H., & Norman, D. A. (1977). *Human information processing.* New York: Academic Press.

Ling, G., & Gerard, R. W. (1949). The normal membrane potential of frog sartorius fibers. *Journal of Cellular and Comparative Physiology, 34*, 383–385.

Livingstone, M., & Hubel, D. H. (1988). Segregation of form, color, movement, and depth: Anatomy, physiology, and perception. *Science, 240*, 740–749.

Lotto, R. B., Williams, S. M., & Purves, D. (1999a). An empirical basis for Mach bands. *Proceedings of the National Academy of Sciences, 96*, 5239–5244.

Lotto, R. B., Williams, S. M., & Purves, D. (1999b). Mach bands as empirically derived associations. *Proceedings of the National Academy of Sciences, 96*, 5245–5250.

Lowe, L. D. (1985). *Perceptual organization and visual recognition.* Dordrecht, The Netherlands.

Luce, R. D. (1959). *Individual choice behavior.* New York: Wiley.

Luce, R. D. (1963). Detection and recognition. In R. D. Luce, R. R. Bush, & E. Galanter (Eds.), *Handbook of mathematical psychology* (Vol. I, pp. 103–190). New York: Wiley.

Luce, R. D. (1995). Four tensions concerning mathematical modeling in psychology. *Annual Review of Psychology, 46*, 1–26.

Luce, R. D. (1999). Where is mathematical modeling in psychology headed? *Theory and Psychology, 9*, 723–737.

Luce, R. D., & Suppes, P. (1965). Preference, utility, and subjective probability. In R. D. Luce, R. R. Bush, & E. Galanter (Eds.), *Handbook of mathematical psychology* (Vol. III, pp. 249–410). New York: Wiley.

MacCorquodale, K., & Meehl, P. E. (1948). On a distinction between hypothetical constructs and intervening variables. *Psychological Review, 55*, 95–107.

Mach, E. (1865). Uber die wirkung der raumlichen des lichtreizes auf die Netzhaut, I. *Sitzungberichte der Mathematisch-Naturweissenschaftlichen Class der Kaiserlichen Akademie der Wissenchaften, 52*, 303–322.

Mach, E. (1886/1959). *The analysis of sensations (C. M. Williams, Trans.)* New York: Dover. Original publication 1886.

Machado, A. (1999). Of minds, brains, and behavior—A review of Uttal's (1998) *Toward a new behaviorism: The case against perceptual reductionism. Behavior and Philosophy, 27*, 51–74.

Mandelbrot, B. B. (1977). *The fractal geometry of nature.* New York: Freeman.

Mandelbrot, B. B. (1983). *The fractal geometry of nature.* New York: Freeman.

Marcus, L. F., Corti, M., Loy, A. L., Naylor, G. J. P., & Slice, D. E. (1996). *Advances in morphometrics.* New York: Plenum Press.

Marr, D. (1982). *Vision: A computational investigation into the human representation and processing of visual information.* San Francisco, Freeman.

Marr, D., & Hildredth, E. (1980). Theory of edge detection. *Proceedings of the Royal Society of London, B207*, 187–217.

Marr, D., & Nishihara, H. K. (1978). Representation and recognition of the spatial organization of three-dimensional shapes. *Proceedings of the Royal Society of London (B), 200*, 269–294.

Marx, M. H., & Hillix, W. A. (1963). *Systems and theories in psychology.* New York: McGraw-Hill.

Matlin, M. W., & Foley, H. J. (1996). *Sensation and perception.* Boston: Allyn & Bacon.

McClelland, J. L., & Rumelhart, D. E. (1981). An interactive activation model of the effect of context in perception (Part 1): An account of basic findings. *Psychological Review, 88*, 375–407.

McCulloch, W. S., & Pitts, W. (1943). A logical calculus of the ideas immanent in nervous activity. *Bulletin of Mathematical Biophysics, 5*, 115–133.

Meyer, A. R. (1975). Weak monadic second order theory of successor is not elementary recursive. In A. Dold & B. Eckmann (Eds.), *Lecture notes in mathematics: No. 453*. New York: Springer Verlag.

Miller, G. A. (1951). Speech and language. In S. S. Stevens (Ed.), *Handbook of experimental psychology*. New York: Wiley.

Miller, G. A. (1954). What is information measurement? *The American Psychologist, 8*, 3–11.

Miller, J. (1981). Global precedence in attention and decision. *Journal of Experimental Psychology, 7*, 1161–1174.

Miyashita, Y., Higuchi, S., Sakai, K., & Masui, N. (1991). Generation of fractal patterns for probing the visual memory. *Neuroscience Research, 12*, 307–311.

Monahan, J. S., & Lockhead, G. R. (1977). Identification of integral stimuli. *Journal of Experimental Psychology: General, 106*, 94–110.

Moore, E. F. (1956). Gedanker-experiments on sequential machines. In C. E. Shannon & J. McCarthy (Eds.), *Automata studies* (pp. 129–153).

Moscovitch, M., Winocur, G., & Behrmann, M. (1997). What is special about face recognition? Nineteen experiments on a person with visual object agnosia and dyslexia but normal face recognition. *Journal of Cognitive Neuroscience, 9*, 555–604.

Murakami, I. (1995). Motion aftereffect after monocular adaptation to filled-in motion at the blind spot. *Vision Research, 35*, 1041–1045.

Myung, I. J., Forster, M., & Browne, M. (2000). Guest editors' introduction: Special issue on model selection. *Journal of Mathematical Psychology, 44*, 1–2.

Nakatani, K. (1980). A model of pattern recognition by binary orthogonal transformation. *Behaviormetrika, 7*, 47–59.

Navon, D. (1977). Forest before trees: The precedence of global features in visual perception. *Cognitive Psychology, 9*, 353–383.

Navon, D. (1981). The forest revisited: More on global precedence. *Psychological Research, 43*, 1–32.

Navon, D. (1991). Testing a queue hypothesis for the processing of global and local information. *Journal of Experimental Psychology: General, 120*, 173–189.

Neumeyer, C., & Spillmann, L. (1977). Fading of steadily fixated large test fields in extra foveal vision. *Pfluegers Archiv, 368*, R40.

Newsome, W. T., Britten, K. H., & Movshon, J. A. (1989). Neuron correlates of a perceptual decision. *Nature, 341*, 52–54.

Nickerson, R. S. (2000). Null hypothesis significance testing: A review of an old and continuing controversy. *Psychological methods, 5*, 241–301.

Nisbett, R. E., & Wilson, T. D. (1977). Telling more than we can know: Verbal reports on mental processes. *Psychological Review, 84*, 231–259.

Nyquist, H. (1924). Certain factors affecting telegraph speed. *Bell System Technical Journal, 3*, 324–346.

O'Toole, A. J., Wenger, M. J., & Townsend, J. T. (2001). Quantitative models of perceiving and remembering faces: Precedents and Possibilities. In M. J. Wenger & J. T. Townsend (Eds.), *Computational, geometric, and process perspectives on facial cognition: Context and challenges* (pp. 1–38). Mahwah, NJ: Lawrence Erlbaum Associates.

Okada, K., Steffens, J., Maurer, T., Hong, H., Elagin, E., Neven, H., & Malsburg, C. v. d. (1998). The Bochum/USC face recognition system and how it fared in the FERET Phase III test. In H. Wechsler, P. J. Phillips, V. Bruce, F. F. Soulie, & T. S. Huang (Eds.), *Face recognition: From theory to applications* (pp. 186–205). Berlin: Springer.

Olivia, A., & Schyns, P. G. (1997). Coarse blobs of fine edges? Evidence that information diagnosticity changes the perception of complex visual stimuli. *Cognitive Psychology, 34*, 72–107.

Olzak, L. A., & Thomas, J. P. (1986). Seeing spatial patterns. In K. R. Boff, L. Kaufman, & J. P. Thomas (Eds.), *Handbook of perception and human performance: Vol. I. Sensory processes and perception.* New York: Wiley.

O'Toole, A. J., Wenger, M. J., & Townsend, J. T. (2001). Quantitative models of perceiving and remembering faces: Precedents and possibilities. In M. J. Wenger & J. T. Townsend (Eds.), *Computational, geometric, and process perspectives on facial cognition: Context and challenges.* Mahwah, NJ: Lawrence Erlbaum Associates.

Oyama, T. (1961). Perceptual grouping as a function of proximity. *Perceptual and Motor Skills, 3,* 305–306.

Pachella, R. G. (1974). The interpretation of reaction time in information processing research. In B. H. Kantowitz (Ed.), *Human information processing: Tutorials in performance and cognition* (pp. 41–83). Hillsdale, NJ: Lawrence Erlbaum Associates.

Page, M. P. A. (2000). Connectionist modeling in psychology: A localist manifesto. *Behavioral and Brain Sciences, 23,* 443–512.

Palmer, S. E. (1982). Symmetry, transformation, and the structure of perceptual systems. In J. Beck (Ed.), *Organization and representation in perception* (pp. 95–144). Hillsdale NJ: Lawrence Erlbaum Associates.

Papadimitriou, C. H. (1994). *Computational complexity.* Reading MA: Addison-Wesley.

Paquet, L. (1999). Global dominance outside the focus of attention. *Quarterly Journal of Experimental Psychology: Human Experimental Psychology, 52A,* 465–485.

Paquet, L., & Merikle, P. M. (1988). Global Precedence in attended and nonattended objects. *Journal of Experimental Psychology: Human Perception and Performance, 14,* 89–100.

Parker, D. M., Lishman, J. R., & Hughes, J. (1996). Role of coarse and fine spatial information in face and object processing. *Journal of Experimental Psychology: Human Perception and Performance, 22,* 1448–1466.

Passmore, P. J., & Johnston, A. (1995). Human discrimination of surface slant in fractal and related textured images. *Spatial Vision, 9,* 151–161.

Pentland, A. P. (1984). Fractal-based description of natural scenes. *IEEE Pattern Analysis and Machine Intelligence, PAMI-6,* 661–674.

Pentland, A. P. (1986). *On perceiving 3-D shape and texture.* Paper presented at the Symposium on Computational Models in Human Vision, Rochester, NY.

Perkins, D. N. (1982). The perceiver as organizer and geometer. In J. Beck (Ed.), *Organization and representation in perception* (pp. 73–94). Hillsdale, NJ: Lawrence Erlbaum Associates.

Perkins, D. N. (1986). Gestalt theory is alive and well and living in information-processing land. A response to Arnheim. *New Ideas in Psychology, 4,* 295–299.

Pessoa, L., Thompson, E., & Noë, A. (1998). Finding out about filling in: A guide to perceptual completion for visual science and the philosophy of perception. *Behavioral and Brain Sciences, 21,* 723–748.

Peterhans, E., & von der Heydt, R. (1995). Subjective contours—Bridging the gap between psychophysics and physiology. In H. e. a. Gutfreund (Ed.), *Biology and computation. A physicist's choice* (Vol. 3, pp. 627–634). Singapore: World Scientific Publishing Co.

Pinker, S. (1997). *How the mind works.* New York: Norton.

Pitts, W., & McCulloch. (1947). How we know universals: The perception of auditory and visual forms. *Bulletin of Mathematical Biophysics, 9,* 127–147.

Poggio, T. (1982). Trigger features or Fourier analysis in early vision: A new point of view. In D. G. Albrecht (Ed.), *Recognition of pattern and form* (pp. 88–99). Berlin: Springer-Verlag.

Pollack, I. (1971). Perception of two-dimensional markov constraints within visual displays. *Perception and Psychophysics, 9,* 461–464.

Pollack, I. (1952). The information in elementary auditory displays. *Journal of the Acoustical Society of America, 24,* 745–750.

Pollack, I. (1953). The Information of elementary auditory displays II. *The Journal of the Acoustical Society of America, 25,* 765–769.

Pomerantz, J. R. (1978). Are complex visual features derived from simple ones? In E. L. J. Leeuwenberg & H. F. J. M. Buffart (Eds.), *Formal theories of visual perception* (pp. 217–230). New York: Wiley.

Pomerantz, J. R., & Kubovy, M. (1981). Perceptual organization: An overview. In M. Kubovy & J. R. Pomerantz (Eds.), *Perceptual organization* (pp. 423–456). Hillsdale, NJ: Lawrence Erlbaum Associates.

Pomerantz, J. R., Sager, L. C., & Stoever, R. J. (1977). Perception of wholes and of their component parts: Some configural superiority effects. *Journal of Experimental Psychology: Human Perception and Performance, 3*, 422–435.

Pratt, W. K. (1991). *Digital image processing* (2nd ed.). New York: Wiley.

Pribram, K. H., Nuwer, M., & Baron, R. J. (1974). The holographic hypothesis of memory structure in brain function and perception. In D. H. Krantz (Ed.), *Contemporary developments in mathematical psychology* (Vol. II, pp.   ). San Francisco: Freeman.

Purcell, D. G., & Stewart, A. L. (1988). The face-detection effect: Configuration enhances detection. *Perception and Psychophysics, 43*, 355–366.

Purves, D., Shimpi, A., & Lotto, R. B. (1999). An empirical explanation of the Cornsweet effect. *The Journal of Neuroscience, 19*, 8542–8551.

Quastler, H. (Ed.). (1955). *Information theory in psychology*. Glencoe, IL: The Free Press.

Rainville, S. J. M., & Kingdom, F. A. A. (1999). Spatial-scale contribution to the detection of mirror symmetry in fractal noise. *Journal of the Optical Society of America (A), 16*, 2112–2123.

Rakover, S. (1986). Breaking the myth that behaviorism is a trivial science. *New Ideas in Psychology, 4*, 305–310.

Rakover, S. (1998). Can mechanistic concepts be applied to part-whole perception? *Psycoloquy, 9*, 1–2.

Rakover, S. S., & Teucher, B. (1997). Facial inversion effects: Part and whole relationship. *Perception and Psychophysics, 59*, 752–761.

Ramachandran, V. S. (1985). The neurobiology of perception. *Perception, 14*, 97–103.

Ramachandran, V. S. (1992). Blind spots. *Scientific American, 266*, 44–49.

Ramachandran, V. S., & Gregory, R. L. (1991). Perceptual filling in of artificially induced scotomas in human vision. *Nature (London), 350*, 669–702.

Rashevsky, N. (1948). *Mathematical biophysics*. Chicago: University of Chicago Press.

Reed, S. K. (1973). *Psychological processes in pattern recognition*. New York: Academic Press.

Reicher, G. M. (1969). Perceptual recognition as a function of meaningfulness of stimulus materials. *Journal of Experimental Psychology, 81*, 275–280.

Reid, T. (1846). *Works: Edited by Hamilton, W.* Edinburgh.

Requicha, A. A. G. (1980). Representations of rigid solids: Theory, methods, and systems. *Computing Surveys, 4*, 437–464.

Rescher, N., & Oppenheim, P. (1955). Logical analysis of gestalt concepts. *Journal for the Philosophy of Science, 6*, 89–106.

Reyment, R. A. (1996). An idiosyncratic history of early morphometrics. In L. F. Marcus, M. Corti, A. Loy, G. J. P. Naylor, & D. E. Slice (Eds.), *Advances in morphometrics* (pp. 15–22). New York: Plenum Press.

Reynolds, R. I. (1985). The role of object-hypothesis in the organization of fragmented figures. *Perception, 14*, 49–52.

Rhodes, G., Brake, S., & Atkinson, A. P. (1993). What's lost in inverted faces? *Cognition, 47*, 25–57.

Rhodes, G., Brennan, S., & Carey, S. (1987). Identification and ratings of caricatures: Implications for mental representations of faces. *Cognitive Psychology, 19*, 473–497.

Roberts, S., & Pashler, L. (2000). How persuasive is a good fit? A comment on theory testing. *Psychological Review, 107*, 358–367.

Rogers, T. D., & Trofanenko, S. C. (1979). On the measurement of shape. *Bulletin of Mathematical Biology, 41*, 283–304.

Rosenblatt, F. (1958). The perceptron: A probabilistic model for information storage and organization in the brain. *Psychological Review, 65,* 386–408.

Rumelhart, D. E., Hinton, G. E., & McClelland, J. L. (1986). A general framework for parallel data processing. In D. E. Rumelhart, J. L. McClelland & the PDP Research Group (Eds.), *Parallel distributed processing: Explorations in the microstructure of cognition: Vol. 1. Foundations.* Cambridge MA: MIT Press.

Rumelhart, D. E., Hinton, G. E., & Williams, R. J. (1986). Learning representations by back-propagating errors. *Nature, 323,* 533–536.

Rumelhart, D. E., McClelland, J. L., & the PDP Research Group (Eds.). (1988). *Parallel distributed processing: Explorations in the microstructure of cognition: Vol. 1. Foundations.* Cambridge MA: MIT Press.

Runeson, S. (1977). On the possibility of "smart" perceptual mechanisms. *Scandinavian Journal of Psychology, 18,* 172–179.

Ryle, G. (1949). *The concept of the mind.* New York: Barnes & Noble.

Sakitt, B. (1972). Counting every quantum. *Journal of Physiology, 223,* 131–150.

Schendel, J. D., & Shaw, P. (1976). A test of the generality of the word-context effect. *Perception and Psychophysics, 19,* 383–393.

Schipke, R. J., & Eberhardt, A. (1999). The forgotten genius of Ubo von Aachen. *Harvard Journal of Historical Mathematics, 32,* 34–77.

Schmidt, H. (1941). Regelungstechnik. *VDI-Zeitschrift, 85,* 81–88.

Schumann, F. (1900). Beitrage zur Analyse der Gesichtwahrnehmungen. Erste Abhandlung. Einige Beobachtungen Uber die Zusammenfassung von Gesichtseindrucken zu Einheiten. *Zeitschrift fur Psychologie und Physiologie der Sinnesorgane, 23,* 1–32.

Schumann, F. (1904). Einige Beobachtungewn uber die Zusammenfassung von Gesichtsein-drucken zu Einhheiten. *Psychologische Studien, 1,* 1–32.

Searle, J. R. (1980). Minds, brains, and programs. *Behavioral and Brain Sciences, 13,* 585–642.

Selfridge, O. G. (1958). *Mechanization of thought processes: Proceedings of a symposium held at the National Physical Laboratory,* London, England.

Sergent, J. (1986). Methodological constraints on neuropsychological studies of face perception in normals. In R. Bruyer (Ed.), *The neuropsychology of face perception and facial expression* (pp. 69–81). Hillsdale, NJ: Lawrence Erlbaum Associates.

Shallice, T. (1988). *From neuropsychology to mental structure.* Cambridge, England: Cambridge University Press.

Shannon, C. E. (1948). A mathematical theory of communication. *Bell System Technical Journal, 27,* 379–423; 623–656.

Shaw, M. L. (1978). A capacity allocation time for reaction time. *Journal of Experimental Psychology: Human Perception and Performance, 4,* 586–598.

Shepard, R. N. (1964a). Attention and the metric structure of he stimulus space. *Journal of Mathematical Psychology, 1,* 54–87.

Shepard, R. N. (1964b). Circularity in judgments of relative pitch. *Journal of the Acoustical Society of America, 36,* 2346–2353.

Shepherd, T. (1999). Object recognition. In W. R. Uttal (Ed.), *Computational modeling of vision: The role of combination.* New York: Marcel Dekker.

Shor, R. (1971). Symbol processing speed differences and symbol interference in a variety of concept domains. *Journal of General Psychology, 85,* 187–205.

Slice, D. E., Bookstein, F. L., Marcus, L. F., & Rohlf, F. J. (1996). Appendix I: A glossary of geometric morphometrics. In L. F. Marcus, M. Corti, A. Loy, G. J. P. Naylor, & D. E. Slice (Eds.), *Advances in morphometrics.* New York: Plenum Press.

Spillmann, L. (1999). From elements to perception: Local and global processing in visual neurons. *Perception, 28,* 1461–1492.

Stebbins, W. C. (1995). Uncertainty in the study of comparative perception: A methodological challenge. In G. M. Klump, R. J. Dooling, R. R. Fay, & W. C. Stebbins (Eds.), *Methods in comparative psychoacoustics.* Basel: Birkhauser Verlag.

Stevens, S. S. (Ed.). (1951). *Handbook of experimental psychology.* New York: Wiley.

Stewart, A. L., & Pinkham, R. S. (1991). A space-variant operator for visual sensitivity. *Biological Cybernetics, 64,* 373–379.

Stewart, A. L., & Pinkham, R. S. (1994). Space-variant models of visual acuity using self-adjoint integral operators. *Biological Cybernetics, 71,* 161–167.

Stockmeyer, L. J., & Chandra, A. K. (1979). Intrinsically difficult problems. *Scientific American, 240*(5), 140–159.

Street, R. F. (1931). *A gestalt completion test: A study of a cross section of intellect.* New York: Bureau of Publications: Teachers College, Columbia University.

Suppe, F. (1984). Beyond Skinner and Kuhn. *New Ideas in Psychology, 2,* 89–104.

Sutherland, N. S. (1957). Visual discrimination of orientation and shape by octopus. *Nature, 179,* 11–13.

Sutherland, N. S. (1958). Visual discrimination of shape by octopus, squares and triangles. *Quarterly Journal of Experimental Psychology, 10,* 40–47.

Sutherland, N. S. (1959). A test of a theory of shape discrimination in octopus vulgaris lamarck. *Journal of Comparative and Physiological Psychology, 52,* 135–141.

Sutherland, N. S. (1968). Outlines of a theory of visual pattern recognition in animals and man. *Proceedings of the Royal Society, 171,* 297–317.

Szilard, L. (1925). *Zeitschrift fur Physiks, 53.*

Takemoto, A., & Ejima, Y. (1997). Retention of local information in generation of subjective contours. *Vision Research, 37,* 1429–1439.

Tanaka, J. W., & Farah, M. J. (1993). Parts and wholes in face recognition. *The Quarterly Journal of Experimental Psychology, 46A,* 225–245.

Tanaka, J. W., & Sengco, J. A. (1997). Features and their configuration in face recognition. *Memory and Cognition, 25,* 583–592.

Tannenbaum, A. S. (2001). The sense of consciousness. *Journal of Theoretical Biology, 211,* 377–391.

Thompson, D. W. (1917). *On growth and form.* Cambridge, England: Cambridge University Press.

Thompson, P. (1980). Margaret Thatcher: A new illusion. *Perception, 9,* 483–484.

Thurmond, J. B. (1966). *Extensions of an informational deductive analysis of form.* Paper presented at the Symposium on Analysis of the Metrics of Form, New Orleans.

Titchener, E. B. (1899). *An outline of psychology.* New York: McMillan.

Tolman, E. (1932). *Purposive behavior in animals and men.* New York: Century.

Townsend, J. T., & Landon, D. E. (1983). Mathematical model of recognition and confusion in psychology. *Mathematical Social Sciences, 4,* 25–71.

Townsend, J. T., & Thomas, R. D. (1994). Stochastic dependencies in parallel and serial models: Effects on systems factorial interactions. *Journal of Mathematical Psychology, 38,* 1–34.

Treisman, A. M. (1986). Features and objects in visual processing. *Scientific American, 255,* 114–125.

Treisman, A. (1988). Features and objects: The 14th Bartlett memorial lecture. *The Quarterly Journal of Experimental Psychology, 40A,* 201–237.

Treisman, A., & Gelade, G. (1980). A feature-integration theory of attention. *Cognitive Psychology, 12,* 97–136.

Treisman, A. M., & Gormican, S. (1988). Feature analysis in early vision: Evidence from search symmetries. *Psychological Review, 95,* 15–48.

Tripathy, S. P., Levi, D. M., & Ogmen, H. (1996). Two-dot alignment across the physiological blind spot. *Vision Research, 36,* 1585–1596.

Turing, A. M. (1950). Computing machinery and intelligence. *Mind, 59,* 433–460.

Turk, M., & Pentland, A. (1991). Eigenfaces for recognition. *Journal of Cognitive Neuroscience, 3,* 71–86.

Uhr, L. (1963). "Pattern recognition" computers as models for form perception. *Psychological Bulletin, 60,* 40–73.

Uhr, L. (Ed.). (1966). *Pattern recognition: Theory, experiment, computer simulations and dynamic models of form perception and discovery.* New York: Wiley.

Uhr, L., & Vossler, C. (1961a). A pattern recognition program that generates, evaluates, and adjusts its own operators. *Proceedings of the Western Joint Computer Conference, 10,* 555–569.

Uhr, L., & Vossler, C. (1961b). Recognition of speech by a computer program that was written to simulate a model for human visual pattern recognition. *The Journal of the Acoustical Society of America, 33,* 1426.

Ullman, S. (1996). *High level vision: Object recognition and visual cognition.* Cambridge MA: MIT Press.

Uttal, W. R. (1958). Cutaneous sensitivity to electrical pulse stimuli. *The Journal of Comparative and Physiological Psychology, 51,* 549–554.

Uttal, W. R. (1971). The effect of interval and number on masking with dot bursts. *Perception and Psychophysics, 9,* 469–473.

Uttal, W. R. (1973). *The psychobiology of sensory coding.* New York: Harper and Row.

Uttal, W. R. (1975). *An autocorrelation theory of form detection.* Hillsdale, NJ: Lawrence Erlbaum Associates.

Uttal, W. R. (1981). *A taxonomy of visual processes.* Hillsdale, NJ: Lawrence Erlbaum Associates.

Uttal, W. R. (1988). *On seeing forms.* Hillsdale, NJ: Lawrence Erlbaum Associates.

Uttal, W. R. (1998). *Toward a new behaviorism: The case against perceptual reductionism.* Mahwah NJ: Lawrence Erlbaum Associates.

Uttal, W. R. (2000). *The war between mentalism and behaviorism: On the accessibility of mental processes.* Mahwah NJ: Lawrence Erlbaum Associates.

Uttal, W. R. (2001). *The new phrenology: Limits on the localization of cognitive processes in the brain.* Cambridge MA: MIT Press.

Uttal, W. R., Baruch, T., & Allen, L. (1995a). Combining image degradations in a recognition task. *Perception and Psychophysics, 57,* 682–691.

Uttal, W. R., Baruch, T., & Allen, L. (1995b). The effect of combination of image degradations in a discrimination task. *Perception and Psychophysics, 57,* 668–671.

Uttal, W. R., Baruch, T., & Allen, L. (1997). A parametric study of face recognition when image degradations are combined. *Spatial Vision, 11,* 179–204.

Uttal, W. R., Kakarala, R., Dayanand, S., Shepherd, T., Kalki, J., & Liu, N. (1999). *Computational modeling of vision: The role of combination.* New York: Marcel Dekker.

Uttal, W. R., Spillman, L., Sturzel, F., & Sekuler, S. (2000). Motion and shape in common fate. *Vision Research, 40,* 301–310.

Valentine, T. (1991). A unified account of the effects of distinctiveness, inversion, and race in face recognition. *Quarterly Journal of Experimental Psychology, 43A,* 161–204.

Valentine, T. (2001). Face-space models of face recognition. In M. J. Wenger & J. T. Townsend (Eds.), *Computational, geometric, and process perspectives on facial cognition: Contexts and challenges* (pp. 83–114). Mahwah, NJ: Lawrence Erlbaum Associates.

Valentine, T., & Bruce, V. (1986). The effects of distinctiveness in recognizing and classifying faces. *Perception, 15,* 525–536.

van der Zwan, R., & Wenderoth, P. (1996). Mechanisms of purely subjective tilt after effects. *Vision Research, 35,* 2547–2557.

Van Orden, G. C., Jansen op de Haar, M. A., & Bosman, A. M. T. (1997). Complex dynamic systems also predict dissociations, but they do not reduce to autonomous components. *Cognitive Neuropsychology, 14,* 131–165.

Van Orden, G. C., & Papp, K. R. (1997). Functional neuroimages fail to discover pieces of mind in the parts of the brain. *Philosophy of Science, Proceedings, 64,* S85–S94.

Van Orden, G. C., Pennington, B. F., & Stone, G. O. (in press). What do double dissociations prove? Modularity yields a degenerating research program. *Cognitive Science.*

Vokey, J., & Read, J. D. (1992). Familiarity, memorability, and the effect of typicality on the recognition of faces. *Memory and Cognition, 20,* 391–302.

Von Neumann, J. (1932). *Mathematical foundations of quantum mechanics.* Berlin: J. Springer.

Vonèche, J. J. (1986). The trouble with Arnheim and Hochberg: A Response to Arnheim. *New Ideas in Psychology, 4,* 303–304.

Watanabe, S. (1985). *Pattern recognition: Human and Mechanical.* New York: Wiley.

Watson, A. B. (1983). *Detection and recognition of simple spatial forms* (NASA Technical Memorandum 84353). Moffett Field, CA: NASA Ames Research Center.

Weaver, W. (1949). Recent contributions to the mathematical theory of communication. In C. E. Shannon & W. Weaver (Eds.), *The mathematical theory of communication* (pp. 3–28). Urbana: University of Illinois Press.

Wechsler, H. (1990). *Computational vision.* Boston: Academic Press.

Wechsler, H., Phillips, P. J., Bruce, V., Soulie, F. F., & Huang, T. S. (Eds.). (1998). *Face recognition: From theory to applications.* Berlin: Springer.

Wegner, D. M. (1994). Ironic processes of mental control. *Psychological Review, 101,* 34–52.

Wegner, D. M., & Wheatley, T. (1999). Apparent mental causation. *American Psychologist, 54,* 480–492.

Weisstein, N., & Harris, C. S. (1974). Visual detection of line segments: An object superiority effect. *Science, 186,* 752–755.

Wenger, M. J., & Townsend, J. T. (2000). Spatial frequencies in short-term memory for faces: A Test of three frequency-dependent hypotheses. *Memory and Cognition, 28,* 125–142.

Wenger, M. J., & Townsend, J. T. (Eds.). (2001). *Computational, geometric, and process perspectives on facial cognition: Contexts and challenges.* Mahwah, NJ: Lawrence Erlbaum Associates.

Werkhoven, P., Snippe, H. P., & Koenderink, J. J. (1990). Metrics for the strength of low level motion perception. *Journal of Visual Communication and Image Representation, 1,* 176–188.

Wertheimer, M. (1912). Experimetelle studien uber das sehen von bewegung. *Zeitschrift fur Psychologie, Part I, 71,* 161–265.

Westheimer, G., & McKee, J. (1977). Spatial configurations for visual hyperacuity. *Vision Research, 17,* 941–947.

Weyl, H. (1952). *Symmetry.* Princeton NJ: Princeton University Press.

Wheeler, D. D. (1970). Processes in word rocgnition. *Cognitive Psychology, 1,* 59–85.

White, M. (2000). Parts and wholes in expression recognition. *Cognition and Emotion, 14,* 39–60.

Whyte, L. L. (1951). *Aspects of form.* New York: Pellegrine and Cudahy.

Widrow, G., & Hoff, M. E. (1960). *Adaptive switching circuits.* Paper presented at the Institute of Radio Engineers, Western Electronics Show and Convention, New York.

Wiener, N. (1948). *Cybernetics or control and communication in the animal and the machine.* New York: Wiley.

Williams, S. M., McCoy, A. N., & Purves, D. (1998). An empirical explanation of brightness. *Proceedings of the National Academy of Sciences, 95,* 13301–13306.

Wilson, H. R., & Gieze, S. C. (1977). Threshold visibility of frequency gradient patterns. *Vision Research, 17,* 1177–1190.

Wittgenstein, L. (1953). *Philosophical investigations (3rd ed.).* New York: Macmillan.

Wolpert, D. H. (1995). The relationship between PAC, the statistical physics framework, the Bayesian framework, and the VC framework. In D. H. Wolpert (Ed.), *The mathematics of generalization* (pp. 117–214). Reading MA: Addison-Wesley.

Wolpert, D. H. (1996). The lack of a priori distinctions between learning algorithms. *Neural Computation, 8,* 1341–1390.

Zhu, S. -C. (1999). Embedding Gestalt laws in Markov random fields. *IEEE Transactions on Pattern Analysis and Machine Intelligence, 21,* 1170–1187.

Zusne, L. (1970). *Visual perception of form.* New York: Academic Press.

Author Index

Subject Index